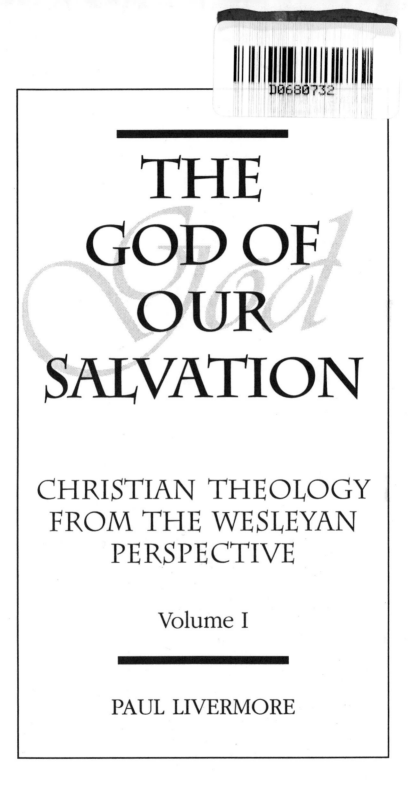

THE GOD OF OUR SALVATION

CHRISTIAN THEOLOGY FROM THE WESLEYAN PERSPECTIVE

Volume I

PAUL LIVERMORE

THE GOD OF OUR SALVATION
by Paul Livermore

ISBN 0-89367-199-1

© 1995
Second Printing 1998
Light and Life Communications
Indianapolis, IN 46253-5002
Printed in the U.S.A.

To the memory of my parents
Dr. Harry E. Livermore
and
Elizabeth Walker Livermore
who loved God
and served Christ's church

CONTENTS

ACKNOWLEDGMENTS

A large number of people have helped to make this work possible. Roberts Wesleyan College and the Free Methodist Church provided for a leave of absence from my teaching responsibilities during the fall semester of 1994. Provost Wayne McCown, President William Crothers, Board Chair David Hoselton, Bishop Gerald Bates and Publisher John Van Valin led in this effort. A list of many friends who contributed generously to this project is included.

Bishop Emeritus Donald Bastian, the chair of the editorial committee assisting me, has given constant encouragement and help since the project was first assigned. The other members of the committee Stanley Johnson, David Kendall, and Donald Thorsen have made valuable suggestions.

Colleagues at Roberts Wesleyan College have entered into lively dialogue on various portions of the work. I mention especially Jeffrey Altman, David Basinger, Elvera Berry, Scott Caton, Joe Coleson, Douglas Cullum, Judson Decker and Harold Hurley. Our division office manager, Karen Wilk, has worked wonders to free me so that I could devote time to writing.

Over the past several years students of mine in seminars on Paul, Wesley and historical theology have taught me much. Susan Armato, Tony Casas, John Hilts, Garry McCaffery, Rodney Mileham, Vicki Payton, Jonathan Rushik, Craig Saunders and Marty Zdrojewski assisted in verifying the Scripture references and in developing the glossaries.

David and Avis Barnes, Bill and Marilyn Christopher, Bob and Mary Jackson and Burton and Ruth Jones, all members of the small group to which Alice and I belong, supported me in word and prayer. The friendship of Gerry and Virginia Atkinson has been a gift from God.

I cherish the encouragement and prayers of my wonderful mother-in-law, Agnes Hoke. Our children, Geoffrey and Alicia, daughter-in-law, Kerry, and granddaughter, Erika, remind me of what is most important. My brother, Harry, who taught me nearly everything I know, and his wife, Janice, have also been exceptional friends.

The wisdom and love of my wife, Alice, continue to amaze me. This extraordinarily gifted person has enriched my life in countless ways and helped me to accomplish my work with her unselfish labor and good humor.

Contributors to the Livermore Project:

Rev. H. Mark Abbott
Dr. & Mrs. Jeffrey Altman
Bishop & Mrs. Robert F. Andrews
Ms. Cheryl Atkinson
Mr. Gerald Atkinson
Miss Carol Bartlett
Bishop & Mrs. Gerald E. Bates
Bishop Donald N. & Kay Bastian
Mr. Verlyn A. Beardslee
Mr. & Mrs. Rudolph Buettner
Rev. & Mrs. G. H. Bonney
Dr. & Mrs. Orrin H. Bowman
Ms. Sharon Brown
Mr. & Mrs. Lawrence Burrows
Dr. & Mrs. Bradford Chaney
Mary Collins
Mr. & Mrs. Paul Cooley
Mr. Guy Delamarter
Dr. William Crothers
Bishop & Mrs. W. Dale Cryderman
Bishop & Mrs. Paul N. Ellis
Bishop & Mrs. David Foster
Mr. & Mrs. Thomas A. Froula

Dr. & Mrs. Bruce Johnson
Rev. David Kendall
Rev. Leslie Krober
Mr. & Mrs. Harry Livermore
Mrs. Virginia Magill
Dr. & Mrs. V. James Mannoia
Dr. & Mrs. Wayne McCown
Nelson & Helen Morton
Bishop & Mrs. Elmer Parsons
Rev. & Mrs. Mitchell Pierce
Rev. & Mrs. Arden Reed
Mr. & Mrs. Wesley Skinner
Rev. & Mrs. Robert L. Smith
Bishop & Mrs. Richard Snyder
Dr. Frank Spina
Spring Arbor College
Dale & Carol Stephenson
Dr. Catherine Stonehouse
Mrs. Audrey Thorsen
Mrs. Una Traver
Dr. Mendal F. Van Valin
Dr. & Mrs. David V. Williams
Mr. & Mrs. Richard Zinck

FOREWORD

The church is a theological institution!

That does not mean it talks to itself in strange, other-worldly language that some scornfully call "god talk." Nor does it mean that the church stands ready to make hasty dogmatic pronouncements on every subject, claiming God as its authority. Good theology leaves room for reflection and mystery.

The church is a theological institution in that it believes it is called to be the servant of God and must always seek to know what God is like, what He has done, and what He wants His people to do. "Christian theology," an old definition has it, "is the science of God and divine things." That's what this book is about.

But, why should theology concern us if secularism has apparently freed Western culture from "superstitions" about God or gods? The truth is that secularism has only freed us for an inrush of neopagan influences – crystal balls, psychics and Lady Luck at the casinos, Buddhas and aboriginal sweet grass. The New Age movement, a quasi-religion laced with ideas imported from the Far East, is proving to be particularly fascinating to growing numbers of the God-starved.

We Christians are not immune to the secular drift. Polls continue to show that many people say they believe in God but do not believe in God as a personal, sovereign being. Could it be that God, for a growing number of people, is no more than "an oblong blue"? For Christians, it's time for a resurgence of theological interest.

By definition, the focus of *Christian* theology is Jesus Christ. Who was He? Where did He come from? What did He do? Can we rely upon His claims about issues of life and death? Most importantly, did He really rise from the dead? Is He alive today? Theology sets these focal questions in a larger context involving all of human existence, both in time and eternity. But for Christian theology, Christ remains at the center.

The Free Methodist Church holds that for answers to ultimate questions the primary source is the Bible. Therefore, the Bible is the focus and norm of theological study. Every issue of ultimate concern is addressed there either in history, poetry, parable, proverb or prophecy. The Free Methodist Articles of Religion on the Scriptures calls the Bible "God's written Word" and Jesus Christ "God's living Word." All the big issues of existence lie embedded in the Bible, and Jesus Christ brings them to focus in Himself.

To be a Christian one must believe in Jesus Christ; to be an informed Christian one must seek understanding by grappling with the questions theology addresses and always holding Christ as the reference point. In layman's terms, theology is what we think and say about God. More properly, it is a systematic attempt to explain our faith. As the medieval theologian Anselm put it, theology is "faith seeking understanding."

The Free Methodist Church, as a branch of the church universal, is a theological institution. So, how does it express its theology? In addition to the printed rituals for baptism and the Lord's Supper, it does so in three particular ways.

First, our church expresses its core beliefs in Articles of Religion. Articles of Religion are terse summaries of theology on particular critical issues, such as creation, salvation or final judgment. Articles historically are not intended as an outline of all things theological. Rather, they are markers to show what orthodoxy says on particular doctrines which heretics across history have put under siege. For example, the doctrine of the Trinity was forged by Christian councils back in the fourth century to answer heresies about Christ that were threatening the very life of the church. Today, the doctrine is shared broadly across Christendom by Protestants, Catholics, Eastern Orthodox and Coptics.

Articles of Religion are footprints of orthodoxy across history. Historic Articles have on them the traces of Augustine, Luther, Cranmer and Wesley, to name a few. Our Articles attempt to mark our church as Wesleyan, historically evangelical and orthodox. They have a certain permanence about them, rooting us in the Reformation and beyond. We lodge them in our constitution, and we open them up for revision reluctantly and only when compelled to do so by critical doctrinal controversies.

Second, the Free Methodist Church expresses itself in what we may call occasional theology. That is, theological responses prompted by particular occasions. If Articles of Religion tend to be fixed, occasional theology tends to be fluid. Because the church is inescapably a theological institution, there is a constant flow of such materials. When a denominational magazine calls Christians to rise above racial prejudice, this is occasional theology. If a conference superintendent asks for support to plant another church, the reasons he gives are occasional theology. When pastors preach about the sanctity of marriage, their appeals, though in contemporary idiom, must be grounded in theology. It's not too much to say that in the church, whatever isn't rooted in theology isn't worth saying.

The flow of occasional theology is endless: bishops' bulletins, letters of counsel, journal articles, sermons, cassettes, videos, seminars, roundtables, devotional books — they are all unavoidably theological. The question is never whether or not we will be intentionally theological. In all we say and do we reflect our understanding of God. The question is only whether our theology will be good or bad theology.

This book is about the third category of theology, systematic theology — so called because it attempts to explore, in a systematic fashion, the content of our faith. Other categories of theology flow into it. It thus has a breadth, a depth and an order which the first two categories do not approach. For example, when it takes up the subject of Jesus Christ, it asks about His humanity and His divinity, His titles given throughout Scripture, heresies about Him that have arisen across history, His role as a mediator between God and humankind, His atoning sacrifice, and the victory He has won for us all.

At the 1989 General Conference, on the campus of Seattle Pacific University, Seattle, WA, the Study Commission on Doctrine (SCOD) was assigned to oversee the writing and publishing of a compendium of systematic theology. The Commission is a standing committee of the General Conference. It in turn asked one of its members, Dr. Paul Livermore, to take up the task.

Livermore chairs the division of religion and humanities at Roberts Wesleyan College, Rochester, NY. The assignment called into play his three decades of study in theology generally and a growing engagement with systematics specifically. He addressed the assignment with characteristic enthusiasm and diligence and in five years of arduous labor – in addition to his teaching load – he produced this first of a two-volume compendium, *The God of Our Salvation: Christian Theology from the Wesleyan Perspective.*

Roberts Wesleyan College itself participated generously. Its president, William C. Crothers, and its provost and senior vice president for academic affairs, Wayne G. McCown, saw to it that the College provided a one-semester leave of absence for Livermore when he was at a critical stage in his work. To them, the project was so important to the church that Roberts Wesleyan College absorbed half the cost. Bishop Gerald E. Bates raised the other half from friends of Dr. Livermore and a wider circle of Christian stewards.

This first volume is now being released in the hope that it will find wide use in the church, standing alongside our Articles of Religion and our flow of occasional theology. It is carefully ordered and clearly written, thus enhancing the substance of our theological beliefs. Laypersons with inquiring minds will find it readable and generously instructive. It should take its place in college and seminary courses as one more effort to aid those whose faith seeks understanding – from a Wesleyan perspective. Free Methodist ministerial candidates may have their first exposure to the stimulation of systematic theology in this volume as they move toward ordination.

It's a serious attempt to interact again with what the great teachers across 2,000 years of church history have said about God's revelation of Himself to humankind. We therefore hope it will also become a basis for dialogue with other Christian bodies in the Wesleyan tradition. Interest in systematic theology has been revived in recent decades, and we all profit when we talk to one another about such crucial matters across denominational lines.

Even farther afield, we may hope representatives of other theological persuasions will see Livermore's work as a serious statement on theological matters.

Theology can erect barriers when it is done with pride or in a sectarian spirit. But done carefully and with appropriate humility, it is equally capable of lowering barriers and bringing serious Christians into better understanding of God and of one another. Through his five years of concentrated effort to state his case clearly, the author has wanted the broader dialogue to ensue.

However wide the arc this first of two volumes cuts, may it find its place on the bookshelves of Free Methodist ministers and laypersons alike – and even on the occasional coffee table. As it goes forth, may it bear witness that whatever our church does to proclaim the gospel of Jesus Christ and build up believers in the most holy faith, it attempts to do so from a base that is soundly theological, because the church is unavoidably a theological institution.

Bishop Donald N. Bastian

PART I.

The Study of God

CHAPTER

THE WESLEYAN PERSPECTIVE ON THEOLOGY

SECTION I. REVELATION
1. The Roots of Theology in Revelation
2. General Revelation and Special Revelation
3. "The Wesleyan Quadrilateral"

SECTION II. THE CHARACTER OF THIS THEOLOGY
1. The Theological Heritage of the Free Methodist Church
2. The Contemporary Theological Scene
3. Special Features of this Theology
4. The Character of this Theology
5. The Outline of this Theology

esus made a solemn observation concerning the nature of study within the church. "Every teacher of the law," He said, "who has been instructed about the kingdom of heaven is like the owner of a house who brings out of his [storehouse] new treasures as well as old" (Matthew 13:52). Theology is the work of servants of the church.[1] It is best accomplished when these teachers draw upon the church's rich treasures to expound the gospel in a fresh way in order to meet contemporary needs.

17

THE GOD OF OUR SALVATION

THE STUDY OF GOD

Theology literally means "the study of God." It has been extended to include the study of humans and the world in relation to God.

Serious theological work has been going on from the beginning of the church and even from the beginning of Israel. Even though the term "theology" was not used by biblical authors, it accurately captures what they were about. They were writing about God, especially about God as He dealt with human beings. This judgment would apply to historical books, such as Samuel and Acts, just as surely as it would to Romans, whose treatise-like form has often been characterized as pure theology. What makes a document theological is the focus of its content – God, the human race and the entire universe in relation to God.

THEOLOGY, A SCHOLARLY DISCIPLINE

Theology requires effort and discipline. It is a study, a task of the mind. It explores, as do all disciplines, questions and answers on a particular topic that we can rationally grasp and comprehend.

In terms of method, theology resembles other disciplines more than it differs from them. For example, we can write about physics because we can study the properties of the physical universe in systematic and orderly ways. Using this method we have developed other sciences of nature and still others of human behavior.

There is also the study of God, theology. When we study about God and the universe in relation to God in systematic and orderly ways, we are thinking theologically. There are ways to do theological work that are correct and true to the discipline. Good theology involves hard work on a specific set of issues and appears when certain rules are followed and rigorous thought is applied to a body of data.

SECTION I. *Revelation*

1. THE ROOTS OF THEOLOGY IN REVELATION

Genuine Knowledge About God, the Foundation of Theology

Theology pursues issues that transcend the material universe. As soon as we say that the main issues of theology pivot on questions about God, we have distinguished it from the physical sciences or from the behavioral sciences in a fundamental sense. God is transcendent and spiritual. We cannot literally see, hear or touch Him. How then can we know anything about God?

Revelation, the Source of Genuine Knowledge About God

The historic church has taught that we have such knowledge and so can properly speak of theology. This knowledge we have received from God is called *revelation.*[2]

The root meaning of both the Hebrew and Greek words "to reveal," *galah* and *apokaluptein,* is "to uncover."[3] Thus, the term "revelation" suggests an uncovering or disclosure of something covered or concealed (Deuteronomy 29:29; Isaiah 40:5; Daniel 10:1; Luke 10:22; Philippians 3:15; 1 Peter 1:12). Thus, we have come to know the essential things we talk about in theology through special, divine activity – revelation – that discloses them to us.[4]

The subject of revelation as well as its object is in the first place God. God reveals Himself; and we, the human family, receive this disclosure. Theology goes beyond our talking about God because we think some things about God that might be true. Revelation implies that God has communicated to us.

In the Christian sense, theology is the study of God and the relation of the human race and the world to God as knowledge about these topics is disclosed in revelation.

19

Revelation, a Divine Gift; Theology, a Human Response

The core in the concept of revelation is that it originates with God; it is a divine act. While human beings play an indispensable role in the theological enterprise, it does not begin with human activity but with God's activity.

But the idea that revelation originates with God carries with it a corollary idea concerning human beings. If God expects us to understand and talk about what He has disclosed, He must also have created us with a capacity to think and articulate specific thoughts. If revelation is to accomplish its goal, the Revealer's intention must have been matched with the Creator's skill. God must have made us so we can think about some things that He thinks about and know in some measure what He is like and what He has done. The human mind must bear some resemblance to the divine mind, so human intelligence corresponds to that degree to divine intelligence.[5]

The fact that we humans can think about God and the things that God reveals to us with some accuracy, though limited, is staggering. But this astonishing confession offers no ground for pride. We know God only in a partial and imperfect way. Our knowledge of God can be real and true, but it is always limited. This calls for humility as well as profound gratitude.[6]

Finally, we add to this an observation concerning our response to the gifts of revelation and our intellectual abilities. We must reflect on the revelation given, develop its implications, and teach its message. We must create theology. Failure to think and talk about revelation short-circuits God's design. Revelation stirs the human mind, but we must do some hard work. Revelation does not turn into theology when it is met with passivity. It offers itself as material that we shape into theological knowledge. Revelation is a divine gift to the church; theology is the human response of the church to that gift.[7]

2. GENERAL REVELATION AND SPECIAL REVELATION

Theology often distinguishes general from special revelation. By this it clarifies the immediacy with which God communicated revelation to us.[8] Though all revelation ultimately originates with God, it does not come to us so directly in all cases.

According to this distinction, God in "special revelation" acted uniquely and savingly in Israel, Jesus Christ and the church. He also inspired chosen people to write authoritatively, explaining His work and will, and in a different though related sense has inspired and has guided the church to interpret what had earlier been written. This revelation is "special" because it has been given only at special times and through special representatives.

In "general revelation" God imprinted upon the physical universe and in human nature knowledge about Himself and His will that He wants us to have. All people, not just those within the history of Israel and the church, have equal access to it. This form of revelation is called "general" because it is equally available, at least in principle, to every member of the human race.

3. "THE WESLEYAN QUADRILATERAL"

During recent years those in the Methodist family have adopted another phrase that distinguishes the various tools we use in writing theology, the "quadrilateral."[9] While general and special revelation emphasize the degree of immediacy in God's action in revelation, the quadrilateral identifies the specific source or resources that theologians use as they work through questions of faith and practice. This is often known as "the Wesleyan quadrilateral," because the term has arisen from an analysis of the theological method used by John Wesley himself, the founder of Methodism.[10]

The word "quadrilateral" indicates that four elements appear in this method. The four are:

- Scripture
- tradition, by which we mean historic Christian teaching
- reason
- experience

The Scriptures as a Source; Historic Christian Teaching, Reason and Experience as Resources for Christian Theology

The four elements in the quadrilateral by no means have equivalent authority. The Scriptures have priority.[11] For this reason a distinction should be drawn among the four. We designate the Scriptures as our source and the other three as the resources for our theological work. Even among the resources that we use, the three do not play exactly the same roles nor are they used in exactly the same ways. These differences will appear as we proceed through a discussion of each of the four in chapters two and three of part one.

SUMMARY: *Revelation*

1. Theology is the study of God and the relation of the human race and the world to God.

2. Christian theology originates in the revelation – disclosure – that God has made to us of Himself and His truth.

3. Theology is the teaching work of the church in which it responds to the gift of revelation by articulating its faith in an orderly and systematic way.

4. While God has revealed Himself indirectly through the physical universe and through human nature (general revelation), Christian theology fundamentally depends upon God's unique disclosure first to Israel, then in Jesus Christ, and finally to the church (special revelation).

5. We can speak of four elements that are used in the formation of our theology. These form a quadrilateral or the Wesleyan quadrilateral. They are:
   • Scripture
   • Tradition or historic Christian teaching
   • Reason
   • Experience

SECTION II. *The Character of this Theology*

1. THE THEOLOGICAL HERITAGE OF THE FREE METHODIST CHURCH

The Free Methodist Church is a member of the great Methodist family, which traces its origin to John Wesley in 18th century England. Benjamin Titus Roberts, the leader in the founding of the Free Methodist Church in mid-19th century America, intended that it continue faithful to the doctrines and practices of Wesley.[12] Thus we Free Methodists look to John Wesley as our theological father.[13]

The Roots of the Free Methodist Church in Historic Orthodoxy

Wesleyanism is a movement within the larger Christian family and teaches the same essential orthodox truths Christians have always believed. We affirm such central doctrines as the holy Trinity, the full deity and full humanity of Christ, the sinfulness of human beings, the transforming grace of God and God's ultimate triumph over sin and evil. These teachings have been believed by millions of Christians over the centuries on every continent, as Wesleyans know very well.

We believe that the teachings just mentioned and other central ones like them are securely grounded within the Scriptures, which we, along with many other Christians, gladly acknowledge as the primary source and final authority of Christian teaching.

23

We look back, as did Wesley and most Christian traditions, to the great teachers of the first centuries. Among these are well-known figures, such as Athanasius, Chrysostom and Augustine. We also include lesser-known ones, such as Irenaeus, Gregory of Nyssa, Basil and Leo the Great. Also, we look to the great councils of the same era, such as Nicea and Chalcedon. We do not try to reinvent classic Christian teaching nor claim that we explain it better than most Christians do, but we gratefully thank God for those who historically stated these doctrines in clear fashion.

The Roots of the Free Methodist Church in Protestantism

However, Wesleyans do more than simply look to the early centuries. We have deep respect for devout Catholics such as Thomas Aquinas (13th century) and Madame Guyon (17th century); for Reformers on the European continent such as Martin Luther and John Calvin; and in England such as Thomas Cranmer and Richard Hooker. We also have high regard for 17th and 18th century Puritans such as Richard Baxter and Jonathan Edwards; and for 18th century pietists such as Peter Böhler and Count von Zinzendorf. The list could go on. We learn from them all, though not all to the same degree nor in the same way.

While Wesleyanism did not arise from one of the three European branches of Protestantism (Lutheranism, Calvinism or the Anabaptists), it does belong to the Protestant family. Wesley was a child of the Church of England and drank deeply from her theology found in the Edwardian and Elizabethan homilies, the Book of Common Prayer and the Anglican respect for primitive Christianity. His early family training also included the influence of English Puritanism. At an important time in his development, Wesley was profoundly influenced by German pietists. Further, after him and on this side of the Atlantic Ocean, we see the rise of camp-meeting revivalism and the holiness movement with leaders such as

Phoebe Palmer and Charles Finney, who have left their marks on the Methodist family. The formation of 20th century Wesleyan theology is multifaceted.

However, we should not assume that mature Wesleyanism is no more than the sum of its parts, a conglomeration from theological eclecticism. No, there is a credible order and logic to the way we gather materials, think about them and work out theology.

In this work I hope to show that the Wesleyan way of thinking about theology contributes to theological discourse. Our primary task is to display the broad sweep of historic orthodox theology as understood from the Wesleyan perspective.

2. THE CONTEMPORARY THEOLOGICAL SCENE

Another purpose of this work is to consider the relation of our theology to the contemporary world. Over the last few centuries the world of ideas has hardly stood still; an explosion of information has ushered in the scientific revolution.

But change has not been limited to the physical sciences and technology. It has also appeared in disciplines closely related to theology such as philosophy and biblical studies. Philosophical atheism – the denial that any supernatural being exists – is commonplace in major universities. In many theological seminaries that train future pastors, it is also common to be instructed in radical biblical criticism. Such an approach to the study of the Scriptures, for example, might say that Jesus of Nazareth did not actually rise from the dead.

Sorting through the different philosophical and theological schools is a complicated task. It has taken place, largely as it should, in the academic world. Most who sit in church pews Sunday after Sunday do not know the details of these schools, nor for that matter do many care to know them. However, none of us has escaped their influence. Outside the church the different philosophies and theologies have worked their way into the popular scene through the media, influencing the way Christians, as well as non-Christians, tend to think about God and Christian teaching.

Challenges of yet another sort confront orthodox Christianity. Cults, such as Jehovah's Witnesses and Mormons, continue to win tens of thousands of followers. The recent growth of new ageism, which once was only on the fringe of society, astonishes us. This movement, which draws on various religions of the East and uses astrology and mediums combined with an optimistic view of human nature, has found a home in the West.

The cults and new ageism, generally speaking, did not originate in the debates in the university. But their actual impact on the masses of modern people often exceeds that of professional philosophers and theologians.

A study of systematic theology that can help us respond to the challenges of contemporary culture must be carefully thought through. History teaches that this challenge presents two dangers, either of which could limit the effectiveness of a theology. The first danger is to ignore these challenges; the second is to be overly impressed with them. Broadside accusations that condemn ideas without understanding their logic or appeal rarely dispel their influence. On the other hand, endorsement without clearly understanding presuppositions and implications usually ends in profound error. All too commonly, theology students turn to questions raised by contemporary culture before they have laid a solid foundation in historic Christianity. Having just begun to know the rudiments of Christian teaching, they assume they understand its logic.

3. SPECIAL FEATURES OF THIS THEOLOGY

A Compendium of Systematic Theology. This work is organized as a systematic theology. That is, it follows a topical arrangement. For example, it discusses all the issues related to questions about Jesus, the Son of God, before it moves on to discuss the issues related to the church.

We distinguish a "compendium" from other kinds of systematic theologies as follows. An outline of theology gives the structure and main points of a theological system but does not enter into full discussion of the issues involved. A multivolume theology explores at great length, the issues involved but has the disadvantage of being too long and too technical to help most students. A compendium seeks to give a full-enough discussion so that the basic issues are exposed and the logic of the theology is clear yet is of manageable length.

Documentation. Since the Scriptures are the primary source for our theology, documentation for them will be included within the text of the book. Documentation for other sources will be given in notes. A study of the notes will indicate a rich use of the principal teachers of the church, as Thomas Oden rightly suggests we should follow. We will depend in particular on those of the early centuries and on those in the Wesleyan family such as Fletcher, Pope and Wiley.

Inclusive Language. We use inclusive language for human beings throughout this work.[14] But we do not apply this rule when speaking of God. Neither the Bible nor the historic church thought of God as having gender,[15] but they also never adopted the position that we ought to use male and female language forms for God interchangeably. That is, they did not speak of God as "Mother" in tandem with "Father" and "she" in tandem with "he." The biblical authors used female and mother imagery for God such as the psalmist describing the relation of God to the humble Hebrew as that of a weaned child with its mother (Psalm 131; see Isaiah 42:13f.). But their refusal to use explicit female names or pronouns for God grew from the struggle within Israel against encroachments by Baalism, a fertility cult in a clearly patriarchal society. The wisdom of Israel and the church in their historical position on this question has yet to be fully appreciated in our own time.

Biblical Criticism. Answers to questions raised by biblical criticism will largely be assumed within this work. For example, this is not an appropriate place to give an extended discussion on whether Paul wrote the Prison Epistles. Those who want to pursue those questions in depth should consult works that address them more specifically.

Format of this Theology. This work has been designed to assist readers in following the discussion as much as possible. Hence, we have included numerous divisions and subdivisions. We have also included summaries at the conclusion of nearly every section within the work.[16] A name and a topic glossary at the end of the book should be consulted when readers come across something unfamiliar. The Scripture and topic indexes can be consulted for the quick location of discussions.

4. THE CHARACTER OF THIS THEOLOGY

Because of the needs that called for this work, it is designed as a teaching and resource document and focuses on building a solid theological system. It therefore emphasizes foundational issues in the broad sweep of Christian teaching. Because the foundation of Christian theology is in the Scriptures, we will think about the relevant Scriptures on which its teachings are based and explore their implications. We will consult the formative theology of the first five centuries of the Christian era. At appropriate places we will talk about the teachings of the great thinkers in the medieval era, the Reformation, Puritanism, and pietism and elsewhere. The Wesleyan roots of this theology will be obvious throughout, at times explicitly and at others times only implicitly. Finally, this work will indicate how our theology responds to questions raised on the contemporary scene.

5. THE OUTLINE OF THIS THEOLOGY

This theology will be divided into six parts. Parts one and two appear in the present volume, parts three through six will appear in a second volume to be published at a later date. The six parts are as follows:

Part I. will treat the task of theology, including the elements in the Wesleyan quadrilateral.

Part II. will consider the doctrine of God, including the Trinity, creation, Christology and Pneumatology.

Part III. will look at the doctrines of human nature and sin.

Part IV. will examine ecclesiology, including the orders of the church, the sacraments, the means of grace and the mission of the church.

Part V. will consider soteriology, including prevenient grace, justification, regeneration and entire sanctification.

Part VI. will explore eschatology, including the doctrines of the return of Christ, the resurrection and the judgment.

SUMMARY: *The Character of this Theology*

1. The Free Methodist Church belongs to the Methodist family whose members look to John Wesley as their founder. Our roots reach back through the Church of England to historic Christian orthodoxy. We have also been significantly influenced by European Protestantism, pietism and American revivalism.

2. This book seeks to respond to religious and theological challenges of the contemporary world, including philosophical atheism, radical biblical criticism, the cults and new ageism.

3. We will use inclusive language when referring to persons and the traditional language when referring to God.

4. Because of the needs to which this work responds, it seeks to be primarily a teaching document that grounds its theology in the Scriptures, the great doctrines of historic Christian and the concerns of Wesleyanism.

ENDNOTES

[1] Pope, *CCT*, 1:14f.

[2] Dunning, *GFH*, 123.

[3] Hendry, *TWBB*, 193-95; Oepke, *TDNT*, 3:571-92.

[4] Hilary, *Trin.* 5:21f., *NPNF* 2:9:91.

[5] Oden, *LG*, 151f.

[6] John of Damascus, *EOF* 1:1, *NPNF*, 2:9:1f.

[7] Barth, *CD* 1/1, 98-111.

[8] Pope, *CCT*, 1:36-41.

[9] Thorsen, *WQ*, 226-51.

[10] Outler, "The Wesleyan Quadrilateral – in John Wesley," *WTH*, 21-37.

[11] Wesley, "Preface" to *Sermons on Several Occasions*, *WJWB*, 1:104f.

[12] "Preface" to *BD*, 1860, iii-xii.

[13] Marston, *FAA*, 19-103.

[14] Roberts, *OW*.

[15] Ambrose, *ECF* 3:63; *NPNF* 2:10:251f.

[16] See *CCC*.

CHAPTER

THE HOLY SCRIPTURES

SECTION I. THE AUTHORITY OF THE SCRIPTURES

1. The Subject Matter of the Scriptures
2. The Authors of the Scriptures
   A. The Source of Authority of Biblical Authors, I. Those Who Describe their Authorization
   B. The Source of Authority of Biblical Authors, II. The Origin of Other Words in Scripture
   C. The Authority of all the Authors Based on Divine Inspiration
3. A Modern Challenge to the Historic View

SECTION II. THE CANON OF THE SCRIPTURES

1. The Old Testament Canon
   A. The Early Church's Acceptance of the Old Testament
   B. The Debate Whether the Hebrew Bible or the Greek Old Testament Should Be Recognized as the Canon
2. The New Testament Canon
   A. Ecclesiastical Debates over Books
   B. Criteria for the Canon

SECTION III. THE RELIABILITY OF THE SCRIPTURES

1. The Truthfulness of the Scriptures
2. The Human Word in the Bible
3. Challenges to the Truthfulness of the Scriptures
4. Accommodation
5. Progressive Revelation
6. The Interpretation of the Scriptures

THE HISTORIC POSITION ON THE AUTHORITY OF THE SCRIPTURES

The historic position of the church has always been that the Scriptures speak the truth and speak authoritatively.[1] For example, when the Scriptures speak about matters we can know only by faith, such as what is the nature of God or when they tell us that a historical event happened, we accept their witness as reliable. And when the Scriptures address ethical questions such as the prohibition against stealing, we heed their words as representing the will of God.

THE MODERN CHALLENGE TO THE STUDY OF THE SCRIPTURES

However, over the past two centuries the study of the Scriptures has taken a new turn. In particular the application of critical historical methods to the study of the Bible has resulted in new views of the Bible. Some of these have been of positive value to the church. But others have questioned the Scriptures' reliability and undermined their authority. As a result this new approach to the Scriptures has challenged teachings that were founded on the belief that the Scriptures are reliable and authoritative.

On the one hand, from a positive side critical studies have enabled us to reconstruct the historical settings of the Bible more clearly. Thus, we can describe, for example, the cultural and religious worlds from which the patriarchs came. Or we can understand the world the early church encountered as it took its message to the Gentiles. This insight into the historical settings of the Bible helps us grasp more clearly its thought forms and hence its teachings.

On the other hand, such critical studies have also cast doubt on scriptural teachings the church has historically taught as true and considered crucial.[2] For example, events the Bible reports as historical, such as the virgin conception of Jesus, have been denied by notable theologians[3] on what they propose are substantial grounds from biblical scholars.[4] Also, skeptical criticism has caused the erosion of the Scriptures' authority to speak clearly on ethical questions. For example, the Scriptures' declaration that certain kinds of sexual activity are in all cases contrary to the will of God is often denied as an absolute and binding standard.[5]

THE FREE METHODIST CHURCH'S VIEW OF THE SCRIPTURES

The Free Methodist Church does not neglect the positive results of historical biblical studies. But it holds to its historic view that the Scriptures are both authoritative and reliable. In 1989 the worldwide church adopted a revised form of its article of religion on the Scriptures. This revised article affirms the following concerning the Bible:

- that it is the trustworthy record of God's revelation completely truthful in all it affirms;
- that its authors were uniquely inspired by the Holy Spirit;
- that it has come to us through human authors who wrote, as God moved them, in the languages and literary forms of their times;
- that it has complete authority over all human life;

- that it teaches the truth about God, His creation, His people, His one and only Son, and the destiny of all mankind.

SECTION I. *The Authority of the Scriptures*

1. THE SUBJECT MATTER OF THE SCRIPTURES

The Scriptures contain two kinds of statements:

- They report historical events in which God acted savingly for humankind. Thus, God disclosed himself uniquely first to Israel, then in Jesus Christ, and then to the early church. Among these three the revelation in Jesus Christ is the central saving and revelatory act of God. The Scriptures are the primary source we have of God's self-disclosure in history, since they report the story of God's saving work.

- Beyond historical events, they also interpret the meaning of God's historical self-disclosure. Thus, they offer theological understanding for these saving events. Also, the Scriptures speak broadly to other questions. They have a good deal to say about ethical questions. They address timeless and enduring issues such as the sanctity of marriage, the nature of the family, the meaning and uses of wealth, the importance of nature and other significant topics.

Revelation in Salvation History

Throughout scriptural history God disclosed Himself as He worked on His people's behalf.[6] For example, the Scriptures frequently speak of God's "arm" to illustrate his powerful intervention (Exodus 6:6; Deuteronomy 5:15; Psalms 44:3; Isaiah 40:11; and Jeremiah 21:5).

But the Scriptures report special events in which God acted uniquely for the ultimate salvation of humankind: the call of the patriarchs, the Exodus from Egypt and the giving of the law at Sinai, the conquest of Canaan, the monarchy, the Exile and return from Babylon; the life, ministry, death, and resurrection of Jesus of Nazareth; and the early days of the apostolic church.

We can focus on two of this great series of events as the core saving events. First, within the Old Testament era our attention centers around the Exodus and the giving of the law to Moses (Exodus 6:6f.). Second, within the New Testament it centers around the ministry, death and resurrection of Jesus (1 John 1:2; Hebrews 1:1f.). In these two especially, God made Himself known through what He did. Biblical revelation finds its center in historical events.

The Interpretation of Saving Events

God's revelation was not confined to the saving events of biblical history. It also came through ideas and words. The meaning of an event was interpreted so that its precise significance was made clear. The Bible is full of these interpretations of God's central, saving acts.[7]

For example, Paul said, "Christ died for our sins according to the Scriptures" (1 Corinthians 15:3). The first part of that statement, that Christ died, announces a historical event. But the bare announcement of a historical event is not enough. A secular, first-century Roman historian, Tacitus, made this point.[8] However, Tacitus could not explain the significance of Christ's death. The second part of Paul's statement, that He died for "our sins," does interpret that great historical event. This interpretation could arise only because God revealed it to the apostle.

Throughout history, the church has taught both. First, the crucial, saving events it reports actually occurred. And second, the meanings applied to them by the prophets and apostles are correct. God is the source of both the events and their interpretations. God revealed Himself in what He did, and He revealed what His acts meant.

Other Words in the Scriptures

Beyond the events of salvation history and the interpretation of these events are a good many things that the Scriptures discuss. For example, they describe for us the origins of the world (Genesis 1-2; Psalm 8). While investigations of physical science can tell us a good deal about our universe, they cannot displace the precious knowledge that the Scriptures alone give of God's creating work and the relationship of His creation to Him.

The discussions in the wisdom literature of the Bible, such as the Proverbs offer insights into human life with immense practical value.[9] They speak about the relationship of humans among one another and about self-control, hard work, integrity and humility. Much the same can be said of the directives of the apostle James. Thus, portions of the Scriptures like these also give us a true, authoritative word from God.

The predictions of the end of history, though by no means easy to explain, teach us that God will sovereignly bring history as we know it to an end and create a renewed world. The historic church has always accepted apocalyptic teachings about such things as God's judgment upon the nations and his promise of the new heavens and the new earth. That is, it has held that these teachings are articles of faith that can be trusted as true and authentic.[10]

2. THE AUTHORS OF THE SCRIPTURES

Because of the importance of the Scriptures, their authors are brought into great prominence. Since the Scriptures are authoritative, those who wrote them have a unique place in the plan of God's revelation to humankind.

Therefore, we should examine the authority granted to the authors of the Scriptures. How can these people speak for God, His acts and His will in a way that other people cannot? Or why do they speak authoritatively and why should we rely upon their witness in a way that goes beyond our trust in what other people might say? Why are they unique in all of history?

Such inquiry into the authority of those who speak for God has been the case from the time of the Scriptures themselves. Even before Moses received the law from God on Sinai, for example, he knew that his leadership would be challenged. Thus, he inquired of God, "Who am I, that I should go to Pharaoh and bring the Israelites out of Egypt?" (Exodus 3:11). The response of God, "I will be with you," (3:12) indicates that Moses acted under divine authorization.

The broad principle that stands behind the authority of the Scriptures is as follows: The Scriptures are the written words of those whom God has authorized and enabled to speak for Him.

A. The Source of Authority of Biblical Authors, I. Those Who Describe their Authorization

Authors of the majority of the Scriptures asserted that they spoke authoritatively, that is, with full and legitimate empowerment from God. They did not enter into their task grasping for power but were granted it from God Himself. For example, Paul, while acknowledging the spiritual maturity of Roman Christians to whom he wrote, still claimed an apostolic authority over them. "I have written quite boldly on some points," he said, "because of the grace God gave me to be a minister of Christ Jesus to the Gentiles" (Romans 15:15f.). This self-conscious authority of the scriptural writers is everywhere evident. What did they point to in support of this authority?[11]

The Unique Calls of Those Who Spoke for God

Moses. God appeared to Moses at Sinai and commissioned him to lead Israel out of Egypt (Exodus 3.2-4:17; 5:22ff.). What Moses said in his debates with Pharaoh and in leading the people from Egypt derived from the authority granted in this theophany (an appearance of God). He had seen God and talked with him.[12]

The Prophets. The three major prophets, Isaiah, Jeremiah and Ezekiel, each encountered God and was called by him to a prophetic ministry (Isaiah 6; Jeremiah 1; Ezekiel 1-3). Thus, like Moses, the prophets' call came in an encounter with God.[13]

The Apostles. The authority of the disciples derived from their time with Jesus during His earthly ministry. Jesus empowered them to do the same kinds of work that He was doing and "appointed twelve – designating them apostles" (Mark 3:14-15; see Mark 6:6b-13; Matthew 10:1-4; Luke 6:12-16). The work of the disciples was then extended beyond the life of Jesus by additional authorization (John 21:15-17).[14]

The appearances of the resurrected Christ to His disciples and to Paul are comparable to the appearances of God to Moses and the prophets – the theophanies. In the case of the apostles, we speak of christophanies (appearances of the risen Christ; Matthew 28:16-20; Luke 24:36-49; John 20:19-23; Acts 1:21-22; 1 Corinthians 15:8; Galatians 1:11-17; 2:1-10).

The difference between Moses' theophanies and the apostles' christophanies should not escape us. The disciples during Jesus' life watched Him minister in Israel; they were sent out by Him to extend His work; they watched Him suffer and die. The risen Christ who appeared to them was also the one who taught them and whose ministry they had observed. Behind the christophany lies the wonder of the Incarnation.

Thus, the appearances of God to the authors of Old Testament books and the appearances of the risen Christ to the authors of New Testament books became the foundation for Israel and Christianity. After God appeared to Moses, we have a nation called Israel and its law. After Christ appeared to His followers, we have the church and its gospel.

The Common Experience of Moses, the Prophets and the Apostles

Moses. After the Lord called Moses to lead Israel from Egypt and the people had crossed the Red Sea, He again appeared to Moses on Sinai and gave him the Torah. Through the long section of Exodus 19-Numbers 10:10, new units of commandments are introduced with clauses like, "The Lord said to Moses" (Exodus 25:1; see 30:17; Leviticus 1:1; 8:1; Numbers 1:1). The text states that Moses first received the Ten Commandments, and then he received many additional statutes and commandments. While still at Sinai, he had renewed theophanies (see Exodus 33:7-11; 34:29-35). Conversations between the Lord and Moses during the wilderness period of forty years seem to occur in theophanies too (Numbers 11:10-23).

The Prophets. Typically, the prophets preface their messages with expressions like "the word of the Lord" (Jeremiah 1:4; Ezekiel 6:1; Hosea 1:1; Joel 1:1; John 1:1; Zephaniah 1:1; Zechariah 1:1) or "the Lord says" (Haggai 1:2; see Isaiah 45:1; Amos 1:9). They also declare on occasion that they have received a "vision" (Ezekiel 1:1) or an "oracle" from God (Habakkuk 1:1; Malachi 1:1). These variant forms in which the prophets describe the source of their messages all emphasize the same two points. First, the message has come from God; second, it therefore has His authority behind it.

The Apostles. Usually, the apostolic letter begins with a reference to its author as a "servant" (Philippians 1:1; James 1:1) or an "apostle" (2 Timothy 1:1; 1 Peter 1:1) or even a "prisoner of Jesus Christ" (Ephesians 3:1). The apostles had roles of continuing service to Christ since they were commissioned as his representatives. John began his first letter pointing to the time he had spent with Jesus during his earthly life as the basis for his authority (1 John 1:1-3). Peter at one point mentions the privilege he enjoyed to see Christ's transfiguration as a source of authority for him (2 Peter 1:16-18; see Mark 9:2ff.). Luke established the authority for his account of the Gospel on his meticulous consultation with those who had been "eyewitnesses and ministers of the word." That is, his sources had seen the events reported in the Gospel and had become their first proclaimers (Luke 1:2f.). Paul believed himself authorized to speak for Christ over the course of his entire ministry. While he taught that all Christians receive the Spirit of God, he also claimed a singular authority for himself (Romans 15:15f.; 1 Corinthians 1:16).

B.   The Source of Authority of Biblical Authors,
II. The Origin of the Other Words in Scripture

Other words appear in the Bible that do not claim for themselves divine origin. As an example, we take the historical writings of the Old Testament. The books of Joshua through Kings are documents that have come to us without any claim to divine authorization. The same applies to the wisdom books of the Old Testament. For example, the introduction to the Proverbs (1:1-7) points to the authority of intellectual activity and tradition. Also, several prominent books in the New Testament do not come from the pen of an apostle. Luke bases his Gospel on his research (1:1-4). No author is identified in the case of the epistle to the Hebrews. These and other portions not attributed to a particular writer found their way into the canonical Scriptures, and the church has always acknowledged that their authority derived from God.[15]

40

C. The Authority of All the Authors Based on Divine Inspiration

Traditional theology has correctly pointed out that Paul's claim in 2 Timothy 3:16 speaks to the authority of all the Scriptures. This passage explicitly states that "all Scripture is God-breathed." In a comparable fashion, Peter writes about the prophets whose words found their way into the Scriptures. Their prophecy, he claims, did not have "its origin in the will of man, but men spoke from God as they were carried along by the Holy Spirit" (2 Peter 1:20f.). Both Paul and Peter had in mind the Old Testament Scriptures when they made their statements. However, as the books of the New Testament became known, they also were accepted as inspired in the same manner as the Old Testament Scriptures. Peter acknowledged this of Paul's letters, even when he found passages within them difficult to understand and which the careless could easily abuse (2 Peter 3:15f.). Thus, all Scriptures within the canon have the authority of God behind them since all of them are inspired.

The inspiration of the Scriptures refers to a unique work of God's Spirit on the authors of the Scriptures. A genuine form of inspiration may be claimed for great hymns or sermons or creeds because God's Spirit assisted the authors in writing them. But the inspiration of the Scriptures is in a class by itself; they are uniquely inspired.[16] There are two dimensions to this work of the Holy Spirit in the cases of scriptural authors, divine authorization and divine guidance. Thus, inspiration relates to:

- divine authorization of the authors of the Scriptures
- divine guidance of the authors so that they wrote clearly and accurately

It is the first of these that we are now considering.

3. A MODERN CHALLENGE TO THE HISTORIC VIEW

The Psychology of Religious Authorities

Some modern critics have attempted to discredit the historic Christian understanding of how those who wrote the Scriptures were authorized. They have done so by pointing to the psychology of religious experiences. They observe that founders of other religions are also often said to have had extraordinary religious experiences. Such applies to Muhammed of Islam and Gautama of Buddhism.[17] By making the experiences of Moses, the prophets, and the apostles fit into the same psychological category, these critics attempt to neutralize the theological value the church has historically seen in the calls of Moses, the prophets and the apostles. Such critics may accept that the Scriptures have value for us today. Often they will refer to the ancient authors as "religious geniuses." But they will deny that God called them or Christ called them in the way the church has always understood. In other words, the critics may claim that the authors of the Scriptures do not have an authorization from God as the church has taught that they do.[18]

The Theology of Authorization

The Scriptures describe their authors as persons uniquely called and inspired to speak for God. Those who received the calls believed in all seriousness that they had encountered God in a special way. Precisely because their experiences were incomparable, they were set apart as those who spoke for God. They had seen God or the risen Lord in a way that normal people do not. He had appeared to them. They did not discover Him nor did they look for Him. Instead, they found themselves drawn into His presence.

Not only the recipients of these calls were convinced that something extraordinary had occurred to them and that this was the source of their authority, people whom they addressed also accepted it. The proper response to the messages of those who had been called and inspired was not imitation but attentive hearing. They were to believe that these people spoke for God because God in His sovereign wisdom and power had chosen to speak through them, had appeared and commissioned them, had given them messages and had inspired them. Thus, their words had a divine origin and authority.[19]

SUMMARY: *The Authority of the Scriptures*

1. The church has historically recognized that the Scriptures are authoritative and reliable.

2. The primary focus of the Scriptures is to report God's saving action in crucial events. The central events in the Old Testament are the Exodus from Egypt and revelation at Sinai; and in the New Testament the life, ministry, death and resurrection of Jesus Christ.

3. The Scriptures also give the authoritative interpretation of the crucial saving actions of God.

4. The Scriptures contain other words beyond those that report and interpret the crucial events of salvation history. These words also are authoritative.

5. Moses, the prophets and the apostles were called of God to speak and hence write for him. Their authorization was these encounters with God and Christ.

6. The Scriptures also teach that all their authors, whether an account of their calling is recorded or not, were inspired and thereby enabled to speak for God.

SECTION II. *The Canon of the Scriptures*

The term "canon" comes from the Greek word *kanon*, which referred to a rod or bar designed to keep things straight. The canon of the Scriptures, thus, denotes those writings that have been accepted as normative.[20]

THE NEW TESTAMENT

Which books are canonical? The answer differs in Christendom for the two Testaments. All Christians accept the same 27 books for the New Testament. Thus, Roman Catholics, Greek Orthodox and Protestants all receive the same list of books as canonical:

- The four accounts of the Gospel
- The Acts of the Apostles
- The 13 letters of Paul
- The eight general letters
- The Revelation of John

THE OLD TESTAMENT

But Christian bodies differ on the books that should be included in the Old Testament list. All accept the 39 books found in the Hebrew Bible (24 as Jews count them):

- There are five books in the Pentateuch;
- The Prophets are divided into two units: the Former Prophets (Joshua, Judges, Samuel and Kings) and the Latter Prophets (Isaiah, Jeremiah, Ezekiel and the Scroll of the Twelve);
- The Writings included the following: the Psalms, two wisdom books (Job and Proverbs), five festival books (Ruth, Song of Solomon, Ecclesiastes, Lamentations and Esther), Daniel and two historical books (Ezra-Nehemiah and Chronicles);

The Roman Catholic and Eastern Orthodox churches, however, accept additional books as canonical, those that are found in the Greek Old Testament Bible.[21] Protestants refer to these additional books as the Apocrypha; Roman Catholics as Deuterocanonical.

1. THE OLD TESTAMENT CANON

A. The Early Church's Acceptance of the Old Testament

The New Testament bears abundant evidence that the early church received the Old Testament in agreement with most Jews of that time. The Pharisees and the common people accepted the threefold form of the Hebrew Bible – that is, the law, the prophets and the writings – (Luke 24:44); the Sadducees accepted only the law (Mark 12:18-23).[22]

The practices of the earliest church established the Hebrew Bible as authoritative. Jesus, Paul, Peter and the author of the letter to the Hebrews all cite from each portion of the Hebrew Scriptures, thus treating all as canonical:[23]

- The law (Mark 12:26 [Exodus 3:6]; Romans 4:3 [Genesis 15:6]; Acts 3:25 [Genesis 22:18]; Hebrews 10:30 [Deuteronomy 32:35])
- The prophets (Mark 7:6 [Isaiah 29:13]; Romans 1:17 [Habakkuk 2:4]; 1 Peter 2:22 [Isaiah 53:9]; Hebrews 10:16 [Isaiah 31:33])
- The writings (Mark 12:36 [Psalms 110:1]; Romans 4:7f. [Psalms 32:1f.]; 1 Peter 1:18 [Proverbs 11:31]; Hebrew 12:5f. [Proverbs 3:11f.])

No New Testament passage can be cited that sets aside a portion of the Hebrew Bible as non-canonical. Jesus' remark, "You have heard that it was said to the people long ago ... but I tell you," does not nullify the authority of the Old Testament. Instead, the New Testament enriches the Old Testament (Matthew 5:21). This is explained by his statement: "Do not think that I have come to abolish the Law or the Prophets; I have not come to abolish them but to fulfill them. I tell you the truth, until heaven and earth disappear, not the smallest letter, not the least stroke of a pen will by any means disappear from the Law until everything is accomplished" (Matthew 5:17f.).

Even Paul's words, which are among the strongest in the New Testament, cannot be understood to neutralize the authority of the Old Testament. His comment in Romans 10:4, "Christ is the end of the law so that there may be righteousness for everyone who believes," can be placed in context by other passages. For example, in Romans 3:31 Paul shows that the Old Testament cannot be set aside when he says, "Do we, then, nullify the law by this faith? Not at all! Rather, we uphold the law." And in Romans 15:4 he shows its relevance when he points out, "For everything that was written in the past was written to teach us so that through endurance and the encouragement of the Scriptures we might have hope."

The only serious challenge to the Christian church's adopting the Old Testament came from a second century heretic, Marcion.[24] Marcion believed himself to be a follower of Paul, but his heresy came about from taking out of context Paul's criticisms of Judaizing Christians. From the earliest records and on through the centuries, we learn that reading from the Old Testament was a regular part of Christian worship – a clear and indisputable witness to the church's acceptance of the Old Testament's canonical status.

B.   The Debate Whether the Hebrew Bible or the Greek Old Testament Should Be Recognized as the Canon

The Greek Old Testament

The Greek version of the Old Testament was actually made by Jews who were of the Diaspora, that is, who lived in lands other than the Holy Land. By the time of Christ, there were large numbers of these Jews who spoke predominantly in Greek. Alexandria, Egypt, had an immense population of non-Hebrew-speaking Jews, and the Jews of this city undertook the task of translating the Bible into Greek in the second century B.C. The completed translation is called the "Septuagint," meaning seventy, named for the 70 men who reputedly worked on the project.[25] Besides offering a Greek translation of the books found in the Hebrew Bible, however, the Greek version also contained a number of new books plus additions to several canonical books. As noted earlier, these are the books that Protestants call the Apocrypha and Roman Catholics call the Deuterocanonical books.

The Early Gentile Church Adopted the Greek Old Testament; this Practice Was Continued by the Roman Catholic and Greek Orthodox Churches

When the early church became predominantly gentile and Greek-speaking, it quickly adopted the Septuagint as its form of the Old Testament. In fact, the New Testament itself reflects the influence of the Septuagint. Paul regularly uses it when he cites from the Old Testament. For him the Greek Old Testament is Scripture.[26]

After the apostolic period, the church fathers rarely noted the differences between the Hebrew Bible and the Septuagint, though the more learned did know they differed.[27] Jerome, Athanasius and Augustine refused to give the apocryphal books the same status as the others. However, common practice prevailed, and the acceptance of the Greek Old Testament rather than the more restricted Hebrew Bible passed into the Roman Catholic Church and Greek Orthodox churches without serious debate.[28]

Protestants Accepted Only the Hebrew Canon

At the time of the Reformation, however, the differences between the two lists of books (the Hebrew and the Greek) came under scrutiny. In most cases, the issue was largely doctrinal. Second Maccabees 12:44-45, for example, supports the practice of praying for the dead. The reformers objected to this teaching along with other teachings and so deleted from the Protestant Bible the extra books found in the Septuagint.[29]

47

2. THE NEW TESTAMENT CANON

The Christian acceptance of the Old Testament canon is based on the usage given it by our Lord and the apostles. The church did not have this advantage when it came to the books it should accept for the New Testament. However, from very early times the church did have documents it turned to because it believed them authoritative.

A. Ecclesiastical Debates over Books

In the earliest years, certain books were accepted and used in the church without serious debate. Justin Martyr tells us, for example, that the typical worship of his time included readings from "the memoirs of the apostles and the writings of the prophets."[30]

However, common practice received its first sharp challenge in the middle of the second century near the time Justin was writing. Marcion, who, as we noted, rejected the Old Testament altogether, also rejected many of the New Testament books. So far as he was concerned, only Paul understood the gospel correctly; the other apostles were captive to Jewish legalism. Marcion chose his own canon – which, he claimed, taught the truth. He accepted ten of Paul's letters and Luke's Gospel. He even edited the books he selected by deleting portions he believed to contain errors.[31]

The response of the church to Marcion was strong. In the first place Marcion's teaching was declared heretical. In the second place, the authority of other books in the New Testament, without his deletions, was confirmed.

The debate raised by Marcion set church leaders to work on identifying the canonical Christian Scriptures. Over the next two centuries, various church leaders offered their lists of canonical books. Among the more important the following three are crucial:

- The Muratorian Canon (late second century)[32]

- Eusebius (early fourth century)[33]
- Athanasius (A.D. 367)[34]

The Muratorian Canon offers the oldest list we have by those who were considered orthodox. Eusebius' list is valuable because it displays the state of the debate at his time. He placed the books in categories that indicated various church leaders' opinions of them. Some books all leaders accepted as canonical, some that all rejected, and some that were accepted by some and rejected by others. Athanasius' list is found in his thirty-ninth festal letter (the letter of the bishop to his congregation at Easter). His is the first list that records precisely the 27 books that became the standard.

However, we should not assume that for the three and one-half centuries before Athanasius there was great instability about the canon. By the middle of the second century, the four Gospels, the Acts of the Apostles, the thirteen letters of Paul, 1 Peter and two letters of John were universally accepted.[35] For various reasons, Hebrews, the book of Revelation, 2 Peter and Jude were disputed, being accepted only by some but rejected by others.[36] From the time of Athanasius on, however, all new lists agreed with the list he had made.

B. CRITERIA FOR THE CANON

Upon what basis did the church decide to include particular books within its canon? That is, why did the church receive the books it did receive while rejecting others?[37]

Apostolicity

For a book to be considered canonical, it had to have apostolic authority. The mark of *apostolicity* could come in more than one way. The work might be directly written by an apostle. Or it might be a book that had his authority behind it. Romans, for example, came from Paul's hand (or at least from the hand of his scribe). But in a number of instances, New Testament books were written by someone other than an apostle, so apostolicity was claimed in other ways. For example, Mark was not an apostle, but he was linked with Peter in the early second century by Papias.[38] Similarly, Luke was linked to Paul. Apostolicity for the early church did not require, then, that a book had to be written by an apostle for it to be included in the canon.

Conformity to the Rule of Faith

From the very first the church had apostolic teaching. This teaching was given in oral form before it was embedded in written form in the books we now have within the New Testament. Luke tells us, for example, that after the day of Pentecost those who made up the church "devoted themselves to the apostles' teaching" (Acts 1:42). This apostolic tradition formed the core of teaching that was given to new converts in new places. It was universally disseminated and universally known as the heart of Christian faith.

Early fathers of the church remark that the apostolic teaching went from apostles to the next generations through successive chains. The bishop of Lyons, Irenaeus (late second century), in particular, provides valuable information on these chains. For example, he notes that Polycarp (early second century) "was not only instructed by apostles, and conversed with many who had seen Christ, but was also, by apostles in Asia, appointed bishop of the Church of Smyrna." Irenaeus goes on to tell us that when he was a young man, he was taught by Polycarp, who was then an old man. Thus, the tradition that Polycarp taught is that which he had learned from the apostles and in turn handed on Irenaeus.[39] Irenaeus used this idea of an apostolic tradition transmitted from the apostles to their successors when he had to debate with heretics. The heretics claimed that their views were found in the Scriptures. Irenaeus countered that he knew these heretical interpretations were wrong because he had direct linkage through his teacher to the authors of the New Testament. Through this teacher he had been taught what the apostles had in mind when they wrote their books.

Similarly, the church could reject a book that claimed to be written by an apostle if it held heretical views. The leaders of the church knew what the apostles taught, and even though a book might ascribe to itself an apostolic origin, if its teaching departed from the "rule of faith," its claim was rejected. Thus, the church was protected from adopting many books into its canon that are attributed to apostles but are clearly inferior in quality and contain teachings contrary to apostolic thought.[40]

The Use of the Churches

During the early centuries of the church, the books we know as canonical surfaced as special because of their prominent use in the churches. That is, most Christian churches over a wide geographical area and over an extended time used these books in worship and in the formation of doctrine. The numerous citations from the canonical Scriptures in the doctrinal arguments of the fathers attest to this use. The same judgment applies to their recorded sermons. Gregory of Nazianzus' five *Theological Orations* are rich in the Scriptures. For the volumes in the *Nicene and Post-Nicene Fathers* devoted to Augustine and to Chrysostom, three belonging to the former and five to the latter offer expository sermons from the canonical Scriptures.

Luther, Calvin and Wesley were all biblical preachers. The documentation of Wesley's use of the Scriptures in his preaching in the recently published bicentennial edition of his works (*WJWB*) demonstrates this.

The Witness of the Spirit

A corollary to this idea of church use arises from God Himself, for God testifies to the canonicity of individual books in the Scriptures. The very concept of *canon* and the use that these books have enjoyed over the centuries arises in no small measure from the fact that they are attested by God. When we read them, we sense that we are in touch with a word that has an authority no human nor group of humans could give by their own action. God speaks in these books. If he had not done so in the past and continued to do so in the present, we would not think of them as the Word of God in the way that we do. This divine witness to the Scriptures by God is the work of the Holy Spirit.

Since the Reformation the precise role of the church in the formation of the canon has been a topic of controversy. In the traditional Roman Catholic view, which was confirmed at the Council of Trent, the church made the judgment concerning those books that belonged in the canon. Calvin objected to the Roman Catholic view taken at Trent by arguing that it subordinated the Scriptures to the institutional church, that is, to the judgment of mere human beings. According to Calvin, "the internal witness of the Holy Spirit" (*testimonium internum spiritus sancti*), which God gives to the true church, verifies the authority of a book.[41]

The historic church has not set the two points, the internal witness of God's Spirit and ecclesiastical action, in tension. It has affirmed that:

- There was an actual, human historical process by which the boundaries of the canon were drawn; the results that we are left with today came from ecclesiastical decisions;
- At the same time, we can accept with confidence the divine authority of the books in the Bible since God Himself, through His Spirit, assisted in the process of selection; and God confirms the judgment of the historic church through the inner witness of His Spirit that the Scriptures give us His Word.

SUMMARY: *The Canon of the Scriptures*

1. The church designates as canonical the Scriptures it has received as authoritative.

2. Because our Lord and the apostles accepted the Old Testament Scriptures, all Christian bodies have received them as canonical.

3. The Roman Catholic and Greek Orthodox churches receive all the books in the Greek Old Testament as canonical, which include the Apocrypha. Protestant churches receive only those in the Hebrew canon since these would have been the Scriptures accepted by our Lord.

4. Without any official ecclesiastical action, early Christians began to receive the writings of the apostles as canonical, to read them in church and to use them as the authoritative Word of God.

5. Marcion's rejection of many books the church received as canonical called forth official statements designating which books were canonical. Athanasius' thirty-ninth festal letter is the document that gives the exact list of the 27 books since recognized by all as the New Testament Scriptures.

6. The criteria for affirming a book as canonical have been:
   • Apostolicity
   • Conformity to the rule of faith
   • The use of the churches
   • The internal witness of God's Spirit

SECTION III. *The Reliability of the Scriptures*

1. THE TRUTHFULNESS OF THE SCRIPTURES

Throughout its long history, the Christian church has accepted the Bible as reliable and true. The assertion of Titus 1:2 that God's promise of eternal life is sure because it comes from "God, who does not lie," represents the common understanding of the historic church concerning the reliability of the Scriptures. They unerringly and infallibly speak the truth for the very simple reason that God is their ultimate author.

Though the Scriptures have God as their ultimate author, He mediated His Word through human authors. Throughout history, the church assumed that since they had God as their ultimate author, the human element did not compromise the Scriptures' truthfulness.

However, since the rise of critical biblical studies around the beginning of the 19th century, the Scriptures have been treated by many scholars, inside as well as outside the church, as fallible works. The historic trust that the church had in the Scriptures was set aside by many as naïve and credulous. These scholars assumed as a matter of course that on many occasions the Scriptures might contain errors of various sorts. In their view the reliability of the Scriptures could be demonstrated only on a case-by-case basis and thus could not be taken for granted.

When we agree in our own time with the view of the historic church that the Scriptures are true and reliable, we are affirming several things about them at the same time:

- We acknowledge God as the ultimate author of the Scriptures and the human element within them as well. The Scriptures were written in particular, ancient, historical eras and social environments that conditioned how their authors wrote and their original readers thought;
- When they wrote, the authors had in mind questions and needs of their own time. These are perennial human questions and needs, but the forms in which they were expressed arose from their own cultural worlds;
- The revelation that God gave to the authors of Scripture was targeted for their own times, their own social environments and their own questions. The Scriptures do not immediately answer our ques-

tions nor do they speak in our terms. Thus, we must read and interpret them to apply them to our situations;

- God worked upon the minds of the authors so that the word that they spoke, the word written in the Scriptures, really did represent what he wanted said to their contemporaries. They unerringly and infallibly make their points.[42]

2. THE HUMAN WORD IN THE BIBLE

Over the past two centuries, scholarship has noted that the human element within the Scriptures takes various forms. It has traced these human sources or parallels to many biblical statements. A few examples will illustrate their varying natures and uses.

Myths of Origin (Theogonies). The *Enuma Elish*, an Akkadian myth of origins from the third millennium B.C., offers intriguing parallels to Genesis 1, the first biblical account of the creation. The theologies of the two have a crucial difference.[43] The myth describes how the physical world was created from a divine body. Genesis, on the other hand, makes a sharp distinction between God and the natural world He created.

Law Codes. Case laws in the Book of the Covenant (Exodus 20:21-23:33) echo some found in the *Code of Hammurabi*, written around 1700 B.C. by a Babylonian king of that name.[44] Israel's statutes are later and are advanced over Hammurabi's Code, moving toward justice and humanitarianism.

Cultic Architecture. The temple of Solomon in 1 Kings 5-8 resembles those of some West Canaanite cities. But Israel's temples made no place for idolatrous representations of God (see Exodus 20:24-26).[45]

Philosophy. Directives similar to the "house rules" of 1 Peter 2:13-3:7 are found in some Stoic philosophers of late antiquity.[46] We still see in Peter the "natural-law" philosophy found in the writings of pagan thinkers. Along with natural law, however, the apostle appeals to distinctly Christian values.

Christian Adoption of Jewish Reasoning. In Romans 4:4-8 Paul follows a technique of interpretation used by the rabbis. This technique, called *gᵉzarah shawa'*, compared two passages of Scripture containing the same word.[47] If the meaning of a crucial word was unclear in one passage, its use in the second passage would illuminate its meaning and thus make the meaning of the first passage clear. While Paul does not come to a conclusion the rabbis would have accepted, he argues as they did.

The Biblical Authors' Use of Sources

No one can claim that we have in the *Enuma Elish* or the *Code of Hammurabi* sources that the biblical authors used. But the authors were certainly aware of ideas such as these sources contained. When they wrote the Scriptures, they were not only teaching the truth, but they were also consciously rejecting pagan errors.

Some have felt that we are left with a contradiction. How can God be the giver of the Scriptures while their authors, at the same time, used human sources? There are three possible resolutions for this dilemma:

- The authors wrote as inspired with no significant input from human sources. They did not write with a conscious awareness of theological ideas available in the pagan world;
- The authors wrote as almost any human would write by using and responding to existing sources and their ideas. Literature is always a dialogue;
- In an integrated manner, the authors used and responded to sources, and the Holy Spirit guided them so that the result was a revelation from God.

Some, using the statements in the Bible that speak of inspiration, adopt the first. Others, using the material evidence alone, have chosen the second answer. If we should adopt the third method, that in an integrated manner the authors of the Scriptures used and responded to human sources as guided by the Holy Spirit, important implications result:

- Divine revelation did not displace the normal human processes of thought that were influenced by a cultural environment. But God guided the scriptural authors as they wrote;
- The biblical authors, by inspiration, responded to materials found in their cultural universes;
- Through the Bible, God speaks in a universal manner, overarching the particular periods in which He gave His Word;
- To interpret the Bible well, we begin with the historical settings of each individual document.

3. CHALLENGES TO THE TRUTH-FULNESS OF THE SCRIPTURES

Historical Accuracy

Questions of the Scriptures' reliability have often focused on the accuracy of their historical reports. Did things happen as the Scriptures report they happened? For example, did Israel cross the Red Sea on dry land (Exodus 14:15-31), and did Jesus raise Lazarus from death (John 11:38-34)? Or did the participants say what the Scriptures cite them as saying? Did Isaiah converse with the Lord (Isaiah 6:8-13), and did Paul witness before Agrippa (Acts 26:2-29)? The debate about the truthfulness of the Scriptures has turned into an examination of the kind of historical data that might support or dispute their reports.

Archaeology

Over the present century the science of archaeology has made great strides. The material at the disposal of archaeologists has increased considerably. Both epigraphic (documents such as the Mari tablets) and non-written items (potsherds, utensils, fragments from garbage heaps, ancient walls) have been uncovered. Archaeologists sift through the data with amazing skill. They decipher and interpret the mounds of data with increasing precision, turning them into intelligible witnesses. A trend in some circles to think of biblical history as highly unreliable has been reversed by the results of archaeology. Stunning support for some biblical accounts has surfaced.[48]

However, though archaeology has confirmed the accuracy of some accounts reported in Scripture once disputed, it has not ended all debate. Nor should we expect it to do so in the near future. And some scholars continue to claim that important archaeological evidence disagrees with biblical accounts.[49]

Multiple Scriptural Accounts of Historical Events

The Scriptures give multiple accounts of certain crucial historical events. The four accounts of the Gospel is a case in point. While there are substantial agreements among the four accounts, differences also occur. For example, was the title on Jesus' cross "This is Jesus, the King of the Jews" (Matthew 27:37) or "The King of the Jews" (Mark 15:26) or "This is the King of the Jews" (Luke 23:38) or "Jesus of Nazareth, the King of the Jews" (John 19:19)? On the one hand, it is obvious that although the precise words differ, the reports essentially agree. On the other hand, we still have to inquire what we mean by reliability and truthfulness. Those for whom reliability can be proved only if the reports would satisfy the standards of a modern stenographer will never find the Scriptures true and reliable. But there may be better ways to account for the differences than attributing them to carelessness or deliberate falsification.

Interpreted History

The term "historiography" refers to the study of particular theories or schools that individual historians adopt and follow when they write history. Historians have been at work for centuries now, but over the last two they have raised certain questions about the discipline of historiography:

- One view of historical writing states that good historians report the "brute facts" of past events.[50] They will not have succeeded, in other words, unless they describe things as they really happened and record words as they were actually said;

- A second view of historical writing argues that good history can be written only by those who are fully conscious of their points of view and can justify them.[51] No one, in fact, reports the brute facts. Historians inevitably have viewpoints and reveal these in various ways. By their selections from the mass of available material, they show what they think is important. Their organization of the materials shows what they think the causes of events were. By their explanations, they set forth what they think events mean. Moreover, this view of historiography believes that a perfectly neutral history – even if it were possible, which it is not – is not desirable. Good historical writing not only attempts to discover what happened in the past but also to understand what it means, and that requires self-conscious subjective judgment.

4. ACCOMMODATION

Studies in rhetoric and intellectual history have advanced our understanding of human language. These studies have shown that cultures develop thought patterns and speech patterns that govern how their peoples process information. On the one hand, the human mind has fixed characteristics so that all people, regardless of time or place, process data in similar ways. At the same time, there also exists a certain elasticity to the mind, and we learn to think in ways taught us by our social environments, both in larger cultural and in smaller familial units.

Scripture clearly reflects the social environments of its authors and readers. God's Word has come through social grids. It was not addressed simply to the human race but to particular peoples who lived in highly developed social environments. Many fine studies have traced the differing characteristics of Hebrew and Jewish-Hellenistic thought patterns of the first century.

Calvin referred to this mode of revelation as the divine accommodation. The term accommodation emphasizes that God has given His word in forms that humans can understand. The Scriptures give us the divine Word in human words and idioms.[52]

5. PROGRESSIVE REVELATION

As we move from the beginning to the end of the Bible, the theological views it reports are constantly undergoing improvement. For example, the patriarchs' views of God are considerably refined by the prophets. The violence against non-Israelites in the period of the conquest (Joshua) is softened by later words that non-Israelites might convert (Ruth and Jonah). Jesus' ethical teaching (Mark 10:2ff.) advances over that of Moses (Deuteronomy 24:1). Paul, writing years after Christ's ascension, shows a greater depth of understanding of the nature of Jesus (Philippians 2:5-10) than does Peter when he first preached after Jesus' departure (Acts 2:22-36).

In a particular sense, the Bible is consistent from beginning to end. In another, one notes continuous growth of understanding and revision. This feature of Scripture we call progressive revelation. The idea that the Scriptures give us progressive revelation does not teach that their earlier parts set forth falsehood and the later ones give the truth. Instead, it teaches that God gradually drew His people to a fuller understanding of his truth as they learned successive lessons, the latter building on the accomplishments of the former. Paul said that "when the time had fully come, God sent his Son" (Galatians 4:4). The teachers of the early church remarked about this divine pedagogy. First, God taught the patriarchs, and then He taught the nation through Moses, through the prophets and through Jesus Christ. The apostles interpreted all that had gone before in the light of Jesus Christ. Nothing is wasted, nothing lost. Each step moves our understanding of God and His will forward, building on the previous step.[53]

6. THE INTERPRETATION OF THE SCRIPTURES

Since its inception, the church has read and believed that the books within the canon give us the Word of God. But it has also interpreted and used them. The earliest record we have outside of the New Testament for a Christian worship service, which was written by Justin Martyr, indicates this.[54]

Ancient Books and Contemporary Meanings

The question of hermeneutics – how we interpret a document – arises from two poles; the one is past and historical, the other is present and contemporary. The documents we have in the Bible were written centuries ago. They reflect in numerous ways that they are ancient documents and respond to ancient historical needs and questions. However, when we read them, we look for more than answers to historical questions. We ask what the Bible has to tell us about the present situation, what we are to believe and how we are to live.

Theological Issues in the Interpretation of the Scriptures

What follows is a brief outline of theological considerations that bear on the interpretation of the Scriptures. The remarks, cursory in nature, will gather a good deal of what has already been said or will be said in future chapters and indicate how they apply to the interpretation of the Bible.

The Canonical Scriptures. The books we read and from which we preach in worship and the books upon which we base our doctrinal formulations are those contained within the canonical Scriptures. Whatever hermeneutical skills we develop are valuable to the degree that they help us understand *the canon* better. We do not study the Scriptures to improve upon them to correct them or to justify positions we might take that in actual fact contradict or compromise them.[55]

The Original Meanings of the Scriptures. Interpretation should begin with an attempt to recover, so far as we are able, the meanings intended by the authors of the Scriptures. The tools scholarship has given us for getting at these ancient meanings are thus a boon since they offer great assistance in that effort. These tools of scholarship such as consulting non-biblical historical records, archaeology and comparative religious studies enable us to reconstruct original settings of the Scriptures to some degree. Through the use of them we can come closer to understanding what their authors meant by their words.[56]

Attention to the Words of the Scriptures. No scholarly tool used to grasp historical settings of the Scriptures can substitute for detailed attention to the words of the Scriptures. Before we look for obscure implications in the Bible, we give priority to the most obvious meaning of their words.[57]

The Historic Understanding of the Church. The previous comments concerning original meanings and attention to the words of the Scriptures might be taken to support a rigidly modern view of hermeneutics that depends upon historical and literary analyses. While we consider these, at the same time we also must listen to the church's historic understanding of the Scriptures. To do so helps us to avoid modern intellectual and theological provincialism. A broad agreement over the meanings of scriptural passages has existed within the church over its extensive history. For nearly two millennia, Christians of each century have seen the same essential truths in the Scriptures.

The Full Meaning of the Scriptures. The principle that we must give attention to original meanings and the words of the Scriptures states that we are not to give interpretations that are foreign to the Scriptures. At the same time, we can use the Scriptures in formulating teachings that go beyond their ancient settings or their explicit words. The early church did this as it worked out the doctrine of the Trinity, which we will take up more fully below. In post-biblical times, the language of the debate shifted from that within scriptural times. This required the church to use terms not explicitly found within the Scriptures. For example, the term "Trinity" itself is not found in the Bible, but it clearly captures the scriptural teaching that God is one yet three, Father, Son and Holy Spirit.[58]

The Guidance of the Holy Spirit. Throughout its history the church has trusted the guidance of the Holy Spirit as it has attempted to understand and apply the Scriptures to its thought and life. Those charged with the task of teaching the Scriptures have needed the special help of the Spirit. This is clearly implied in the list of the gifts that the Spirit grants the church (Ephesians 4:11-13).[59] The proper interpretation of the Scriptures requires the exercise of the intellect, but it also requires much more. Paul teaches that the aid of God's Spirit is absolutely essential for us to understand the things of God (1 Corinthians 2:14f.). Since the Scriptures are the Word of God, their meaning can be grasped only as God enlightens our understanding through the work of the Spirit. He who inspired the authors of the Scriptures to write them in the first place will also enable us to understand them.

SUMMARY: *The Reliability of the Scriptures*

1. Throughout its long history, the Christian church has correctly accepted the Bible as reliable and true.

2. There are many evidences of a human word within the Scriptures. These reflect the thought forms and cultural environments in which the Scriptures were written. The authors of the Scriptures regularly used cultural modes of expression to declare their words.

3. Recent studies, such as archaeology, have consistently shown that the Bible reports accurate history, so far as it can be tested.

4. In the writing of history, all historians, including biblical authors, do more than simply report data. They also write from a particular perspective.

5. In revealing his truth to us through the authors of Scripture, God accommodated His message to human language and culture. Even with this limitation, however, what He revealed is timeless and saving truth.

6. When we compare the end of the Scriptures with the beginning, we can point to a progressively clearer and fuller enunciation of God's truth – progressive revelation.

7. Our contemporary task with respect to the Scriptures is to find the present meaning of the ancient word. This task of interpretation involves:
   - Using the canon of the historic church
   - Beginning with the original meaning
   - Attending to the very words of the Scriptures
   - Listening to the church's historical understanding of the Scriptures
   - Searching for the full meaning of the Scriptures
   - Relying on the guidance of the Holy Spirit

ENDNOTES

[1] Hilary, *Trin.* 4:14, *NPNF* 2:9:19.

[2] Shanks, *SJ* 120-26.

[3] Brunner, *Med.* 322-327; Pannenberg, *ST* 318f.

[4] Bultmann, *HST* 291f., 295f.; see Brown, *BM* 516-31.

[5] Lebacqz and Barton, *SP* 114ff.; Scroggs, *NTH* 109-18.

[6] Wright, *GWA* 59ff.; Cullmann, *SH* 19-24.

[7] Cullmann, *SH* 88-114.

[8] Tacitus, *Annals* 15:44 in *DCC* 2.

[9] von Rad, *WI* 113-37.

[10] Justin, *Second Apology* 9, *ANF* 1:191; Irenaeus, *AH* 4:40, *ANF* 1:523f.; Cyril of Jerusalem, *CL* 15, *NPNF* 2:7:104-14.

[11] Wesley, "A Clear and Concise Demonstration of the Divine Inspiration of the Holy Scriptures," *WJW* 11:484.

[12] Payne, *TOT* 46-48.

[13] Heschel, *Prophets* 431-33; Skinner, *PR* 201ff.; Payne, *TOT* 49-53.

[14] Machen, *OPR* 58-68; Bruce, *CG* 92-95.

[15] Pope, *CCT* 1:172f.

[16] Pope, *CCT* 1:92-95; Moore, *Jud.* 1:234ff.

[17] Livingston, *AS* 139f.

[18] Cunningham and others, *SQ* 87-90; Bianchi, *ER* 6:407.

[19] Theophilus to "Autolycus" 2:9, *ANF* 2:97; Chrysostom, *Homilies on First Corinthians* 7:7, *NPNF* 1:12:36f.; Wiley, *CT* 1:182-84; Young, *SP* 57-61; Abraham, *DIHS* 63f.

[20] Pope, *CCT* 1:203-5.

[21] Sanders, *ADB* 1:846f.

[22] See Josephus, *Wars,* 2:165, *Jos.* 2:386f.

[23] Pope, *CCT* 1:153-68.

[24] Tertullian, *AM* 2, *ANF* 3:297ff.; Kelly, *ECD* 57.

[25] See *Letter of Aristeas* 301-16, *APOT* 2:120f. and Philo, *Moses* 2:25-44, *Philo* 6:460-71.

[26] Swete, *IOTG* 381-401.

[27] Swete, *IOTG* 406-33.

[28] Turro and Brown, *Jerome* 2:515-24.

[29] Zahn, *NSH* 2:392f.

[30] *First Apology* 67, *ANF* 1:185f.

[31] Tertullian, *AM* 3-5, *ANF* 3:321ff.

[32] *NTA* 1:42-45.

[33] *CH* 3:25:1-7, *NPNF* 2:1:155-57.

[34] "Thirty-ninth Festal Letter" 5, *NPNF* 2:4:552.

35 Metzger, *CNT* 199-201.

36 Metzger, *CNT* 201-7.

37 Metzger, *CNT* 251-54; Shelton, *ABC* 32f.

38 Eusebius, *CH* 3:39:14-16, *NPNF* 2:1:172f.

39 *AH* 3:3:4, *ANF* 1:416; see Tertullian, *PAH* 20f., *ANF* 3:252f.

40 Eusebius, *CH* 6:12, *NPNF* 1:257f.

41 *Inst.* 1:7:1-5 (1:68-73); Wiley, *CT* 1:164-66.

42 Pope, *CCT* 1:186-92.

43 Lambert, *ABD* 2:526-29.

44 Oppenheim, *IDB* 2:517-19.

45 Myers, *ABD* 6:355f.

46 Fitzmyer, *Jerome* 2:366f.

47 Strack, *ITM* 94; Barrett, *EPR* 89.

48 Albright, *NHBR.*

49 Dever, *ADB* 364-66.

50 See North, *IDB* 2:607f.

51 Kähler, *HJHBC* 123-48; Rottenberg, *RHR* 52-93.

52 Calvin, *Inst.* 1:8:1-2 (1:74-76).

53 Pope, *CCT* 1:95-97.

54 *First Apology* 67, ANF 1:186.

55 Wesley, Sermon 12, "The Witness of Our Own Spirit," 6, *WJWB* 1:302f.

56 Wesley, *The Principles of a Methodist Farther Explain'd* IV.3, WJWB 9:158f.

57 Wesley, "Letter to Samuel Furly," May 10, 1755, *WJWB* 26:557.

58 Brown, *Jerome* 2:615-19.

59 Wesley, "A Letter to the Reverend Mr. Porter," 17, *WJW* 9:94f.

CHAPTER

3

RESOURCES FOR THEOLOGY

SECTION III. EXPERIENCE
1. Religious Experience
2. The Contribution of Religious Experience to Theology
3. The Interpretation of Religious Experience
4. The Teaching Value of Religious Experience
5. The Scriptures and the Interpretation of Religious Experience
6. Corporate Rather Than Individual Religious Experience
7. The Use of Experience as a Theological Resource

SECTION I. *Historic Christian Teaching*

1. VARIOUS KINDS OF HISTORIC CHRISTIAN TEACHING

A. The "Rule of Faith"

The Kerygma or Proclamation of the Apostles' Earliest Preaching

hen we go back to the earliest days of the church, we see that the apostles proclaimed a message with a few core teachings. This central core of teachings has been called the *kerygma,* from the New Testament Greek word for "proclamation". Certain teachings predominated in the sermons reported in the early chapters of the Acts of the Apostles, that is, in its *kerygma* (see Acts 2:14ff.; 3:12ff.; 7:2ff.; 10:34ff.). They include the following:[1]

- The time of fulfillment that God had promised has dawned;
- This has taken place in the life, ministry, death, and resurrection of Jesus of Nazareth;

- In virtue of His resurrection Jesus has been exalted to the right hand of the Father;
- The Holy Spirit is the sign of Christ's present power and glory;
- The messianic age will soon be consummated in the return of Christ;
- All people are called to repent and believe, being promised that they will be forgiven and receive the Holy Spirit and the promise of life in the future age.

Catechesis or Teaching in the Early Church

After exposure to the *kerygma* of the church, those who responded were grounded in essential Christian teaching. This teaching has been referred to as *catechesis*, a Greek word for "teaching", or *didache*, another Greek word for "teaching". Jesus instructed His disciples, and they in turn instructed the earliest converts to the gospel. So the church has through its long history trained its members in fundamental Christian teachings. Paul explicitly refers to such teaching in Romans 6:17 and 1 Thessalonians 4:1. We can see the elements of such early Christian catechesis in such passages as 1 Thessalonians 4:1ff. and much of 1 Peter. This elementary teaching focused on three items:[2]

- On God, that He was living, spiritual and one (unlike the multiple gods of the pagans);
- On the doctrine of retribution, that all would ultimately be judged for their actions;
- On Christian virtues, that Christians should abandon pagan practices of idolatry, sexual immorality and cruelty and should worship only the true and living God, and that they should be sexually pure, and should live by the perfect law of love.

A. The "Rule of Faith"

The post-apostolic "rule of faith," then, is built on the early church's *kerygma* and catechetical teaching. The *rule of faith* refers to a succinct list of items that Christians believe and teach.[3] It resembles the *kerygma*, which outlined the fundamental core beliefs of the most primitive Christian preaching and the catechesis of the most primitive teaching. The rule does not elaborate or develop the Christian faith but rather declares its essential elements.

Forms of the rule of faith can be seen in two places within early Christian worship: in the baptism ritual and in the weekly celebration of the Lord's Supper. As a part of the baptism ritual, the rule would appear in question-and-answer form.[4] This ancient procedure has continued into the present. Thus, candidates for baptism have been asked for two millennia now whether they believe in God, the Father Almighty, maker of heaven and earth, in Jesus Christ his only Son and in the Holy Spirit. Those who answer the question affirmatively are to be baptized.[5]

As a part of the ritual of the Lord's Supper called the Eucharist, the rule would appear in the form of prayer. The worship leader would recite the great saving acts of God and the central core beliefs of the Christian church.[6]

The Apostles' Creed

The rule of faith gradually took the shape of what we now know as the Apostles' Creed.[7] This creed is called apostolic, not because the apostles themselves wrote it, but because it gives in concise form the essential core teachings that derive from the apostles.[8] The creed as we presently know it can be traced to the fifth century. But earlier forms of the creed are found in the fourth century, and its fundamental elements derive from the early church's *kerygma* and catechism. The central teachings of the Apostles' Creed are built around the Persons of the Trinity, the Father, the Son and the Holy Spirit.[9] Thus, it affirms of God the Father, that He is:

- Almighty;
- The Maker of heaven and earth;

And of Jesus Christ, that He:

- Is the only Son and our Lord;
- Was conceived by the Holy Spirit and born of the Virgin Mary;
- Suffered under Pontius Pilate, was crucified, dead and buried;
- Descended into Hades;
- Rose on the third day and sits at the right of the Father;
- Will come to judge the living and the dead;

And of the Holy Spirit that through His work there is:

- The holy catholic church;
- The communion of saints;
- The forgiveness of sins;
- And the resurrection of the body and life everlasting.

B. Councils

The Early Ecumenical Councils

A council is a convened meeting in which church leaders come together to deliberate on a question of theology or policy, reach a decision by vote, and publish the results of the decision as the official viewpoint of the church.

Soon after its founding, the church held a council and took *official* action on a pressing issue. Some Jewish Christians were alarmed at the growing number of gentile converts. And they questioned whether Gentiles should not become Jewish proselytes by being circumcised and adhering to all the commandments in order to become full Christian converts. Acts 15 reports about this first council, the Council of Jerusalem, which met around the year A.D. 48. The apostles and elders of the church came together in Jerusalem, discussed the issue, reached a decision and published the results as official.

For more than two centuries following the Jerusalem Council, there were no universal councils though there were regional councils. The first universal council was called by Emperor Constantine and took place in Nicea, a city of Asia Minor in A.D. 325. During the fourth century and the next few centuries, seven universal councils were held. We call these seven "ecumenical councils" since leaders from the entire or *worldwide* church met to discuss the issues and debate the options.

The results of the ecumenical councils were published as creeds or definitions of the creeds. The word "creed" comes from the Latin word *credere* which means "to believe." Those who confessed the creeds or definitions were the faithful and thus could be distinguished from the heretics who would not.

The first four ecumenical councils in particular were critical in the defining of classic Christian teaching about Jesus Christ and about the Trinity. They were as follows:

- The Council of Nicea (A.D. 325), which affirmed that the Son was truly God;
- The First Council of Constantinople (A.D. 381), which affirmed the true humanity of Jesus;
- The Council of Ephesus (A.D. 431), which affirmed that the two natures of Jesus Christ (His humanity and His deity) were not mingled and thus not diluted but united so that each nature was kept in its integrity;
- The Council of Chalcedon (A.D. 451), which further clarified the two natures and yet one person of Christ.

Denominational Councils, Synods, Conferences and Conventions

Throughout church history and up to the present time, councils have continued to meet. Since the division between Eastern and Western Christianity in 1054, councils of one branch of the church body have set themselves in opposition to another. Thus, the Eastern church has condemned views taken by the Western church, and likewise the Western church has condemned views of the East.

The "ecumenical councils" of the twentieth century, though they do include large numbers of various denominations, have also not reached the "catholic" or *universal* consensus that the councils of the early centuries did.

Likewise, Protestant bodies have had their conciliar meetings. Thus, the Lutherans have synods, the Methodists conferences, and the Baptists conventions.

The Protestant bodies have published their conciliar decisions that touched on doctrinal questions in official documents. From the Lutherans came the "Augsburg Confession" (1530), from the Presbyterians the "Westminster Confession" (1646), from the Anglicans "the Articles of Religion" (1571), from the Methodists the "Articles of Religion" (1784) and from the Free Methodists the "Articles of Religion" (1860).

The Articles of Religion of the Free Methodist Church

A study of the Articles of Religion of the Free Methodist Church reveals our parentage and our viewpoint on important doctrinal issues. For example, Article One "On faith in the Trinity" in the Free Methodist Church (1989, 1860) can easily be traced to Article One of the Methodist Episcopal Church (1784), to Article One of the Anglican Church (1571), to Article One of the Augsburg Confession (1530), to the Definition of Chalcedon (451), to the Nicene Creed (325). Thus, we stand in agreement with the church universal on this important question of Christian teaching.[10]

Article Eleven "Of the Justification of Man" in the Free Methodist Church (1989 [Article Nine, 1860]) can be traced to Article Nine of the Methodist Episcopal Church (1784), to Article Four of the Augsburg Confession (1530) and no further in official church documents.[11] But the themes of this article appear in Augustine's debate with Pelagius (around A.D. 400).[12] The doctrine of justification by faith touches on a matter of controversy during the Reformation era.[13]

The language of Article Twelve on entire sanctification in the Free Methodist Church (1989 [Article Thirteen]) can be traced to John Wesley. Ideas within this teaching can be traced much further back to teachers of the medieval church such as Thomas à Kempis[14] and of the early church such as Gregory of Nyssa (fourth century).[15] Still, this is the one article that represents Methodist teaching in its most distinct form.

The Articles of Religion of the Free Methodist Church reveal the actions of General Conferences in deciding a theological position. Our church agrees with the church universal on the matters of the Trinity and our understanding of Christ, the central and core issues of Christian faith. We agree with the Reformers on the matter of justification by faith, the church and the sacraments. Our articulation of the doctrine of sanctification finds echoes in the broad universal church, though there is a special Methodist way of explaining it.

C.   Teachers of the Church

Both informal teachings (the rule of faith) and formal ones (the creeds) are relatively brief statements. Historic Christian teaching has taken still another form beyond these two that has played an important role in the theological enterprise. This is found in the vast body of material written by the church's great teachers.

The authority attributed to these lengthy works is generally of a different sort from that belonging to the shorter forms of tradition. These teachings are given in full-length documents and major books. Some, such as *Why the God-Man?*, on the atonement, by Anselm (a late medieval teacher), discuss only one particular theological issue. Others are more comprehensive such as *The City of God* by Augustine. What binds this wide range of material into a single category is this: These works reach conclusions on controversial theological topics by systematically working through an entire set of questions related to them. That which makes them so valuable, therefore, is not merely the solutions they reach, though conclusions could find their way into creeds, but the reasoning by which the teachers reached them. These works do more than express the Christian viewpoint; they also reflect the Christian way of thinking and wrestling with enduring and perplexing questions.

The works of these great teachers of the church have a quality that endures far beyond their own times. One can still read with great profit Athanasius and Gregory of Nazianzus, who wrote in Greek during the fourth century, and Hilary of Poitiers and Augustine, who wrote during the same century. We can all learn from the great medieval scholars Aquinas and Anselm. And Luther, Calvin and Arminius have something to teach all Protestants.

John Wesley

We can also read with great profit to all the works of John Wesley, the father of Wesleyan Methodism. This brilliant and clear-thinking 18th century Englishman wrote in a manner that cuts through the intervening years and still speaks directly to the mind and heart.[16] Protestants from other traditions, who have often ignored him, would find a catholicity and breadth in his thought that would inform their theology and nourish their souls.

Certainly we do not agree with all things that all of these teachers said. We could not because they did not entirely agree with one another. But there is far more agreement among these classic Christian teachers than is often supposed. And there is a richness to their teaching and thinking that rewards the church when it delves into their works. They are truly the "doctors" (teachers) of Christian faith.

2. THE GUIDANCE OF THE HOLY SPIRIT

When the church is at work as a body of believers, seeking to know the mind of God and to follow His truth as it comes to know that truth, the Holy Spirit is at work to guide it into truth. Thus, the decisions of the church in council are not simply the work of human beings, but the decisions of humans guided and illumined by the Holy Spirit.

"He Will Guide You into All Truth"

Jesus promised His disciples that after His departure the Spirit would grant them spiritual illumination. "But when he, the Spirit of truth, comes," Jesus said, "he will guide you into all truth" (John 16:13). While Jesus certainly had His disciples in mind – the Spirit would give them assistance for their great apostolic work – He also included those who would believe through their work.[17] Thus, the Spirit continues to guide His people as they seek to know His truth and follow it.

"It Seemed Good to the Holy Spirit and to Us"

The council of Jerusalem, the very first universal council of the church, after it had deliberated on the matter for which it was called, drafted a letter to publish its decision. The letter included the note that both God and human beings shared in the decision-making process, "It seemed good to the Holy Spirit and to us" (Acts 15:28). This reference to the Holy Spirit, then, suggests that the church believed God's Spirit directed the members of the council as they debated and worked through the issue at hand. While human beings were using their best skills, God was guiding and overruling in their thoughts.

"But You Have an Anointing"

Very late in the apostolic period, the Apostle John had to address the question raised by certain heretics who claimed that an anointing gave them special insight into God's truth and they could require "ordinary" Christians to accept their peculiar teachings. John instead pointed out that all Christians have received the Holy Spirit, the anointing, and do not have to take the claim of these teachers (1 John 2:20-27).

This passage does not support the view of an individualistic anointing but individual anointings within the collective body of the church. The Spirit teaches what the church has always taught (2:24). The individualistic view that counters the teachings of the church is under suspicion. The Spirit of God who taught the disciples one thing would not teach a modern person another. The Spirit of God who led the church and its great teachers to understand one thing in past eras would not lead it in the present to adopt a view that contradicts its ancient understanding. The Spirit is consistent. Thus, there is an inner affirmation of the Spirit confirming that the historic understandings of the church are the truth of God.[18]

3. THE CANON OF VINCENT

A fifth century monk, Vincent of Lérins, articulated in clear form the canon, as it is usually called, or rule that defines which teachings belong to the universal church. The canon reads:[19]

> Moreover in the Catholic [universal] Church itself, all possible care must be taken, that we hold that faith that has been believed everywhere, always and by all.

Vincent's canon states that we must consider three areas when we seek to define precisely what the universal Christian faith holds: geography, chronology and universality.[20] Thus, for example, according to his rule, it would be wrong to claim that an essential Christian truth has been discovered in the 20th century that was unknown or unacknowledged throughout the majority of Christian history. Neither can we argue that something is an essential Christian teaching that is believed in North America but denied by orthodox believers in Europe, Africa and Asia.

4. HISTORIC CHRISTIAN TEACHING AND THE SCRIPTURES

The Priority of the Scriptures

The Protestant Reformation in the sixteenth century brought into sharp focus the value of historic Christian teaching in relation to the Scriptures. The Roman Catholic Church stated its position at the Council of Trent in the "Decree Concerning the Canonical Scriptures" (1546).[21] The Roman Catholic Church continues in that position to this day.[22] According to the Decree of Trent, the "truth and discipline" that our Lord Jesus Christ taught his disciples "are contained in the written books, and the unwritten traditions." The decree went on to say that the council "receives and venerates with an equal affection of piety and reverence all the books both of the Old and of the New Testament ... as also the said traditions."

On the other hand, the historic Protestant position placed the Scriptures in clear priority over church tradition. This viewpoint is reflected in Article Four in the Free Methodist Constitution. The article states in language that goes back to the earlier form of Article Six of the Church of England, "Whatever is not found in the Bible nor can be proved by it is not to be required as an article of belief or as necessary for salvation."[23] Protestant churches have grounded their view that the Scriptures take priority over church tradition in two factors:

- The authors of the Scriptures were closer to the formative salvation-historical events;
- The authors of the Scriptures were inspired in a way that church teachers were not.

Historic Protestantism has stated the matter correctly. While church teaching will sometimes go beyond the explicit words of the Scriptures, it should still remain in harmony with them. Church teaching is an interpretation of the Scriptures; the Scriptures give the norm for tradition. Tradition is judged by the Scriptures; the Scriptures are not judged by tradition. The historic tradition does judge us (contemporary Christians and denominations) and sets a guide for us. The Scriptures stand above the teachings of the historic church. Ideally, they should be in agreement. However, if we claim to stand with the teachings of the Scriptures and against the teachings of the historic church, the burden is upon us to prove that we understand them both correctly.[24]

5. METHODOLOGICAL PRINCIPLES IN THE USE OF HISTORIC CHRISTIAN TEACHING AS A THEOLOGICAL RESOURCE

Much of Protestantism, while holding the correct view that the Scriptures have priority, have gone on to ignore or pay slight attention to historic Christian teaching. They have done so even with regard to teaching that conforms to the Vincentian Canon. This has often resulted in theological rootlessness. While holding to the primacy of the Bible, a delicate balance between Scripture and historic Christian teaching is required if we are to keep our theological roots. Here are principles that will help in this task.[25]

- The Scriptures are their own best interpreters. Before we consult other authorities, we ask what the Scriptures have to say. For example, Matthew and Luke provide the first context for understanding Paul.[26]
- In accordance with the Vincentian Canon, early ecumenical creeds take precedence over later confessional traditions and more widely accepted teachings take precedence over more narrowly accepted ones.
- The great teachers are more useful than the lesser teachers. And even the greater teachers are to be measured by their care in following the Scriptures.

Of course, we will hardly reach a point at which all Christians agree on who the great teachers are and who the lesser teachers are. But time and patience have sifted out who the historically great and helpful teachers are from those who are the clever and popular teachers.

SUMMARY: *Historic Christian Teaching*

1. The core elements of historic Christian teaching can be found in:
    *   The apostolic proclamation (*kerygma*) and doctrinal teaching (*catechesis* or *didache*).
    *   The post-apostolic "rule of faith" and the Apostles' Creed.
2. The essential teachings of the historic Christian church were hammered out in the seven early ecumenical councils. They centered on teachings about the Trinity and the nature of Christ.
3. Later denominational councils have also played an important role in defining Christian doctrine.
4. The great teachers of the historic church can still be read with great profit. They not only teach us what Christian truth is but also how to think in a Christian manner.
5. Our Lord promised that the Holy Spirit would guide the church as it sought to understand and proclaim the truth.
6. Following the Vincentian Canon, we safely embrace the truths that Christianity has always endorsed and thus is protected from doctrinal provincialism.
7. The Scriptures remain our primary and normative source of theology.

SECTION II. *Reason*

1. THE DEBATE OVER THE PLACE OF PHILOSOPHY IN THEOLOGY

Early in the history of the church, the relation of philosophy to theology became a matter of controversy. On the one hand, some important Christian teachers such as Tertullian (late second century),[27] Luther (16th century)[28] and Karl Barth (20th century)[29] have placed a high wall of division between philosophy and theology. Philosophy, they contend, does not help the church develop correct teaching.

On the other hand, other important Christian theologians have made much use of philosophy, deliberately including it in their work. Justin Martyr (middle second century) believed the contribution of philosophy could be great. He said that the same Word (Logos) that inhabited Jesus in its fullness and inspired Abraham also inhabited the philosopher Socrates.[30] Clement of Alexandria (late second century) also acknowledged that the Logos indwelt some pagan philosophers.[31] Yet he believed that the endowment of the Spirit in the prophets was greater than that in the philosophers. While much more cautious than Justin and Clement, Augustine (late fourth and early fifth centuries)[32] and John Wesley consistently used formal philosophy in their work and each, on occasion, spoke positively of its use.[33]

2. HUMAN KNOWLEDGE

Theology requires the use of the mind, and good theology requires disciplined thinking. For example, the ability to interpret the Scriptures with success depends upon the mastery of human language. Only those who have thought deeply about the ways in which humans put words together to express feelings and to articulate shades of meaning can enter the world of precise interpretation. Clear and accurate interpretation of the Scriptures depends upon the ability to think clearly and logically.[34]

Though one theologian grants more importance to one mode of knowing such as Thomas Aquinas emphasizing empirical knowledge,[35] Christian theology as a whole has recognized that the various ways in which humans come to know are all indispensable. These epistemologies include:

- Intuition, which refers to the innate knowledge that humans have or the direct grasp of knowledge by the mind;
- Empirical knowledge, which refers to knowledge gained from reflection on sensory experiences;[36]
- Discursive reasoning, which refers to the knowledge gained from an orderly and progressive sequence of thoughts.

Discursive Reasoning

Discursive reasoning is particularly important for theology. Careful human discourse must be logical; it must go from one point to the next in an orderly progression. The second thought must follow the first because it makes sense to do so. The two thoughts must be connected by more than simple sequence; they must build to a conclusion. Disconnected thought is haphazard and cannot be trusted; discursive thought is logical and reliable.

By using the simple procedure of going from one thought to the next, analyzing, comparing, contrasting, adding or subtracting, we can move the discussion forward to reach clear, logical and convincing results. When thought breaks down and one idea has no relation to the one preceding it or the relation that is really there differs from the one we think is there, the results are illogical.

3. THE CONTRIBUTION OF REASON TO THEOLOGY
Human Thinking Inevitably Involves Critical Thought

It is impossible to desist from all use of reason and critical thought. To do so would stop thinking mid-stream. In many respects critical thinking is simply directing the mind forward in an orderly and systematic way. To think clearly and precisely is to think critically. To distinguish one thing from another, to see that the first thing logically follows the second or to say that if one thing is true then a second cannot be true – these are not intrinsically acts of unbelief but of simple human thought. If we are not allowed to think in these ways, then we are not allowed to think.

The Contribution of Reason to Theology

Human reason plays three critical roles in the work of theology:

- It offers us material from reason or life experiences that must be included in our theological thinking;
- It helps us organize and interpret data, whether drawn from the Scriptures, from historic Christian thought or from reason and life experiences;
- It enables us to sort through the data critically.

Theology Uses Intuition, Perception and Discursive Reasoning as Well as the Scriptures

Theological reasoning requires analysis (breaking an issue into its several parts) and synthesis (constructing the parts into a meaningful whole). It depends on knowledge gained from both intuition and sense experiences. We do not intuit theological truths purely and simply or experience them purely and simply. Nor do we learn them solely from the Scriptures or historic Christian teaching.

For example, to conclude that certain kinds of actions such as promiscuous sexual conduct are wrong may involve several interrelated steps. Empirical knowledge could tell us that such behavior exposes one to highly contagious diseases. It also tells us that such conduct results in enormous personal chaos, self-contempt and possible marital disaster. Statistical data from medical care givers and social scientists can predict the risks involved in both cases. Intuition tells us life is valuable. Intuition further tells us that the protection of our life and the lives of others is a moral duty. It also tells us that sexual loyalty is also a moral duty. Thus, we can combine empirical knowledge and intuition to conclude that promiscuous sexual conduct is both foolish and wrong.

But the Scriptures likewise treat the topic of promiscuous sexual conduct. The creation account tells us that God made us male and female for marriage and that this relationship is sacred, requiring the greatest loyalty of all our relationships (Genesis 1:27; 2:24). This gives a context for the implicit prohibition of defiling marriage through unfaithfulness. The seventh commandment explicitly articulates this prohibition (Exodus 20:14). Proverbs 5:1-14 observes how the immediate pleasure of promiscuous sexual conduct is followed by bitter regret and domestic chaos.

What we know by the use of reason, then, converges with the witness of the Scriptures. The Scriptures speak with more sharpness and detail, but they do not speak to us in a vacuum. Rather, they address us as creatures with rational ability who are already thinking about the data life offers, and our intuitions perceive what is true and false and what is right and wrong.

4. "I BELIEVE IN ORDER TO UNDERSTAND"
The Problem Of Credulity

Careful reasoning protects us from credulity. "Credulity," related to the word "creed," comes from a Latin word meaning "one who easily believes." A credulous person is someone who believes easily, perhaps too easily. Thus we can make a distinction between types of belief. One kind of belief is serious and thoughtful. The other is adopted without serious reflection and thus is capable of misleading the one who holds it.

In the strict sense, credulity is the kind of belief that affirms propositions without subjecting them to careful

84

thought. It does not try to understand or make sense of them because it may assume the human mind has no capacity ever to understand theological truth. Human reason and Christian faith, in this view, run on separate tracks.

The critical use of the mind does not necessarily mean that we are eager to reject propositions, though we may very well have to rethink them. It means that we are trying to understand precisely what they mean and how they relate to other theological truths that we already know and understand.

"Faith Seeking Understanding"

Augustine of Hippo's (354-430) unique way of explaining the relation of faith and reason has made a permanent contribution to theology. Though he was raised in the church, his early education included large installments of classic pagan literature. At that time in his life, Augustine believed that the Christian faith, including the Scriptures, was intellectually inferior to paganism. Gradually, however, his confidence in pagan thought declined because of its failure to answer life's perplexing questions. Then Augustine reconsidered the Scriptures. This change in attitude did not arise quickly. He came only gradually to the point where he fully accepted the Scriptures and understood them.[37]

The unfolding of understanding resulting from the exercise of faith is the critical point in Augustine's view of the theological enterprise. Through faith, he taught, we open ourselves to searching for answers and truth on a certain path. This path is found in the Scriptures and the historic Christian faith. Once we are on it and begin to look earnestly for the answers on the path of faith, understanding comes.

The sequence of the Augustinian method can be described as follows: God moves the heart to love and search for Himself, for He is the source of wisdom. This in turn brings happiness. Previously, according to Augustine, we sought for happiness through self-sufficiency (pride) and self-gratification (lust). By humbling ourselves and looking for answers where God has provided them, in the Christian Scriptures as understood by the church, we grow to love God more and more. God then illumines the mind increasingly, and the mind begins to understand more and more.[38]

Theology as the sequence of faith leading to understanding has been given classical expression. Anselm later refined this in the formulations: "faith seeking understanding" (*fides quaerens intellectum*) and "I believe in order to understand" (*credo ut intelligam*).[39]

5. THE LIMITS OF REASON

Three limits can be assigned to reason. They are:
- The limitations of our senses and reasoning ability;
- The provincialism of our intellectual environment;
- The bias of sin.

A. Human Finitude

Human beings are by definition finite. Because of this our senses can never perceive all of the relevant data nor can our minds sufficiently comprehend with absolute clarity all of what our senses perceive.

For example, those who cannot see cannot know what the Grand Canyon looks like. We may describe it to them at length, and, since they have had experience of depth and ruggedness, they can imagine it somewhat. But our description does not have the same effect as their actually seeing the Grand Canyon.

But even those with sight can hardly claim they have really seen the Grand Canyon. This natural wonder stretches far beyond our panoramic grasp. A wide sweep gives us the first sense of its greatness. Tourists stay all day to view it in different lights and ride or walk to the bottom for different vantage points. Still, the most persistent see only a fraction of it.

Our capacity to reason is similarly limited. This can be explained on several counts, such as the fact that we have only a limited amount of the relevant data. Or the fact that at one time we can process only a limited amount of the data that we have.[40]

B.   The Social Conditioning of Reason

Our thinking is also conditioned by the social milieu in which we live. The history of ideas shows that the ways in which people perceive the sensory world and the manner in which they process data are conditioned by the view of reality inherited from their social environment. Our intellectual framework does not arise from sheer biology, formal education, or personal choice. It also comes as a result of our living in a certain social and intellectual milieu.

In some respects East Africans as a group think alike and so do North Americans as a group. Though reality is the same for both, the grids through which the two social milieus view reality have been conditioned differently.

Furthermore, views of reality are always in a state of change. Thirteenth-century European thought grew from 12th century thought. Worldviews evolve slowly, almost imperceptibly from one generation to the next. Most youth know they see things differently from the way their parents saw them, but it is difficult to note the shift from one day to the next or even one year to the next.

All of this suggests that when we approach theology, we come to our task within a philosophical framework. We have a view of reality inherited to a greater or lesser degree from the intellectual milieu we inhabit. Some intellectual worldviews are better that others; that is, they come closer to comprehending the real world. But none is perfect.

C.   The Bias of Reason by Sin

We cannot trust reason without qualification on another count. This belongs to a different order from the limitations we have just discussed. The third limitation is the flaw in our will, our sinfulness. This has several aspects.

Sin Predisposes Us to Pride and a Selfish Use of Reason

Augustine described pride as the primary form inner sin takes.[41] While we often think of pride as public ostentation or vanity, it also attacks our minds so that we develop a swollen opinion of ourselves. Pride moves us to attribute to our perceptions and reasoning a skill they do not possess.

In some respects the sinful mind seems to work as well as it would if there were no bias to sin. But in other respects pride runs the mind off course with disastrous results. Brilliant and gifted persons use their intellectual powers for rebellious and selfish purposes. Their reasoning ability may dazzle us, but the potential results of it terrify us. The worst tyrants of the world have rarely been persons of average intellectual ability.

We common people also twist our perceptions and reasoning to achieve sinful, self-serving goals. It happens with subtlety. At a critical moment the illusive and inordinate love of self, that fierce desire to protect and promote our own interests, moves us to rationalize and distort truth.[42]

Sinful Pride Joins the Limitation of a Social Environment to Create Even Larger Problems

Sin insinuates itself into a social environment just as surely as it does into an individual's self-will. But given social form, the results can be even more frightening.

For example, racism, an inflated social ego, has roots in both our fallen nature and our intellectual environment. Personal selfishness can be, to some degree, held in check by our immediate circle. But when those in this circle share the view that "my" people – whatever group that means – are superior, the deception becomes more illusive. Passed through generations, a growing set of rationalizations reinforce social pride and self-will. The faulty logic gives racism an intellectual framework that is then transmitted from parents to children. The children grow up believing it represents the way things really are; they assume they have intuited this judgment, which is really a prejudgment or a prejudice. The inherited value seems untestable and self-evident, though continuous energy is subconsciously spent to maintain the fiction. This social view feeds personal pride while other factors such as low self-esteem may drive us to compensate by finding victims we can justifiably lord it over.[43]

The Limits of Overcoming the Limitations

If we take these three limitations together, the finitude of our reason, the social conditioning of our reason, and the bias of reason by sin, we can see that human thinking cannot be trusted to accomplish its task without error. The first two of these, our finitude and social conditioning, can be corrected to some degree with education. But education, as far as the church is concerned, cannot attack and solve the problem of sin. Since this problem is of a different order, it requires a correction of a different kind.

6. LIMITING REASON'S AUTHORITY

The real problem is whether, in theological matters, we will limit reason's authority. There are two possible sides we might take:

- The one says that reason legitimately contributes to theology so long as it works under the authority of the Scriptures;
- The other says we can trust the Scriptures only so far as they agree with reason, that is, reason is our final authority.

Reason's primary function in theology is to serve a critical faculty, not as a source. To read and understand the Scriptures at the most elementary level requires an ability to reason. To organize scriptural teachings on fundamental theological issues such as on the nature of God requires reason.

To apply the values of scriptural teachings to contemporary issues that the Christian must face also requires careful use of the mind.

"The Fear of the Lord is the Beginning of Wisdom"

The wisdom literature of the Old Testament consciously follows the path of reason. But by itself it gives no blanket endorsement to reason as a safe guide. Four times the Scriptures explicitly state the idea that "the fear of the Lord is the beginning of wisdom" (Psalms 110:10; Proverbs 1:7; 15:33; Job 28:28). Thus, they seek to inculcate a certain humble attitude or disposition as the essential predisposition to the use of the mind.[44] Reason is a wonderful and indispensable tool; it is also a dangerous lord.

SUMMARY: *Reason*

1. The contribution of philosophy to theology has long been a matter of debate. Many important theologians have distrusted it; others have given it high standing.

2. The various modes of reason, that is, intuition, empirical knowledge, and discursive thought, all contribute to theology in that they:
   - offer us material to be included in our thinking
   - help us organize and interpret material
   - enable us to sort through and critically judge material

3. The careful use of reason can protect us from credulity and poorly thought-out faith. However, the Christian looks into the Scriptures with trust for answers, and listens with confidence to the teachings of historic Christianity.

4. The ability of human reason to function is limited by its:
   - finitude

- social conditioning
- bias toward sin

SECTION III. *Experience*

1. RELIGIOUS EXPERIENCE

Religious experiences are common to all peoples in the human race. The Scriptures report that the neighbors of Israel and of the church were as deeply influenced by religious experiences as were the Israelites and the members of the church. For example, the 450 prophets of Baal and the 400 prophets of Asherah, who contested with Elijah on Mount Carmel, had experiences they believed derived from their god and his consort (1 Kings 18:19ff.). Or in New Testament times the devotion of the Ephesians to Artemis, goddess of the hunt, is obvious (Acts 19:23ff.).

Similarly, in contemporary times the followers of the various religions of the world describe their religions in terms of the religious experiences that they have. These experiences vary from one religion to another, each determined by the characteristics of that particular religion. But in all of them devotees take the experiences seriously, believing that they genuinely come from the god or gods they worship.

Religious Experience and Spirituality

Religious experiences or the religious dimension of life is often referred to as "spirituality." This term in popular parlance acknowledges the reality of a spiritual dimension to life without at the same time endorsing the Christian God.

Thus, the term "spirituality" suggests that we humans are more than animals with highly developed minds. We also have an inner dimension, that is, a spiritual dimension that seeks answers to ultimate questions such as the meaning and destiny of life. The term "spirituality" points to inner experiences that resonate with the ultimate questions.

The scope of vision in the term "spirituality" may be broad. The more traditional may use it to mean that the ultimate reality is God as Christians have understood him. The term may also include something more vague such as persons receding into their inner selves to be in touch with a universal life force.

Religious Experiences and the Nature of God

Classic Christianity has always acknowledged this universal human experience. But it has denied that all explanations of human spirituality are equally valid (Acts 17:26ff.). The distinct character of religious experiences in Christian teaching arises from the Christian view of God. Because of the nature of God and because God has made us so that we can relate to him, we humans have particular kinds of spiritual experiences.

The Scriptures describe these religious experiences in rich detail covering a wide range of possibilities. Adam and Eve hid from God's presence because of their shame for disobeying him (Genesis 3:7ff.). The psalmist rested in God though he was assaulted (Psalm 62). Jonah made a futile attempt to escape from God's presence and the task God had assigned him. The criminal crucified with Jesus repented and received the promise of everlasting life (Luke 23:40-43). Lydia had her heart opened by God to respond to Paul's preaching (Acts 16:13-15). Each one of these had a profound religious experience, each experience was unique to the individual person's situation, and each reflected the Christian view of God.

Thus, the Christian understanding of a religious experience can be described in two propositions:

- People may have religious experiences that are an integral part of their lives;
- These religious experiences are grounded in the nature of their personal relationships with the God

whose true character the Scriptures reveal and Christian teaching explicates.

2. THE CONTRIBUTION OF RELIGIOUS EXPERIENCE TO THEOLOGY

But in what sense do religious experiences provide knowledge that serves as a resource for theology? Or how do religious experiences contribute to that theology? There are two possibilities:

- Religious experiences may confirm a theological understanding that is securely grounded in the Scriptures;[45]
- Religious experiences awaken us to scriptural teachings that we had not heretofore been aware of or adequately understood.

3. THE INTERPRETATION OF RELIGIOUS EXPERIENCE

Personal experiences are real events. However, the experiences include meanings given to them either by the persons themselves or by others. Thus, subjective experience does not give us theological knowledge that we can set alongside the Scriptures or the teaching of the historic church. Experiences do not answer our questions; they themselves require answers and explanations. That is, they are real but do not satisfy our desire to understand.

The Complexity of Religious Experience

A religious experience is not merely a simple event caused by an encounter with God. Rather, it arises from a complex of factors. These factors coalesce to form the experience. We would include the following in religious experience:

- Theological ideas that have taken shape through teaching and reflection such as ideas about the nature of God or how one can enter into a right relationship with Him;

- An event that bears on ultimate questions, such as the birth of a child, a critical sickness, a death of a loved one, a moral failure or an inexplicable tragedy;

- Religious action that is based on the theological ideas that have been embraced such as repentance for sin, trust in God or continued rebellion against God;

- Emotions that arise from having succeeded or failed such as the fear of judgment for sin, the hunger for forgiveness from sin or the peace that comes from forgiveness;

- The actual relationship or the lack of a relationship with God such as a sense of His presence or of His absence.

4. THE TEACHING VALUE OF RELIGIOUS EXPERIENCE

Experience and Cognitive Dissonance

Religious experience can be unsettling. It can unsettle not only because it involves physical discomfort or pain but also because it may be difficult to reconcile the experience with the theological ideas the subject has embraced. Thus, the experience creates cognitive dissonance in the theological realm. That is, the mind is thrown into internal conflict.

For example, ancient Job, prior to his misfortune, had an understanding of the world and God that was perfectly satisfactory. Everything fit into its proper place and worked adequately for him (Job 1:1-5). Then he experienced a series of events that did not fit into his scheme, and he hardly knew what to make of them (Job. 1:6-2:8). This forced him to reconsider his understanding of God.

Advice given Job was of little help. We can divide the advice into two categories. Job's wife gave one type of advice by suggesting that he "curse God and die" (Job 2:9). Job's friends gave him a second type by suggesting that the old way of understanding the world was still adequate in spite of his distress (Job 2-37). Thus, two inappropriate answers to an experience in which a theological heritage fails, or appears to fail, in the time of crisis can be:

- rejecting the theological heritage without exploring its riches that may lie below the surface;
- denying the reality of the experience and blindly holding to inadequate theological understanding.

The Heuristic Role of Religious Experience

Experiences that excite cognitive dissonance should bring about deepened thought. They should not result in abandonment of faith nor the continued adherence to an inadequate understanding of faith. Instead, the religious experiences that create cognitive dissonance with regard to theological ideas should lead us to explore the deeper riches of Christian truth. They have *heuristic* value. The term "heuristic" comes from the Greek word that means "to find" or "to discover." The heuristic value of experience refers to its way of propelling us into deeper thought on truths we have embraced but have not fully understood. Thus, one of the principal ways in which experience contributes to theology is its pressure upon us to explore the Scriptures and historic church teaching to find clearer ways of understanding both Christian truth and the experience.

5. THE SCRIPTURES AND THE INTERPRETATION OF RELIGIOUS EXPERIENCE

The relation between experience and the Scriptures can be stated in two propositions:

- The Scriptures interpret and explain experience;

- Experience does not interpret or explain the Scriptures, but it does awaken us to explore the deep teachings of the Scriptures.

The Scriptures provide the theological norm and are our ultimate source of understanding because they have depths of wisdom for all the complex experiences of life. However, though we may believe this, we cannot say at the same time that we fully grasp the insight the Scriptures give.

"God ... Showed that He Accepted Them"

Acts 15 reports on the Council of Jerusalem in which the church leaders reflection on experience played a role in the debate. The question concerned whether gentile Christians needed to be circumcised and keep the law of Moses in order to be saved. Some Christian members of the party of the Pharisees argued that it was necessary, and Paul and Barnabas argued that it was not (vv.1-5).

Those who argued that circumcision was required could point to the one passage from the Old Testament that explicitly treats the issue of circumcision. They could claim that it supported their view (Genesis 17:9-14). Those who disputed the necessity of circumcision could not point to such an explicit Old Testament passage, but they could cite the recent experience of the successful gentile mission and also point to other Scriptures that were implicitly relevant. This is precisely what they did.

Peter recounted the case of Cornelius. Cornelius was a Gentile who had honored the God of Israel but had not become a full proselyte to Judaism. When Peter preached the gospel to him, Cornelius and his whole family accepted the message, received the Holy Spirit and were baptized. That is, they became full Christians (see Acts 10:1-11:18). Alluding to Cornelius at the Council of Jerusalem, Peter observed that "God, who knows the heart, showed that he accepted them by giving the Holy Spirit to them, just as he did to us" (Acts 15:8). From this he drew the deduction that the council should not require circumcision.

As the discussion at the council continued, Barnabas and Paul reported about their success in the gentile mission (Acts 15:12), referring to the work described in Acts 13:4-14:28. Thus, they pursued the same line of reasoning that Peter followed by pointing to religious experience.

Finally, James, who was presiding at the council, returned to the Scriptures. He cited Amos 9:11-12 in which the prophet foretold the time when God would take for Himself a people from the Gentiles (Acts 15:13-18). Thus, James argued that the Scriptures supported the side of those who favored lifting the circumcision requirement.

The Council of Jerusalem, then, did not set the Scriptures aside and take only the witness of experience. Instead, they looked at the total witness of the Scriptures in greater depth. The Scriptures interpreted and explained what they had seen but had not fully understood. Thus, the Scriptures remained normative but were understood more clearly through the heuristic force of new experiences.

6. CORPORATE RATHER THAN INDIVIDUAL RELIGIOUS EXPERIENCE

Many experiences described in the Scriptures are personal and individual in character. That is, they are described as happening in the life of a person. The general rule, however, is that these experiences are valid grist for the theological mill because they have a universal quality about them. For example, the psalmist may use the first person singular "I," since some psalms grew from personal experience and were thus autobiographical. But these psalms speak with such power because they match universal experience. In fact, as modern readers go through experiences such as those the psalmist went through, they are awakened to the riches of these psalms. These may include experiences of sickness (Psalm 41), guilt (Psalm 130) or danger and deliverance (Psalms 34:1-7). The universal character of these autobiographical psalms adds to their compelling truth.

On other occasions the psalmist explicitly refers to the experiences of others. These psalms express wisdom gained from reflection on common human experiences such as sickness and guilt (Psalms 107:17-22) or danger and deliverance (Psalms 107:23-32).[46]

John Wesley

One pioneering aspect of John Wesley's theology (and also of his contemporary, Jonathan Edwards) was the systematic way in which he studied the experiences of many people and considered their theological implications. His theological statements drawn from experience were not based solely on what went on in the lives of individuals, even his own. Rather, he carefully reflected on the complex spiritual experiences of people and studied the Scriptures to explain and make sense of them. Scriptures were not made to conform to experience but studied to illuminate experience. In a manner that resembles some features of the work of modern social scientists, Wesley observed what people did in a variety of circumstances. When he sought to understand what they did, however, he explored the Scriptures for clear explanations.[47]

7. RELIGIOUS EXPERIENCE AS A THEOLOGICAL RESOURCE

When we say that experience is a resource for theology, we must note at the same time that it is a different kind of resource. Experience does not offer us theological knowledge in the same way that the Scriptures do. Nor does it give us the kind of help in understanding the Scriptures and Christian truth that historic Christian teaching does. And finally, experience does not give us the tools for interpreting the Scriptures and historic Christian teaching the way that reason does. Instead, experience gives the data of real life, which themselves must be thought about and understood.

SUMMARY: *Experience*

1. People have universally had religious experiences. The unique contribution that Christian teaching makes to understanding these experiences grows from its unique view of God.

2. Experience does not offer theological understanding. Rather experience itself must be thought about and understood.

3. Religious experience can contribute to theology in that it confirms a theological understanding.

4. When experience results in cognitive dissonance in theological thinking, it should awaken us to consider the riches of the Scriptures and historic Christian teaching that up till then we had inadequately understood.

5. We should study the Scriptures to interpret experience, not experience to interpret the Scriptures.

6. When we use experience as a resource for our theological work, we think primarily of corporate or common human experience rather than individual, isolated experience.

ENDNOTES

[1] Dodd, *APD* 21-24.

[2] Carrington, *PCC* 14-17; Selwyn, *FESP* 383ff.

[3] Tertullian, *PAH* 13, *ANF* 3:249.

[4] Hippolytus, *AT* 21:12-18, pp. 36f.

[5] *1989 Book of Discipline* A/904, pp. 185f.

[6] Hippolytus, *AT* 26:21-27, p. 51.

[7] Wesley, Sermon 70, "The Case of Reason Impartially Considered," 1:5, *WJWB* 4:591f.; "A Letter to a Roman Catholic," 5-11, *JW* 494-96.

[8] *CC* 1:14-23 and *CC* 2:11-41.

[9] Fletcher, "The Portrait of St. Paul," III.V, *WJF* 3:209-11.

[10] Wheeler, *HETFAR* 47ff.

11. Wheeler, *HETFAR* 199ff.
12. Augustine, "On the Spirit and the Letter," 45, *NPNF* 1:5:102.
13. Wesley, Sermon 5, "Justification by Faith," *WJWB* 1:182ff.
14. Wesley, entry for May 24, 1738, *JJW* 1:466f.
15. Wesley, "An Address to the Clergy," 2, *WJW* 10:484; Outler, *JW* 9f., note 26; Flew, *IPCT* 118-88.
16. Outler, "Introduction" II and V, *WJWB* 13-29, 66-96.
17. Wesley, *FAMRR, I,* 5:6, *BWJW* 11:144f.
18. Augustine, *Reply to Faustus, the Manichean* 7:2, *NPNF* 1:4:174; Brown, *EJ* 368-76.
19. *A Commonitory* 2:6, *NPNF* 2:11:132.
20. Wesley, Sermon 39, "Catholic Spirit," III, *WJWB* 2:92-95.
21. *CC* 2:80.
22. *CCC* 80-83.
23. A/108, *BD 1989* p. 10; *CC* 3:489f.; see Wheeler, *HETFAR* 121-24.
24. Augustine, *On Baptism, Against the Donatists* 1:4. *NPNF* 1:4:427.
25. Oden, *WL* 14f.
26. Wesley, Sermon 16, "The Means of Grace," *WJWB* 1:386-89.
27. *PAH* 7, *ANF* 3:246.
28. Drewery, *HCD* 323-34.
29. Kent, *HCD* 581f.
30. Justin, *First Apology* 46, *ANF* 1:178.; see Tillich, *ST* 1:18-28.
31. Clement *Stromata* 1:19-20, *ANF* 2:321-23.
32. Brown, *AH* 101ff.
33. Wesley, "An Address to the Clergy," 2, *WJW* 10:483f.
34. Wesley, Sermon 70, "The Case of Reason Impartially Considered," I, *WJWB* 2:589-93.
35. Thomas, *ST* 1:32:1, *BWTA* 1:315-18.
36. Hilary, *Trin.* 1:46, *NPNF* 2:9:216.
37. Augustine, *Conf.* 3:9-11; 6:7f., *NPNF* 1:1:62f., 92f.
38. Madame Guyon, "God Known by Loving Him," *EC* 1:315.
39. *Pros.* 1, *Anselm* 5-7; Pope, *CCT* 1:43-45; Oden, *LG* 25.
40. Wesley, Sermon 69, "The Imperfection of Human Reason," *WJWB* 2:568-86.
41. Augustine, *Conf.* 10:36-42, *NPNF* 1:1:158-61.
42. Wesley, *EAMRR* 31-36.
43. Wesley, Sermon 38, "A Caution Against Bigotry," *WJWB* 2:63ff.; Casserley, *GR* 54-57.
44. Heschel, *GSM* 118f.; von Rad, *WI* 67f.
45. Wesley, Sermon 11, "The Witness of the Spirit," IV-V, *WJWB* 1:293-98.
46. Wesley, *JJW* 9, 110.
47. Cell, *RJW* 72-93.

PART II.

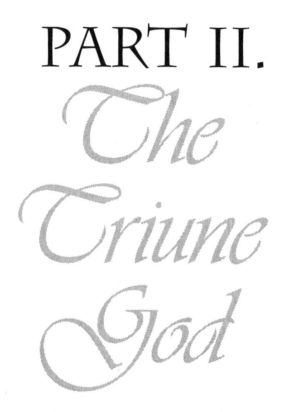
The Triune God

CHAPTER

1

THE GOD OF ISRAEL AND THE CHURCH AND THE GODS OF THE NATIONS

SECTION I. THE UNIQUENESS OF THE CHRISTIAN VIEW OF GOD

1. God, the Central Figure in the Scriptures
2. The Question in the Scriptures and the Early Church of Whether God Exists
3. The Uniqueness of the Christian View of God
4. The Question in the Scriptures and the Early Church on the Nature of God
5. The Priority of the Question of God's Nature Over Ethical Questions
6. Debates Within the Scriptures and Christian History
7. The Exclusive Nature of the Christian View of God

SECTION II. THE QUESTION OF GOD'S EXISTENCE

1. Modern Skepticism on the Question of God
2. The Persistence of Belief in God
3. The Arguments for the Existence of God
   A. The Ontological Argument
   B. The Cosmological Argument
   C. The Teleological Argument
   D. The Moral Argument
4. The Results and Limits of the Arguments

THE GOD OF OUR SALVATION

SECTION I. *The Uniqueness of the Christian View of God*

1. GOD, THE CENTRAL FIGURE IN THE SCRIPTURES

The entire Bible focuses on God as the chief actor.[1] The Old Testament begins with the statement that God created the heavens and the earth (Genesis 1:1). Immediately after giving a genealogy, Matthew, the author of the first book in the New Testament, recounts Jesus' birth as Immanuel, "God with us" (Matthew 1:23). And the story of the earliest church commences with Jesus telling His disciples that the Father would send His Spirit after His departure so that they could witness to the world (Acts 1:8).

God is the central figure in the story of Israel, in the account of Jesus of Nazareth and in the message of the early church. At the core of Christian faith is a firm belief in God.

2. THE QUESTION IN THE SCRIPTURES AND THE EARLY CHURCH OF WHETHER GOD EXISTS

The Psalmist stated: "The fool says in his heart, 'There is no God'" (Psalms 14:1). The fool he may have had in mind was a practical atheist. Some lived as if God did not exist and they would never have to answer to him. There were theoretical atheists in ancients times, too, but they were by far in the minority.

Hence, we rarely see within the Scriptures an argument for the existence of God. Paul's words in Romans 1:19f. approach this argument, but even this passage does not have the appearance of the traditional arguments for God's existence.

3. THE UNIQUENESS OF THE CHRISTIAN VIEW OF GOD

Belief in a supreme supernatural being is not unique to the Scriptures nor to Christian faith. The fact that the Scriptures speak constantly about God does not, in itself, set them apart.[2]

However, the particular view of God that Christians have sets the Christian faith apart from all other faiths. No other religion thinks of God in the way that Christians do.[3] Closest to the Christian view is that of Judaism.[4] At a much greater distance is that of Islam. The views of the other religions depart even more from Christian truth.

Distinguishing the Christian View of God from the Jewish View

The Christian view of God is closer to that of Judaism than to that of any other religion. Since both Jews and Christians accept the Old Testament as canonical, they agree on the teaching of God's transcendence, unity and spirituality.[5] But Judaism does not accept Jesus as the incarnate Son of God nor does it accept the Christian understanding of the Spirit of God. That is, it rejects Christian teaching on the Trinity.[6]

Distinguishing the Christian View of God from the Pagan View

When the Christian church began to preach to Gentiles, the church could not assume that the listeners understood the meaning it gave to the term "God," even in an elementary sense. And after Gentiles had come to understand the Christian view, they did not necessarily agree with it.

Christians have always had to define sharply who God is and what He is like, and thus set the Christian view in distinction from pagan views. Paul, for example, acknowledged that the Athenians were very religious people who believed in gods and observed religious practices, but he said they were still ignorant of the truth about God and failed to worship Him as they ought (Acts 17:22ff.).

4. THE QUESTION IN THE SCRIPTURES AND THE EARLY CHURCH ON THE NATURE OF GOD

During the time the Scriptures were being written, the major problem its authors had to deal with concerned the nature of God. They constantly debated with other religions whose views of God differed radically from the Christian view.

In some cases these false views of God were adopted only by those outside of Israel and the church (Psalms 115:2ff.; 1 Corinthians 8:4-6). At other times the false views were embraced not only by non-Israelites or non-Christians but also by God's chosen people. In these cases false views threatened the integrity of the faith (Exodus 32; Revelation 2:14f.).

5. THE PRIORITY OF THE QUESTION OF GOD'S NATURE OVER ETHICAL QUESTIONS

Both the Scriptures and the great teachers of the church have assumed that the question about God's nature is the first question of theology. If people adopt a true view of God, they then have a foundation upon which ethical questions can be dealt with. But if they embrace a false view of God, it is impossible to turn the tide against evil behavior.[7]

"Be Holy Because I, the Lord Your God, am Holy"

The detailed instructions on holiness recounted in Leviticus 19-26 are introduced with an observation about the character of God: "The Lord said to Moses, 'Speak to the entire assembly of Israel and say to them: "Be holy because

I, the LORD your God, am holy""" (Leviticus 19:1-2; see 1 Peter 1:15f.). The holiness of God is the standard and the ground for holiness in God's people.[8]

"Destroyed from a Lack of Knowledge"

The prophet Hosea preached to the people of Israel, who had become Baal worshipers. Hosea catalogued how they were guilty of great injustice and wickedness, but he noted that the source and foundation of evil practices lay in a view of God that was false. "My people," Hosea said, "are destroyed from lack of knowledge" (4:6). Hence, they stumbled and their prophets stumbled (4:5). They consulted idols rather than God's law and engaged in the prostitution sponsored by the Baal cult. They sacrificed to idols and gave their very children to this vile worship of Baal (4:11-13; see 1 Thessalonians 4:4f.).[9]

Early Church Apologies

In its attempts to win the world to Christianity, the same sequence was observed by teachers of the early church. Before they would try to instruct Gentiles on how to live, they debated with them about their views of God.[10]

These teachers wrote "apologies."[11] An apology gives a reasoned argument why heathen views are wrong and the Christian view is right. The apologies of these ancient teachers pointed out that pagan myths described their gods as deceitful, murderous, adulterous and cruel. Those who believed the myths would behave as the gods did, as reported in the myths. Apologies also pointed out that the myths were self-contradictory and nonsense. Wise pagans and the better philosophers did not even believe the myths were true.

On the other hand, the apologists reasoned, the Christian God is righteous, merciful and redemptive; and the biblical story is well-supported and full of good sense. Those who abandon the false views of God and adopt the Christian view begin to live life differently. The correct view of God becomes the foundation of a better life.[12]

6. DEBATES WITHIN THE SCRIPTURES AND CHRISTIAN HISTORY

The Scriptures report strong debates about God and His nature. Those who spoke for God delineated the truth about God and explained why it is true. They also refuted what is false and explained why it is false. For example, Isaiah (44:9ff.) jeered at the idols of pagans. Jesus told the woman of Samaria that the Jews knew the truth about God and the Samaritans did not (John 4:22). Immediately after his conversion, Saul preached in the synagogues of Damascus that Jesus was the Son of God and the Christ, and for that Jews tried to kill him (Acts 9:20-31).

Similarly, Christian leaders after the New Testament books were all written also engaged various persons in rigorous debate. Justin Martyr[13] argued with Jews that Jesus was the promised Messiah and the Son of God. Justin[14] and Tertullian[15] debated with Roman officials that Christian belief in Jesus as the Son of God did not threaten the well-being of the empire. And Athanasius[16] and Augustine[17] argued with other learned philosophers that the Christian view of God made better sense than did any other view.

7. THE EXCLUSIVE NATURE OF THE CHRISTIAN VIEW OF GOD

Historically both Israel and the church defined their views of God by distinguishing them from pagan views. They declared what they believed by setting it over against what they did not believe. The Christian view represented the true view of God, and the others represented the false view.

This method of debate, by its very nature, is exclusivistic. It claims to know the truth in the question under discussion.

Persons who intend to become genuine Christians must surrender other views of God.

The exclusivistic strain in biblical religion has excited strong objection. The idea has commonly been claimed in both the ancient and modern worlds that no position so grips the truth that it can rightly exclude all contradictory statements as inherently wrong. The Christian view does this.

Neither Israel nor the church asked people to sacrifice the integrity of their intellects when they called them to faith in the true God. Instead they spent enormous energy clarifying what they meant when they talked about God and explaining why their view was logical and true. Still, the essential element in Christian teaching is that a Christian view of God is incompatible with a non-Christian view. One cannot at the same time believe in the Christian God and hold a view of God that departs from the historic Christian understanding of God. To do so is illogical and inconsistent.

SUMMARY: *The Uniqueness of the Christian View of God*

1. Virtually all peoples in the past and in the present have believed in a supreme being.

2. The predominant question within ancient times was not whether a supernatural being, God, exists; the question concerned his nature. Thus the Scriptures and historic Christian teaching offer a unique view of God.

3. Both Jews and Christians emphasize God's transcendence, unity and spirituality. But Judaism rejects Christian teaching on the incarnation of the Son of God and on the Trinity. Other religions and philosophies offer views of God that depart much more radically from the Christian view.

4. When Christian teachers have encountered those who belonged to other religions or have held non-

Christian views of God, a consideration of God's nature has always been an important part of their conversation.

5. Classic thinkers within the Scriptures and the church believed that the question of God's nature preceded questions about ethics. Thus, before we can determine what is right and wrong and what Christian behavior ought to be, we have to determine the correct understanding of God.

6. When the gospel was proclaimed, one important first step was to raise the question of God's nature. Within the Scriptures and the early church, Christian teachers engaged in apologies, that is, demonstrations of the weakness of the logic in false views about God and defenses of the Christian view.

7. Christian teaching on God is exclusivistic. That is, one cannot accept the Christian view and another view at the same time.

SECTION II. *The Question of God's Existence*

1. MODERN SKEPTICISM ON THE QUESTION OF GOD

The classic Christian view of God prevailed for centuries in the church. But a new challenge was introduced at the end of the medieval era and remains with us today. This is the challenge of modern skepticism.

Modern skepticism of the historic church's view of God was founded in the revolution in philosophy leading to the change in natural sciences. Important thinkers, such as Roger Bacon, who initiated the change in the sciences, continued to embrace the Christian view of God. These men had in mind only that when we investigate the material world, we must rely solely on empirical evidence. But in time the new philosophical method began to impact the way people thought about God.

Modern skepticism has spread widely as agnosticism and atheism, especially in certain circles such as institutions of higher education. Agnosticism states that we can never know whether God exists or what He is like, even if He does exist. Atheism is bolder and denies God's existence altogether.[18]

2. THE PERSISTENCE OF BELIEF IN GOD

In spite of the influence that agnosticism and atheism have gained, belief in God persists. Historically such belief was nearly universal in the many religions of the world, but the persistence of faith in spite of the present environment of skepticism is an important phenomenon. This continuing faith in God is not confined to one segment of society. Believers include many members from across the general population, rich and poor, educated and uneducated, laborers and professionals.[19]

3. THE ARGUMENTS FOR THE EXISTENCE OF GOD

Christian thinkers across the centuries have argued for God's existence. Through these arguments they have sought to demonstrate the existence of a supreme supernatural being consistent with the historic Christian view of God. This method proceeded through the use of reason alone without a basis in the Scriptures. That is, it sought to show that the Christian view of God, while depending upon revelation, does not violate or contradict the best use of human reason.

Thomas Aquinas (1225-1274) gathered several of these arguments into an organized system that has been widely adopted as a model since his time.[20] We can group the various arguments into four basic types: the ontological, the cosmological, the teleological and the moral arguments.

A. The Ontological Argument

The term "ontological" comes from the Greek verb "to be" and thus refers to "that which exists." Anselm (1033/34-1109) originally developed the ontological argument in the form with which we normally associate it. Anselm stated his thesis in a simple formula, but it is still not easy to grasp. The best way to understand the ontological argument is to read and then reread his words. They run as follows: "There exists a being, than which nothing greater can be conceived, and it exists both in the understanding and in reality."[21]

Anselm anticipated possible objections to this argument. For example, someone might claim that to think of God as the greatest of all beings cannot prove His existence. For at the same time we think of such a being, we can also think that such a being does not exist, that is, He is only a thought. But, responded Anselm, it is illogical to say that we can think of a being that is the greatest of all beings but does not exist. Since existence is surely a characteristic of the greatest of all beings, when we think of the greatest of all beings, we are thinking of one who must exist.

The ontological argument is deceptively simple in form. Upon first reading it may seem to be nothing more than a game of logic, as critics of Anselm have claimed.[22] Many seem to have missed its main point. It does not argue that because I can imagine something, it must exist. Rather, it claims that the reason the mind intuits or senses a supreme being is because this supreme being really exists and really must of necessity exist.[23]

B. The Cosmological Argument

The cosmological argument goes back as far as the church fathers.[24] However, it is most generally linked with Thomas Aquinas who offered variations of the argument. He argued from the principle of causation, pointing to the sequence of effects resulting from causes. For example, a daughter is born of a father and mother, who in turn were born of their fathers and mothers, and so on. Thus, each effect has a cause.

To explain the full story, Thomas said, we have to posit one of two things. Either there is an ultimate, non-contingent and necessary cause that is not caused by anything else but causes other effects and we call that God; or there is an infinity of intermediate and contingent causes that may cause other effects but were also themselves the effects of other causes.

Within our world, the material world, we know intermediate or efficient causes. Nothing in our natural experience causes itself. As stated above, daughters are born of mothers and fathers, and so on back as far as we can go. But was there ever a first mother and father; and, if there were, where did they come from? Either there is an infinity of efficient causes and effects, which Thomas believed is plainly illogical, or there is an ultimate first cause, God.

The persistent objection to the cosmological argument is that it claims to know something we simply cannot know. The cosmological argument claims that we can mentally step outside of the chain of intermediate causes and effects to posit an ultimate cause. But the critics state that we simply cannot do this. We do not have any experience of an ultimate cause. It is purely a hypothetical construct. When we jump from intermediate causes, which are what we experience day in and day out, to the ultimate cause, we project something outside of our world.[25]

But the main question of the cosmological argument maintains its force. To ask why there is something and not nothing in the world is worth pondering. The criticism of the cosmological argument merely reflects the limits of empirical knowledge. Empirical knowledge, the knowledge we can gain from the study of physical evidence, confines us to the causal link within the material world. The cosmological argument claims that we can think beyond the empirical realm, and those who oppose the argument have never shown why such thinking is not legitimate.[26]

C. The Teleological Argument

The teleological argument, also called the argument from design, points to the intricate way in which complex parts of our world work together to achieve goals. William Paley (1743-1805) gave the argument popular form by using the watch and the eye as examples. If we should stumble on a watch, Paley reasoned, with its wheels, springs and levers of various sizes and shapes all perfectly adjusted to one another so that exact measurement of time can be made, we would not suppose the watch just happened. There must have been a watchmaker who originally designed the instrument to achieve a purpose and who then executed the design. Likewise, the human eye reflects enormous complexity in purpose, design and execution. And when we add the many parts of nature together and reflect on how wonderfully they are coordinated, we must assume that there was an original purposer, designer and creator – God.[27]

Philosophers often claim that the theory of evolution refutes the teleological proof. The theory of evolution states that new and more complex forms of life developed by adapting to their environments by "natural selection." Rather than accept the notion of an original designer who at the beginning created complicated creatures, these opponents of the teleological argument claim that the complex creatures gradually evolved as the weaker, nonproductive forms became extinct and the hearty ones arose.

The teleological argument emphasizes the complex of intermediate causes. The world with its multiple causes and effects works with stunning precision. For example, vegetable life depends upon an intricate balance of light, air, moisture and chemical. Or humans are not only living creatures but highly complex living creatures. The statistical chances of all this occurring by accident or, according to the theory of evolution, by natural selection, are infinitesimal. It is simpler and more credible to acknowledge that a wise God made this complex creation.

D.   The Moral Argument

The moral argument arises from the innate sense we have that some things are good and others evil. We, as human beings, all possess this moral sense; and thus we know that we should act in certain ways and avoid other acts. Since this is how we are, the logical conclusion is that God has made us this way and we will ultimately have to answer to him.[28]

Two major criticisms of the moral argument have been put forward. The first criticism acknowledges claims that the sense of right and wrong, which all human beings admittedly have, results from social influence such as parental training. If this is the case, then we cannot look to a transcendent being, God, as its source.

However, most critics of the moral argument join the rest of us in presuming that some values are universal and that all of us, when we think about them, know what they are. That is, these values are not imposed by mere social influence but belong to the very nature of human beings and reflect how they are made. Historians hold individuals and nations accountable for failing to live up to certain ideals. For example, condemnation of war criminals for "crimes against humanity" depends upon the universality of the moral sense. The most logical source of this universal moral sense is God, the Creator, who made us with the capacity to make moral judgments.

The second criticism of the moral argument takes up the problem of evil. It asks why so many innocent persons suffer if God is both the sovereign of the world and good. A sovereign God who allows such tragedy, it is argued, cannot have a very well-developed moral character. Certainly he is many steps behind the average human who does not claim moral perfection but would not permit a child to endure misery.[29]

The answer to this second criticism of the moral argument looks more fully at the kind of world we live in. We live in a moral universe; therefore, we are more than simply individuals or social units in an amoral and strictly material universe. The network of what we do and how it affects our environment is complex. If God constantly interfered to ensure that evil deeds did not bring evil consequences on the innocent, the processes of this world would break down. It would no longer be a moral universe.

Immanuel Kant himself, a critic of the other three arguments for the existence of God, accepted the moral argument as valid. He appealed to the doctrine of the afterlife. He proposed that there the accounts are fully settled. Now we are in a time of testing and trial. Then evil will be finally dealt with, and righteousness will be vindicated. That great judge and settler of the accounts is God.

4. THE RESULTS AND LIMITS OF THE ARGUMENTS

By themselves the arguments rarely bring skeptics to faith. But their inability to persuade skeptics is not simply because the arguments are flawed. In terms of their logical consistency, the arguments are every bit as cogent as their critiques. While they may not compel belief, they show with real force that Christian belief in God is rational and consistent with thoughtful investigation of the world outside of special revelation.

But the arguments for the existence of God are far from offering a full-orbed Christian understanding of God.[30] For that we depend upon the revelation that God has given us in his work with Israel and in Jesus Christ as recorded in the Holy Scriptures.

SUMMARY: *The Question of God's Existence*

1. Modern skepticism, born of a thoroughgoing empirical method, has cast doubt on the existence of God. Disbelief in the forms of agnosticism or outright atheism has become prominent, especially in certain circles.

2. Even in modern times, however, belief in God persists across the general population.

3. Classic arguments for the existence of God have been offered that describe God in a manner consistent with his nature as we know it from the Scriptures.

4. The ontological argument describes God as the being who is greater than any other conceivable being.

5. The cosmological argument describes God as the original and necessary cause of all things that are in the chain of secondary causes and effects.

6. The teleological argument emphasizes the complex world in which we live, how wonderfully all its parts coordinate and the obvious conclusion that a great designer has created everything within the world.

7. The moral argument points to the innate sense that all humans have that certain things are right, others are wrong and that we are all accountable for our behavior.

8. The arguments cannot prove the existence of God in a way that will force skeptics into belief. But they do show that belief in God is logically consistent and makes sense.

9. The arguments for the existence of God do not offer us a full-orbed Christian view of God. For that, revelation is absolutely necessary.

ENDNOTES

1. Heschel, *GSM* 136-43.
2. Ringgren, *IR* 66f.; Wright, *OTAE* 16-29.
3. Clement of Alexandria, "Exhortation to the Heathen," *ANF* 2:171ff.
4. Buber, *TTF* 7-12.
5. Epistle to Diognetus 4, *AF* 252f.; Novak, *JCD* 36-41; Oden, *WL* 49.
6. Knight, "Building Theological Bridges," *JC* 109-23; Novak, *JCD* 59-72.
7. Eichrodt, *TOT* 1:282-86.
8. Eichrodt, *TOT* 1:278.
9. Snaith, *DIOT* 56f.
10. Grant, *AC* 101-19.
11. Lactantius, Clement of Alexandria, Tertullian.
12. Pellegrino, *ECC* 1:60.
13. *Dialogue with Trypho* 1, *ANF* 1:195.
14. *Apologies* 1:1-3 and 2:1, *ANF* 1:163, 188.
15. *Apology* 1-4, *ANF* 3:17-21.
16. *Against the Heathen* 1, *NPNF* 2:4:4 and *On the Incarnation of the Word*, *NPNF* 2:4:36ff.
17. *The City of God* 1:1, *NPNF* 1:2:1.
18. Wiley, *CT* 1:262-67.
19. Wiley, *CT* 224-26.
20. *ST* 1:2:3, *BWTA* 1:21-24.
21. *Pros.* 2, *Anselm* 8.
22. Gaunilon, *Anselm* 145-53; Kant, *EG* 39-40.
23. Oden, *LG* 174-79.
24. Hilary, *Trin.* 1:4, *NPNF* 2:9:3f.
25. Hume, *EG* 93-98.
26. Russell and Copelston, "A Debate on the Existence of God," *EG* 167-91.
27. Paley, *EG* 99-103.
28. Kant, *EG* 137-43.
29. Mill, *EG* 114-20.
30. Hill, *ER* 12:5-7.

CHAPTER

2

THE TRUE
AND
LIVING GOD

SECTION I. THE NAMES OF GOD
1. God
2. Yahweh
3. The Lord

SECTION II. THE ATTRIBUTES OF GOD
1. Categories of God's Attributes
2. The Spirituality of God
3. The Personality of God
4. God as Self-caused and Self-sustaining
5. The Unity of God
6. The Immutability of God
7. The Sovereign Power of God
8. The Sovereign Knowledge of God, His Foreknowledge and His Wisdom
9. The Sovereignty of God Over Time
10. The Sovereignty of God Over Space: Immensity, Infinity and Omnipresence
11. The Holiness, Righteousness and Truthfulness of God
12. The Goodness, Love and Mercy of God

SECTION III. THE HOLY TRINITY
1. The Old Testament Witness to the Trinity
2. The New Testament Witness to the Trinity

3. The Trinitarian Controversies of the Early Church
   A. Three Early Heresies
   B. Two Later Heresies
   C. The Definition of Orthodoxy
4. The Controversy between the East and West
   on the Procession of the Spirit
5. Essential Features of Trinitarian Thought

onversation about God is possible with those who do not accept Christian revelation, and this conversation can make some progress. But the unique Christian understanding of God cannot be discerned, let alone believed, until we turn to the Scriptures and examine them with the aid of historic Christian teaching.

The unique Christian teachings about God appear in three areas: in the names chosen to denote God, in characteristics attributed to Him and in the Trinity.

DIVINE NAMES THAT DESCRIBE THE CHARACTER OF GOD

A few divine names appear repeatedly in the Scriptures: God, Yahweh and the Lord. Each of these makes a unique contribution to our understanding of God's character. Other divine names appear in the Scriptures with low usage, and the meaning of them is obvious. Among these rarely used names are titles such as the Holy One of Israel or Savior, and metaphors such as the Rock or Shield. Because the meanings of the latter are obvious, we will not examine them but give attention to the three most frequently used names.

ATTRIBUTES THAT DESCRIBE THE CHARACTER OF GOD

God's attributes are qualities we attribute to him. They represent an understanding of God's character. Most terms adopted for these attributes such as righteousness or mercy, appear explicitly within the Scriptures. Others such as omnipotence or aseity (that is, underived existence), though not found explicitly within the Scriptures, grow from their teachings and draw together ideas found within them.

THE HOLY TRINITY

The teaching that God reveals himself as Father, Son and Holy Spirit, that is, the Trinity, became explicit in the New Testament and was articulated by the early church. This teaching sets Christianity distinctly apart from Judaism, with which it has much in common. Early credal forms of this teaching are found in the rule of faith[1] and eventually developed into the well-known Apostles' Creed. This great affirmation of Christian faith is structured around the three Persons of the Trinity. Thus, the teaching of the Trinity forms the climax of the Christian understanding of God.

SECTION I. *The Names of God*

1. GOD

The most common divine name in the Scriptures is God. Both the Hebrew word used most frequently, *elohim*, and the Greek word, *theos*, designate the supreme supernatural Being.

The Scriptures also use these words for the gods whom pagans worship. The root from which the Hebrew word derives, *el*, appears in other Semitic languages; and *theos* is the common Greek word for a divine being. Still, the Scriptures do not consider this pagan usage as wholly proper (1 Corinthians 8:5). While they acknowledge that such beings might exist; these gods do not challenge the supremacy of God. He alone is truly God (Isaiah 45:18-25). On the other hand, the expression "living God" (Deuteronomy 5:26; Psalms 42:2; 1 Thessalonians 1:9) affirms that the God of Israel and the church is real and implicitly denies the reality of any being behind pagan idols; they are merely wood or stone.

2. YAHWEH

The other most common divine name in the Old Testament is Yahweh. As far as we know, this name was unique to Israel. It came to serve as the proper name for Israel's God.

In His theophany – that is, His appearance – to Moses, God identified himself as the God of Abraham, Isaac and Jacob (Exodus 3:6) and revealed his name as Yahweh (Exodus 3:14), relating it to the verb "to be," *hayah*, saying, "I am who I am" (Exodus 3:13f.). The origin of the name Yahweh is uncertain; but it clearly expresses the idea that the God of Israel is the truly, eternal existing One.[2]

Both Jews and Christians understood "Yahweh" to signify that God was the eternal Being. When Greek-speaking Jews translated the Bible into the Greek language, they rendered the crucial revelation to Moses as *ego eimi ho on*, which literally means "I am the One who is."

Jesus referred to Himself using the same language; sometimes with a predicate, such as "I am the bread of life" (John 6:48) and sometimes without a predicate, simply "I am" (John 8:58). In the latter case, the Jews who heard Jesus understood Him to be identifying Himself with Yahweh (John 8:59).[3]

3. THE LORD

The divine name "Lord" also appears in both Testaments. The Hebrew word *adonai* and the Greek *kurios* both suggest sovereignty. Thus, those in covenant with God are not his equals but his subjects, and they should render him obedience and service.

After the Babylonian exile Hebrew-speaking Jews no longer read the divine name "Yahweh" aloud. It became the unspeakable name and was highly revered. In synagogue worship, when readers came to the name "Yahweh" in the Scriptures, they substituted *adonai* in its place. Similarly, in almost all cases Greek-speaking Jews who translated the Old Testament used the word *kurios*.

Likewise, "Lord" became one of the most common divine names for Jesus after the Resurrection (Acts 2:36). In part Christians used this name to reject efforts of Rome to force a confession that the emperor was *dominus* (Lord). The courageous stand of the early Christians arose because they understood it to be a divine name, one that they must deny to an emperor and ascribe only to Jesus (1 Corinthians 12:3).[4]

SUMMARY: *The Names of God*

1. The divine names serve as concise indicators of God's character.
2. The name "God" signifies the supreme supernatural being who alone is to be worshiped.
3. The name "Yahweh" suggests that God is the eternal existing One. Because the name "Yahweh" was revealed only to Israel, it signifies that true knowledge of God comes through His self-revelation.
4. The name "Lord" calls us, as subjects, to obey and serve our divine Sovereign.

SECTION II. *The Attributes of God*

1. CATEGORIES OF GOD'S ATTRIBUTES

The divine attributes are the characteristics God has. Christian teaching has developed different kinds of categories to distinguish these attributes. One kind of category distinguishes absolute from relative attributes; another natural from moral attributes.[5]

Absolute and Relative Attributes

We can think of God in relation to two separate spheres: first Himself and second the world He has created, especially human beings whom He governs and redeems. The first focuses on God alone and the second on God and everything else.

God's absolute attributes refer to the qualities God has in relation to Himself. For example, even if there were no world or no human beings, God would be spiritual and perfectly wise.

God's relative attributes refer to God in relation to the created world and people. To the created world, for example, God is almighty and omnipresent. That is, He exercises His power in relation to the world He has created and thus is almighty; and He spans all time and thus is omnipresent. To human beings God is loving, merciful, just and redemptive.[6]

The distinction between God's absolute and relative attributes has limits. If there were no created world, for example, we would still say God is good, though we largely think of His goodness in relationship to His creatures.

Natural and Moral Attributes

The relative attributes of God can be further divided into two classes: those that relate God to the whole of the created world, and those that relate Him to moral creatures in that world as their judge and redeemer.

As the governor of the whole world, God exercises absolute sovereign power. He is greater than His creation in terms of time, space and knowledge.

With respect to the moral creatures He has created, whether supernatural or human, He also governs as their sovereign. Though He grants them limited freedom, all moral creatures still must answer to God. He gives the standard for truthfulness and righteousness. As their sovereign judge, He also is the one who can effectively grant mercy and spiritual renewal.

The Transcendence and Immanence of God

The transcendence of God in the first place speaks of God as greater than anything else in the world, seen or unseen, natural or supernatural. The only language that we can use to describe this characteristic of God is that of metaphor: "Do not I fill the heaven and earth?" (Jeremiah 23:24).[7]

When the Scriptures describe the heavenly court they strike the transcendent note. The Old Testament pictures God as a monarch being worshiped by heavenly creatures (Isaiah 6:1-7), and the New Testament also sees Him on the throne where He is worshiped by the church (Revelation 4-5).

Most commonly, however, the Scriptures refer to God in relation to the world, that is, in His immanence. Even in His immanence, God remains Spirit. We cannot see or concretely sense His involvement, though we can see the effect of it (John 3:3-8). In various ways God participates in the events that take place within the world. For example, God sustains the natural order by regulating the seasons of the year (Acts 14:17) and providing for the fruitfulness of living creatures (Deuteronomy 26:10). Also, He intervenes in the natural course of events, what the Scriptures call signs and wonders and we refer to as miracles (Psalms 78:4, 11;

125

John 2:11). Finally, God moves directly on human wills, such as guiding and overruling in the decisions people make. For example, the brothers of Joseph had sold him into slavery with the intention of getting him out of their lives, but God intended for him eventually to become the means of saving the family of his father Isaac (Genesis 50:20).

2. THE SPIRITUALITY OF GOD

The Hebrew and Christian understanding of God reflected in the Scriptures is utterly distinct from that of the other cultures round about Israel. With few exceptions, ancient peoples imagined divine beings in material terms. These beings were large and gigantic, as Baal who rode the clouds. Still, they were material.

In the most succinct statement of this truth, Jesus declared that God is Spirit (John 4:24). When we say that God is absolutely spiritual, we think of His actual being as totally independent of the material world, though He can relate to the world and use it as He designs. In no way does God depend upon any creature, seen or unseen.

Scriptural Images of God as Material or Human

The Scriptures often picture God in concrete or human terms; therefore, they may use features of nature to personify God's person. For example, the clap of thunder, God's voice, is powerful (Psalms 29:3-9). His strong arm delivers from enemies (Psalms 44:3), and His face turned toward us shows His favor (Numbers 6:25). And God grows hot with anger (Exodus 4:14).

We call the human images that the Scriptures use of God "anthropomorphisms." This term comes from two Greek words: *anthropos*, the human being, and *morphe*, form. Thus, to speak of God anthropomorphically is to speak of Him as possessing human form.[8]

In its boldest form the Scriptures state that God made us in His image and likeness (Genesis 1:26f.). Though the terms "image" and "likeness" can also be used of idols, Genesis 1 does not suggest that God has a physical image, nor does the dignity humans possess lie in their physical resemblance to God. The church has understood this language used of God as metaphorical. That is, since God is Spirit, He cannot be represented by any image made from matter (Exodus 20:4, 23; Deuteronomy 5:8),[9] and humans bear God's likeness in some spiritual way.

3. THE PERSONALITY OF GOD

Because human beings are made in God's image, they have special qualities that other creatures do not have. They have the powers of intelligence and choice so that they can consciously direct their actions toward goals. God also has intelligence and will, and He can purposefully think and choose. For example, the Scriptures speak of God's counsel and choice, which suggest that He has thought a matter entirely through, come to a decision about the best course of action, and is systematically effecting His will (Psalms 33:11; Isaiah 19:17; Ephesians 1:11).

Also, because humans are made in God's image they can talk with others in ways that lower creatures cannot. So God also communicates.[10]

God's personal relational qualities are shared internally within the Godhead before they are shared externally with creatures He has made. And all of God's personal relationships with His creatures are grounded in the relationships of the Father, Son and Holy Spirit within the Godhead. The Father loves the Son and has put all things into His hands (John 3:35). The Spirit, who is God, intercedes for the saints (Romans 8:26). The Son, who is God, also intercedes for the saints (Hebrews 7:25). The Persons within the Trinity profoundly relate to one another. These inter-trinitarian relationships within the Godhead indicate the personal quality of God.

The Pathos of God

The Scriptures speak of God as possessing emotions that human beings possess, such as compassion (2 Kings 13:23; Psalms 86:15), wrath (Nahum 1:2-6; Revelation 16:19) and grief (Genesis 6:6; Ephesians 4:30). The prophets in particular go farther and note shifts in God's emotions as He responds to human beings and their self-inflicted tragedies. For example, Hosea describes the change of God's wrath to mercy. The Israelites clearly merit wrath, the prophet notes, but even before their repentance God shows pity: "My heart is changed within me; all my compassion is aroused. I will not carry out my fierce anger (Hosea 11:8f.; see Joel 2:13f.). [11]

Human emotions may be complex, especially when we are dealing with others in personal relationships. What one does responds to what another does. The love one offers may awaken a responding love in the other. The rejection one gives may be answered with grief or anger in the other. One may even recoil from allowing the results of sin to go on without some relief. There are no simple explanations for this complex of emotions and the actions they elicit.

Some theologies have described God as "impassible." This word comes from the negative form of the Latin word *passus* and means "incapable of being affected" or "incapable of suffering." The concept cannot apply to the God of Israel and the church; He is deeply involved in the human story. Though God is perfectly righteous, He cannot be described as an unaffected judge who has no stake in the matter. Jesus knew the end that would fall on the city of Jerusalem and would not prevent it, but He mourned for the city with a longing heart (Matthew 23:37-39).

To Know God as Personal

Because God is personal, we can relate to Him as persons. The Bible often uses the expression "to know God" to describe this personal relationship. However, because of our finiteness we can know God only in a limited sense, and it is more proper to say that we are known by God (Galatians 4:9). We will know Him more fully only after the resurrection (1 Corinthians 13:12).

Still, in this restricted sense, both the Old and New Testaments speak of limited, finite human persons as knowing God.[12] When we say that we know a person, we say both that we know certain facts about that person, and that we share with that person in interpersonal ways so that the relationship can have genuine depth. The Old Testament often refers cautiously to knowing something about God that has, or ought to have, a profound effect upon the entire life (Exodus 16:11; Psalms 41:11; see Romans 2:18).

But the Scriptures also speak in terms of the personal relationship a person can have with God. The direct petitions of the psalmist portray this intimate knowledge of God. For example, he can pray: "To you, O Lord, I lift up my soul; in you I trust, O my God" (Psalms 25:1-2a; see 63:1-7). The closest analogies to this relationship between God and his servants are found in human relationships such as that of husband and wife (Ephesians 5:25-27) or mother and child (Psalms 131:2) or father and children (Romans 8:15) or that of friends with one another (James 2:23).

When we say that God is supremely personal, we include several thoughts. We mean that God is infinitely wise and free to choose according to His good pleasure. In the context of His wisdom and His freedom, He has chosen to relate in a personal way with creatures He has made.

The personhood of God, then, makes possible the relationship God has with Himself through the Persons of the Trinity, and the relationship He can have with His creatures, both supernatural (angels) and human.

4. GOD AS SELF-CAUSED AND SELF-SUSTAINING

God does not depend upon anything outside of Himself either for His original existence or for His continued existence. God has life in Himself and has granted to the Son that He have life in Himself (John 5:25f.). This is fundamentally assumed in the Scriptures, not discussed. For everything that exists does so because God causes it to exist. But nowhere do we have an account of how God came to exist; He simply is.

We refer to this self-caused quality of God as His aseity. The term "aseity" comes from two Latin words: the prefix *a*, meaning "from," and the pronoun *se*, meaning "oneself." Thus God's aseity refers to His "being from himself" alone. It emphasizes that He does not depend on anything or any one else. He was caused by nothing outside of Himself and continues to exist by nothing beyond Himself.

When we say that God is self-caused, we do not mean that He once was not and then at some later point caused Himself to be, for that is an obvious contradiction. But He always has been and always will be because He is and chooses to be.

Such teaching takes us to the frontier of our understanding and even beyond it. It is an issue of faith in a revelation. We speak here of what we have never experienced and cannot experience. The idea has clear meaning but describes what is incomprehensible to finite beings.

5. THE UNITY OF GOD

Both the Decalogue, that is, the Ten Commandments (Exodus 20:3; Deuteronomy 5:7) and the *Shema*, the basic confession of Israel (Deuteronomy 6:4), required that only one God be worshiped. The Old Testament commanded this in the face of pagan polytheism, the belief that there are many gods. Polytheism not only acknowledges that many gods exist but allows for each to be worshiped.

In New Testament times the young Christian church also challenged the polytheism of a pagan environment. At times Christians did so with great risk to personal life. Pagans did not always object to the worship of a new deity (Acts 17:18f., 23). But they often did object to the Christian teaching that forbade the continued worship of their favorite deities and thus presented a threat to their cults (Acts 19:27).[13]

The belief in God's unity and singleness is a foundational truth, one from which other truths derive.[14] If God is One, then He is the sole creator whom all should seek and find (Acts 17:24-27). If God is One, then He is the God of the Gentiles as well as the Jews, and they also can become His children by faith (Romans 3:29f.).

6. THE IMMUTABILITY OF GOD

God remains completely and entirely consistent with Himself. That is, He is immutable. This is what Malachi meant when he said, "I the Lord do not change" (Malachi 3:6).

Immutability differs from inflexibility.[15] God responds to human decisions in various ways. He can send blessing or judgment, depending on whether He is responding to good or evil. The Scriptures are even bold enough to say that God changes His mind (Genesis 5:5f.). This does not mean that God has moved from His ultimate purposes but that He responds to the situation brought on by human choices in an appropriate way. [16] From the human view God may appear to have changed, from the divine perspective He never departs from His own counsel or changes His mind.[17]

The character of God remains constant. He is always loving (Psalms 106:1), always righteous (Psalms 103:17), always wise and powerful (Daniel. 2:20). In dealing with us God is always effecting His good will. Thus, He may comfort (Psalms 23:4) or afflict (Psalms 90:15), reward (Psalms 18:20) or punish (Jeremiah 21:14), make His presence known

(Exodus 33:14) or conceal it (Psalms 10:11). The constancy of God reveals itself in His appropriate responses.

7. THE SOVEREIGN POWER OF GOD

God is utmost and supreme in His power; we say He is omnipotent, all-powerful. The Scriptures typically describe God as almighty. God exercises His power in three ways: through natural law, through miraculous events and through human history.

The large view of the Scriptures is that God is patiently and systematically exercising His sovereignty through the natural forces. The cycles of nature such as the movement of the sun (Psalms 19:1-6) and the seasons (Psalms 74:17) witness to God's guidance of the physical universe for our good.

At times God may intervene through a sign or wonder, a change from the normal course of events, to achieve His purposes. By this means He can save His people through miracles (Exodus 13:17-14:22), punish their enemies (Exodus 7:8-11:10) or answer the cry of a helpless person (2 Kings 4:8-37).

God also exercises power through human decisions. This issue is delicate since it raises the question whether humans have any significant freedom. The large historical view of the church is clear. The church has believed the Scriptures held together two items that seem irreconcilable: On the one hand, all people have an essential freedom to make their own decisions and be held responsible for them (James 1:13-15). On the other, God moves and directs people to accomplish His sovereign will. He plans and provides for the salvation of all humankind (2 Peter 3:9), and He hardens whom He will and has mercy upon whom He will (Exodus 33:19; Romans 9:14-18). Even evil that we mortals plan and execute and for which we are rightly judged, may become a means by which God effects His plan (Genesis 50:20; Acts 2:23).

8. THE SOVEREIGN KNOWLEDGE OF GOD, HIS FOREKNOWLEDGE AND HIS WISDOM

God knows all things, understands all things and acts out of infinite wisdom.

The Scriptures refer to God's knowledge of the facts of nature (Psalms 50:11). More often, however, they refer to His knowledge of the inner thoughts of people (Psalms 94:11). Psalm 139 describes the wonder of God's detailed knowledge of people; it extends in all directions, including before conception (vv. 15-16), before action (vv. 3f.) and before any exposure (v. 2).

Because God exists within the eternal "now," there is no past or present to him as there is to us. As a result God's knowledge of the future is complete and includes future choices that decide eternal destiny.[18] He knows who will be His own and predestines them to be conformed to the image of His Son (Romans 8:29). One essential foundation of prophetic predictions within the Scriptures is that the events of the future are as present realities to God. He reveals them to His servants as something to be seen now (Revelation 1:19), though as historical facts they have not yet occurred.

We humans assume we are wise. We gather counselors and helpers to protect us from making errors. But human wisdom invariably fails. For example, God foiled the plan of Absalom, King David's son, by deceiving him through the brilliant adviser Ahithophel (2 Samuel 15:14). Thus the advice of the Scriptures to us mortals is: "Let not the wise man boast of his wisdom or the strong man boast of his strength or the rich man boast of his riches, but let him who boasts boast about this: that he understands and knows me" (Jeremiah 9:23f.). Paul can say in irony that God's foolishness is wiser than man's wisdom, and thus the message of the Cross becomes a means of salvation to those who hear and believe (1 Corinthians 1:18-2:8).

9. THE SOVEREIGNTY OF GOD OVER TIME

In reflecting upon God's sovereignty over time, the psalmist voiced this acclamation, "Praise be to the Lord, the God of Israel, from everlasting to everlasting" (Psalms 41:13; cf. 90:2). Similarly John describes God as He "who is, and who was, and who is to come" (Revelation 1:4). When we think of God and time, we look back to the endless past and forward to the endless future.

God made everlasting covenants, that is, covenants that will never wear out, with the entire human family (Genesis 9:17) and with the patriarchs (17:7f.). His promise to David that a son of his will always rule (2 Samuel 7:16) was finally reached in Mary's Son (Luke 1:33). God installed the sons of Levi in an everlasting priesthood (Exodus 40:15). God can make such extensive promises because He dwells from the everlasting past to the everlasting future.

The scriptural language of God's sovereignty over time looks at the issue from within time, though it always takes God to the boundaries. "In the beginning God created the heavens and the earth" (Genesis 1:1). God was there when it all began. We have no way to conceive of what precedes the beginning, but God obviously was there. In this fashion the church uses the term "eternal" to suggest two things of God: first, that He endures through all time, from the very beginning to the very end; and second, that He endures beyond time.[19] Teachers of the church have suggested, in fact, that God created time when He made the world, since time really is a way of marking the sequence of events in creation.[20]

10. THE SOVEREIGNTY OF GOD OVER SPACE: IMMENSITY, INFINITY AND OMNIPRESENCE

The Scriptures speak similarly of God's relation to space as they do of His relation to time. His presence is everywhere. "If I go up to the heavens, you are there; if I make my bed in the depths [Sheol, the place of the dead], you are there" (Psalms 139:8). We call this God's omnipresence. [21]

The knowledge of this omnipresence of God, which both comforts and disturbs, can take several forms. Generally, the Scriptures think of the sense of God's presence as a comfort. It heals the broken hearts of repentant sinners, for God turns His face from the sin and restores the sinner (Psalms 51:10f.). On the other hand, unrepented sin can result in banishment from God's presence (Psalms 5:5). Other passages state that when God makes His judging presence known, the wicked, who had presumed they would not be held accountable, will perish (Psalms 68:2).

11. THE HOLINESS, RIGHTEOUSNESS AND TRUTHFULNESS OF GOD

The Scriptures use several terms to describe the righteousness of God, terms that when applied to human beings refer to their moral rectitude. No trace of evil or sin can be found within Him. Thus, we say that God is holy, righteous and truthful.

The Holiness of God

From a human perspective the basic meaning of holiness is that which is separated from the common and ordinary unto God. God is essentially separate and unique. He is the "Holy One of Israel" (Isaiah 1:4; Jeremiah 50:29). When the prophet Isaiah saw the Lord, high and exalted, he heard the seraphim chant, "Holy, holy, holy is the LORD Almighty; the whole earth is full of his glory" (Isaiah 6:3). In response the prophet was immediately shaken with awareness of his mortality and sin (Isaiah 6:5).[22]

Because God's character is holy, holiness comes to describe that which is upright and perfectly pure. The conduct of those who belong to God should be modeled after God's character. The code of laws in Leviticus 18ff. brings this out clearly. Israel is not to follow the customs of the Egyptians or Canaanites. Rather, Israel is to obey God's laws and decrees, for He is the Lord their God (Leviticus 18:1-5). The holiness code of Leviticus then enunciates the solemn commandment: "Be holy because I, the LORD your God, am holy" (Leviticus 19:2). This expectation that God's people should be holy – that is, patterned after God – is later repeated by the apostle (1 Peter 1:15f.).

The Righteousness of God

The root idea of righteousness derives from the terms of a covenant in the ancient Near Eastern world. Members of a covenant bound themselves by mutually accepted terms: The righteous adhered to the terms; the unrighteous did not.

The covenant that God made with Israel was not between equals but between a sovereign and His subjects. Still, God never acted arbitrarily. He was perfectly righteous and always righteous, and whatever He did was righteous.

Thus, the righteousness of God is often described as an inner divine standard against which human actions are measured and judged. Pharaoh admits that the Lord is righteous and His people have been evil (Exodus 9:27). The psalmist notes that the righteous God tries human hearts (Psalms 7:9). Human righteousness is always measured against this divine standard (Psalms 9:8). Although no one can be judged as absolutely righteous (Romans 3:10); even so, in a relative sense, the Scriptures often refer to certain persons as righteous (Psalms 1:5; 5:12).[23]

The Truthfulness of God

God's truthfulness emphasizes His utter reliability. The word of God (Psalms 119:43) and His law (Psalms 119:142) are true and hence reliable, because they express the inner integrity of God; He cannot lie (Titus 1:2) because for God to lie would contradict His nature. The psalmist says of God that with "the crooked you show yourself shrewd" (Psalms

18:26). However, this does not describe a deceptive side to an otherwise truthful God. Rather, it simply means that God returns upon the heads of those who practice systematic deception the fruits of their work.

What God says by way of speech or promise will be in complete accord with reality because God is absolutely truthful. When we reflect upon His words, we gain insight and illumination (Psalms 43:3). Likewise, His judgments are righteous and true (Psalms 96:13).

12. THE GOODNESS, LOVE AND MERCY OF GOD

The Goodness of God

God's goodness is reflected to us first in the story of creation. Seven times in the opening chapter of the Bible, God pronounces what He has made as "good" (Genesis 1:4, 10, 12, 18, 21, 25, 31). The psalmists pick this note up and repeatedly offer praise to God for His goodness (Psalms 25:7, 8; 34:8; 52:9; 73:1; 100:5). In the New Testament, Peter bears witness to the goodness of God, reminding Christians of this, even when they are persecuted (1 Peter 2:3).

We draw from all this that God will not do anything that is contrary to His goodness. For example, for Him to lie would be inconsistent with His goodness. His goodness is consistent.

The Love of God

Closely related to God's goodness is God's love. The idea of God's love for human beings suggests both a positive affection for us and a covenant commitment. The general Hebrew word that translates into love, *hesed*, emphasizes the love God has for His people that persists through all circumstances. According to the repeated refrain in Psalm 136 the fact that God's "love endures forever" explains Israel's remarkable history.[24]

137

Even at the origin of the nation, God's choice of Israel as His people was grounded in His love, not in some inherent merit of theirs that drew His attention to them (Deuteronomy 7:7-10). Ultimately, because of His love for the world God gave His Son so that we might live through faith in Him (John 3:16).

God's love is enduring but demanding. It brings forgiveness but also demands loyalty (Exodus 34:6f.) and brooks no rivals (Exodus 20:5-6; 34:14). The apostle John made the profound observation that "God is love" (1 John 4:8), but this cannot be reversed to say that love is God. The character of God finally defines love, not the opposite. God's love is a holy love, as His holiness is a loving holiness.

The Mercy of God

God's love includes His mercy, the undeserved favor with which He views us. Mercy particularly emphasizes that God looks kindly upon us and not according to our merits. God's mercy is closely related to His grace. Mercy emphasizes God's attitude toward us in spite of our unworthiness; grace draws attention to the work He does for us and issues from His mercy. Mercy and grace together identify the mystery of our salvation, which originates in God. Sinners suffering for their misdeeds appeal to God's heart. "Restore us again, O God our Savior, and put away your displeasure toward us. ... Show us your unfailing love [mercy], O LORD, and grant us your salvation" (Psalms 85:4, 7). Paul describes the profound redemptive changes that Christians enjoy and upon which they should base their new lives as "the mercies of God" (Romans 12:1).

SUMMARY: *The Attributes of God*

1. Christian teaching describes God's character through identifying His essential attributes. We can speak of God's absolute and relative attributes and of His natural and moral attributes. However, within God

all divine attributes form a perfect unity.

2. God is transcendent. He is greater than anything He has made, whether seen or unseen, in part or in whole. He is also immanent and thus can relate perfectly and completely to His creation, as He chooses, to accomplish His will.

3. The living God is spiritual, that is, nonmaterial. Even so, He has revealed Himself in material form in Jesus of Nazareth, who was the Word of God incarnate. When the Scriptures describe God, they use metaphors and analogies, especially those from the human sphere of existence.

4. God is personal. Therefore, He understands, chooses and communicates. The most profound form of communication is within the Trinity itself. But God also communicates with human beings, creatures whom He made with personhood. In His relationship with humans God experiences divine emotions such as compassion, wrath and grief.

5. God is prior to all other beings, seen or unseen. He is responsible for His own existence. All else exists because He has brought it into existence for His good pleasure.

6. There is one God. He is the Lord and there is no other (Isaiah 45:18-25).

7. God is constant and unchangeable. Yet the ways in which He responds are varied.

8. God's power, knowledge, foreknowledge and wisdom are infinite. He is completely sovereign over time and space, possessing eternity, immensity and omnipresence.

9. God is perfect in holiness, righteousness and truth without any sin, evil or deceit whatsoever. God is also perfect in goodness, love and mercy. He knows our frame and weakness. His plan of salvation grows from His compassionate and powerful love for us.

THE GOD OF OUR SALVATION

SECTION III. *The Holy Trinity*

THE DISTINCTLY CHRISTIAN DOCTRINE OF GOD

The Christian understanding of God arises most distinctly out of the doctrine of the Trinity.[25] This teaching helps us define what it means to be Christian, since all other Christian teachings such as those on salvation or on the church grow out of the teaching on the Trinity.

THE ACCEPTANCE OF THIS DOCTRINE BY NEARLY ALL CHRISTIANS

The doctrine of the Trinity forms the outline for the Apostles' Creed. Its core features have been accepted by Christians on every continent, in every century, from nearly every church. A short list of the older witnesses would include: Irenaeus (ca. A.D. 180 in Lyons, France)[26], Tertullian (ca. A.D. 200 in Carthage, North Africa);[27] and of later witnesses we can include Thomas Aquinas,[28] Calvin,[29] Arminius,[30] Wesley,[31] Hodge,[32] Pope[33] and Strong.[34] The seven truly ecumenical councils of the early church specifically adopted this teaching, and it was a main feature in the first of these, the Council of Nicea (A.D. 325),[35] the First of Constantinople (A.D. 381),[36] and Chalcedon (A.D. 451).[37] The Niceno-Constantinopolitan Creed was reaffirmed by the Roman Catholics at Trent (A.D. 1564),[38] the Russian Orthodox (A.D. 1643),[39] and the Lutherans (A.D. 1530).[40] The older creeds clearly shaped statements on the Trinity hammered out later by other Christians of the West: the Church of England (A.D. 1562),[41] the Presbyterians (A.D. 1647),[42] and the Methodists (A.D. 1784).[43] It appropriately serves as the First Article of Religion in the *Book of Discipline* for the Free Methodist Church.[44] The doctrine of the Trinity is the central teaching of the Christian faith.

1. THE OLD TESTAMENT WITNESS TO THE TRINITY

The Old Testament makes no explicit reference to the Trinity, such as that in the baptismal directive of Christ (Matthew 28:19.). The Old Testament's reserved treatment of this teaching grew from the unfolding nature of revelation.[45] Before God could teach about the distinctness of the Son and of the Spirit, Israel had to be purified of polytheism and idolatry. As Augustine said: within the Old Testament the Gospel is latent, within the New Testament it is patent.

There are indications of the "threeness" of the one God within the Old Testament, but it does not teach it explicitly. The church, noting these indications, has argued that they are consistent with the doctrine of the Trinity, and their meaning is made clear by that teaching.

The Plural Forms of Divine Action

The creation account reports: "Then God said, 'Let us make man in our image, in our likeness'. ... So God created man in his own image, in the image of God he created him, male and female he created them" (Genesis 1:26f.). The account then reports a conversation with shifts between plural and singular forms while noting the fact that God alone created human beings in His image. Tertullian and Augustine held that Genesis 1:26f. reflects the relationship between the Persons of the Trinity and foreshadows the relationship between the deity and humanity of the incarnate Son.[46] This view has considerable weight.

Anticipations of the Incarnate Son in the Old Testament

The Old Testament reports appearances of God in human form to the patriarchs Abraham (Genesis 17:1ff.; 18:1ff.) and Jacob (Genesis 32:22ff.). It also notes such an appearance to the three Hebrews in Nebuchadnezzar's fiery furnace (Daniel 3:25). The Scriptures present these as genuine theophanies – appearances of the divine Person to human beings (Genesis 17:1; 32:30). Because they were not merely messengers from God, we can say that an essential feature of the Incarnation is already indicated within the Old Testament: The Sovereign God had come among us in a truly human form.[47]

Proverbs 8:22ff. describes Wisdom which was with God before creation and had a principal role in creation. The Wisdom theme reappears in the New Testament and is applied to the Son in John's description of the Word (John 1:1ff.) and Paul's description of the Image of the invisible God (Colossians 1:15ff.).

Anticipations of the Gift of the Spirit

In the Old Testament the Lord sent His Spirit upon His servants to enable them to do His work. Moses needed assistants, so the Lord put His Spirit upon those set apart (Numbers 11:25). The Spirit of the Lord came upon the judges of Israel (Judges 3:10; 6:34). In a corresponding fashion the Old Testament has promises of the gift of the Spirit for a future time, a time that the church saw as fulfilled in its life and ministry (Ezekiel 37:27; Joel 2:28; Acts 2:17f.).

2. THE NEW TESTAMENT WITNESS TO THE TRINITY

While the Old Testament's witness to the Trinity is latent, in the New Testament it is patent. The term "Trinity" itself did not appear until two centuries later. Tertullian appears to have been the first one to use that term precisely.[48] But the central elements of that teaching are clearly present within New Testament books.

The Baptismal Directive and the Pauline Doxology

Christ's final directive to His disciples was that they were to go into the world and make disciples of all nations, baptizing them in the name of the Father and of the Son and of the Holy Spirit (Matthew 28:19f.). He did not command His disciples to baptize in the "names" of the Father, Son and Holy Spirit. This might have suggested a plurality of deities. The singular "the name" and the plural "the Father, Son and Holy Spirit" suggest threeness in oneness. This baptismal directive of Jesus has been adopted by virtually all Christian churches: Those who have been baptized as Christians have been baptized in the name of the Trinity.[49]

Though many introductory prayers and concluding doxologies of New Testament letters have a two-person form (God the Father and the Son), 2 Corinthians ends with a Trinitarian form that has served as one of the classic Christian benedictions (13:14): "May the grace of the Lord Jesus Christ, and the love of God, and the fellowship of the Holy Spirit be with you all."

The Relation of the Son to the Father

The deity of Christ defined as the deity of the Son of God was the foundation for understanding all the relationships within the Godhead. Explicit Trinitarian thought began with reflection on scriptural statements that Jesus Christ is the unique Son of the Father. Precisely this occurred during the first centuries as the church worked through Christological and Trinitarian questions at the same time.

Jesus in His prayers addressed God as Father (Matthew 11:25; John 17:1, 24-26; Matthew 26:39-42). He also taught His disciples to pray to God as their Father (Matthew 6:9). Moreover, He constantly referred to God as their Father (Matthew 5:16, 45, 48; 10:20 and so forth). But there is a difference, best understood by the historic explanation of the church: Jesus is God's Son by nature; we have that relationship by grace.[50]

This special relationship of the Son to the Father appears when He is described as the "only begotten Son" of God (John 1:14, 18; 3:16, 18). This means He is uniquely God's Son. None other shares that relationship. He was born of the will of God alone and not the will of a man (John 1:13). Gabriel explained to Mary more explicitly that, because of Jesus' virgin birth, He would truly be the Son of God (Luke 1:35).

Thus, the foundation of Trinitarian thought is laid in the unique relationship that exists between the Father who generated the Son and the Son who is generated, not created, by the Father. To generate means to transmit one's essential nature, and thus Jesus Christ is God of God.

The Relation of Spirit to the Father and the Son

The final step in the development of the doctrine of the Trinity required the clarification of the relation of the Spirit to the Father and to the Son. The term the historic church adopted to describe this relationship was the "procession" or the going forth of the Spirit (John 15:26).

In the last hours before His passion, Jesus told His disciples that in answer to His request, the Father would send the Paraclete, the Spirit, whom the world could not accept (John 16:15-17). But the Spirit's coming, He explained, required His own departure, so it would be better for them that He go, even though this thought caused sorrow (John 16:5-11).

Between His resurrection and ascension Jesus instructed His disciples to wait for the "promise of the Father" – the Spirit – who would empower them for their work (Luke 24:49: Acts 1:5, 8). The promised Spirit was then sent on the day of Pentecost (Acts 2).

Paul does not offer us a historical account of the relationship between the times of the Son and the Spirit, as Luke and John do, but He links the Father and the Son to the present ministry of the Spirit. The Spirit works out in human lives the grace of Christ Jesus (Romans 8:2). He is the basis on which we belong to Christ (Romans 8:9). He assures us that we are children of God (Romans 8:16). The Spirit is the enabler by whom we confess Jesus as Lord (1 Corinthians

12:3). He is also the power by whom we can mortify the deeds of the flesh (Romans 8:13) since those in whom God's Spirit dwells are liberated from the power of sin in the flesh (Romans 8:9). Finally, the Spirit is the down payment of our eternal inheritance (Ephesians 1:13f.). He Himself will raise our mortal bodies from death as He raised that of Christ Jesus (Romans 8:11).

3. THE TRINITARIAN CONTROVERSIES OF THE EARLY CHURCH

During the first centuries after the apostles the church dealt with several major heresies. Some of these profoundly threatened the faith and were successfully overcome only after long and protracted conflicts.

When taken together these heresies illustrate virtually every possible variation of misunderstanding regarding the Trinity. When all the heresies are considered, the basic issue that keeps resurfacing is the need to find a way to maintain a strict monotheism – the belief in one God – with the firm Christian conviction that the Father, Son and Holy Spirit are each truly God.

A. Three Early Heresies

Ebionism: The Question Whether Jesus Was Really Divine

Ebionism, which flourished during the century after Jesus' life, represented a vigorous attempt to be Christian and remain Jewish, but it did so at a heavy cost: It simply denied that Jesus was the unique Son of God. Some Ebionites accepted His virgin birth but still refused to confess His deity. Others did not accept the Gospel accounts of His virgin birth, claiming He had a human father. Ebionites honored Jesus as a virtuous man but denied that He was the incarnate Word.[51] They solved the Trinitarian question by striking out the Son and the Spirit in the Godhead, retaining only the Father.

Marcionism: Whether the God of the Old Testament Was the Same as the God of the New Testament

Marcion, a teacher in Rome who was excommunicated ca. A.D. 144, rejected all vestige of Israel's heritage.[52] He made a vigorous attempt to join Gnostic ideas to Christian teaching. His theological system was a full dualism. That is, he had a good god and an evil god equally poised against each other in perpetual conflict. The God of Israel – the evil, materialistic and judgmental god of his system – opposed the good god who had sent one of his offspring into Jesus of Nazareth. Marcion rejected the Old Testament, and he further rejected all the New Testament except Luke's Gospel and ten of Paul's letters. Marcion even edited the biblical books he had kept to insure that they would conform to his doctrine.[53]

Unlike the Ebionites, Marcion attracted many followers among the growing number of gentile Christians and proved to be a short-lived but serious threat. However, the rejection of the canon of the Holy Scriptures by both heresies limited their enduring influence.

Sabellianism: The Question Whether there Are Three Distinct Persons or God Has Only Three Modes of Being

Heretics who argued on the basis of the received Scriptures proved more formidable. Such was Sabellius, a Libyan of the early third century. He emphasized such Scriptures as those that say the Father and the Son were one (John 10:30). Thus, Sabellius reduced the threeness of God to a strict oneness. Crass forms of Sabellianism taught that God came in three modes through the three stages of history: the Father in Old Testament times, the Son during the time of Jesus, and the Spirit during the time of the church. Thus, his heresy goes under the name of modalistic monarchianism. Sabellius himself had more sophisticated explanations for his view, though he did teach that there was only one person in the Godhead who appeared in three modes.[54]

B. Two Later Heresies

Arius: The Question Whether the Son Is of the Same Nature as the Father

Arius, an early fourth century heretic from Alexandria, Egypt, was far more dangerous than any other. For a time he could count a near majority of the Christians among his disciples. Arius dealt mainly with the relation of the Son to the Father. He taught that the Word is the Father's first creation, not His actual Son. This Christology does not descend so low as the Christology of the Ebionites because Arius also taught that the Word is above all heavenly and earthly creatures and became incarnate in Jesus and brought salvation by His death and resurrection. Hence Jesus is to be worshiped and adored. Even so, according to Arius, the Word does not have the same nature as the Father, who alone is truly God.[55]

Arius argued from the received Scriptures to develop his case. He pointed to passages that describe the subordination of the Son or His dependence on the Father, such as Matthew 28:18; John 5:22, 19.[56] Another crucial passage he used was Proverbs 8:22. Wisdom here was generally understood by Christians as an Old Testament reference to the Word of John 1:1-18. Arius claimed the passage confirmed his viewpoint, since it states that God created (Gk., *ektisen*) Wisdom before any other creature.[57]

Eunomius: The Question Whether the Spirit Is of the Same Nature as the Father

Eunomius, a mid-fourth century disciple of Arius, took his master's view to the next logical step. He added new arguments to deny the Son was of the same nature as the

Father. But he extended the discussion to the Spirit and taught that the Spirit was a creation of the Son just as Arius had taught that the Son was a creation of the Father.[58] Hence, the followers of Eunomius became known as pneumatimachians from a Greek word that means "Spirit-makers."[59] We are presented, then, with the picture of a heavenly chain of beings, a virtual pantheon.[60]

C. The Definition of Orthodoxy

Principal Teachers in the East: Athanasius and the Cappadocians, Basil, Gregory of Nazianzus and Gregory of Nyssa

Athanasius was slightly younger than Arius but also from Alexandria. Though only a deacon at the time of the Council of Nicea, he served as secretary to the aged archbishop of Alexandria at the Council and was the principal architect of the decision given by the Council. The anti-Arian thrust of the Nicene Creed reflects the influence of Athanasius in several places.

Two principal flaws in the thinking of Arius can be mentioned. First, Arius confused the issue of the relationship between the Father and the Son with that of the nature of the Persons of the Godhead. When we speak of the relationship of the Father to the Son, we speak of the one being the Father and the other the Son, and by that fact the Father has a priority. Athanasius pointed out that the Son was generated by the Father and thus was derived from the Father. But when we speak of the nature of the Father and the Son, we cannot speak of priority or difference. Both are truly God, both truly eternal. Thus, the Son does not have a different nature from the Father nor did He come into existence after the Father as a result of His being generated by the Father. The Father was *always* the Father because He always had His Son who was of the same divine nature as the Father.[61]

Second, Arius pointed to passages that describe the dependence of the Son upon the Father. But, Athanasius said, these passages refer to the humanity of the Christ.[62] In overlooking the relationship of our Lord's humanity to His deity, Arius and his followers falsely attributed to the eternal Word characteristics that belong to the man Jesus.

In response to Arius' teaching, the Nicene Creed articulates a clear statement about the Son. First, it declares that the Lord Jesus Christ is "begotten, not made." Second, it says that He is of "one substance" (*homoousion*) with the Father. Third, it rejects as heretical the idea that "there was a time when the Son of God was not."[63]

The battle with Arianism did not go away merely because the Council of Nicea had given its decision against it. Over the next two generations after A.D. 325 followers of Arius exerted great effort to propagate his view. They had periodic successes.

Three great Cappadocian fathers along with the now older Athanasius continued the struggle against the views of Arius and his disciples on the doctrine of the eternal Word. These three were Basil and Gregory of Nyssa, who were brothers, and their personal friend, Gregory of Nazianzus. Their work played a significant role in the recasting of the Nicene Creed at the First Council of Constantinople in A.D. 381. In particular this revised creed affirmed the equality of the Spirit with the Father and the Son in the crucial words: "And in the Holy Ghost, the Lord and Giver of life, who proceedeth from the Father; who, with the Father and the Son together is worshipped and glorified."

Principal Teachers in the West: Ambrose, Hilary and Augustine

Athanasius and the Cappadocian fathers worked in the Eastern church where Greek was predominantly spoken. Discussions on the Trinity in the Western church, where Latin was predominantly spoken, paralleled those in the

East. The Western church would have included North Africa except for Egypt but including Italy, France and Spain. Arianism had also made tremendous inroads into the Western church. During the same time that Athanasius and the Cappadocians were writing in Greek, several great teachers were also writing in Latin: Ambrose of Milan,[64] Hilary of Poitiers (France)[65] and Augustine of Hippo (North Africa).[66]

The Language of the Trinity

During the fourth century certain terms evolved to convey the church's understanding of the Trinity. The teachers fully realized that they used analogies and metaphors that could not completely articulate reality,[67] but they also believed these words accurately reflected the truth and hence were more than mere reflections of their own biases.

They developed a Latin vocabulary parallel to the Greek. The Orthodox teachers recognized that the words they chose did not necessarily have the same denotations in one language that they had in the other, though the connotations were the same. When we compare the writings of Greek authors on the Trinity with those of Latin authors, a considerable precision and unity emerge.[68]

The crucial words chosen, which identify that which makes the Father, the Son and the Spirit fully and equally God, are *ousia* (literally, "being") in the Greek and *substantia* (literally, "substance") in the Latin. The fierce battle with the Arians over whether to use *homoousios* (of the same substance) or *homoiousios* (of a similar substance) – a difference of only one letter – in the Nicene Creed, thus, turned on a single point: Is the Son God in very being or only like God? The church chose to say that He is God in very being. The terms that distinguish the Father from the Son and from the Spirit are *hypostasis* (literally, "substance") or *prosopon* (literally, "face") in the Greek and *persona* (literally, "face") or *subsistentia* (literally, "subsistence") in the Latin. A precise review of the Definition of Chalcedon will show how carefully the church used these terms to say exactly what it meant.[69]

4. THE CONTROVERSY BETWEEN THE EAST AND WEST ON THE PROCESSION OF THE SPIRIT

The debate in Trinitarian thought on the procession of the Spirit came to fruition after the classical period had passed, though its seeds were sown at that time. The issue was over the relation of the Spirit to both the Father and the Son: Does the Spirit come from the Father or does the Spirit come from both the Father and the Son?

The original form of the clause in the Creed of Niceno-Constantinople says that the Spirit "proceeds from the Father" (John 15:26). This wording is still followed by the Eastern Church. But the Third Council of Toledo (A.D. 589) added *filioque*, to say that the Spirit "proceeds from the Father and the Son," and this has since become the common reading in the West. Scriptural support for the Western reading depends upon the emphasis placed upon the Son's involvement in the coming of the Spirit. The Scriptures say both that the Father will send the Spirit through the intervention of the Son (John 14:16, 26) and that the Son Himself will send the Spirit (15:26; 16:7).

This difference – the absence or presence of the *filioque* phrase – has remained one of the main sources of division between Eastern and Western Christianity. All churches of the West that use the Creed, including Protestants, have kept the *filioque* phrase.[70]

Eastern thought emphasizes that within the Godhead the Father is the source of both the Son and the Spirit. The Son is eternally generated by the Father, and the Spirit eternally proceeds from the Father. The Eastern view is a kind of inner-trinitarian reflection on the matter. That is, apart from God's historical saving work for the human race, what is the relation among the three Persons of the Trinity?

151

Western thought reflects the historical action of God for our redemption. The Father sent the Son and by the Virgin Mary He was incarnated within time; the Spirit now proceeds from the Father and from the Son to bring us redemption. The Western view represents the Trinity as the Godhead works out from itself to us.[71]

5. ESSENTIAL FEATURES OF TRINITARIAN THOUGHT

The Vital Relationship of the Doctrine of the Trinity to the Doctrine of Salvation

The classic definitions of the Trinity, it has been earlier observed, are stated in ontological language. That is, they describe the being of God. On the other hand, the Scriptures, with some exceptions, teach a functional or economic Trinity by which God reveals himself in relational terms.[72]

But the classic definition accomplished something of immense value. This grew from the valid impulse of the church to keep its theology biblical. There were various misunderstandings that contradicted the gospel. Some of these were promoted with great vigor and with appeals to the Scriptures for support. It was against these that the church carefully fashioned its understanding of the self-revealed God. This becomes clear as we trace the history of the Trinitarian debate. Each new challenge brought forth a sharper definition of what is orthodox and what is not.

In this process of reaching a correct understanding of God, the doctrine of salvation was at stake. The early teachers fought so vigorously for an orthodox statement because they correctly sensed that the Christian doctrine of salvation could not survive with a sub-Christian view of God. False teachings on the Trinity undermine the doctrine of salvation by weakening God into only one among other supernatural beings or removing Him from the saving actions of the Scriptures. If our Lord Jesus Christ is not truly God of God – as the creeds confess – but only a god of God; then the

152

atonement we have through His life, death and resurrection is still no more than the work of a creature for other creatures.[73]

One God in Three Persons

The church struggled to keep two convictions together: that God is one; and that the Father, Son and Holy Spirit are each truly God. In upholding the oneness of God, the church resisted the perils of tritheism, the belief that there are three gods, which essentially leads to polytheism, the belief in many gods. The church insisted the three Persons of the Trinity are still one God. At the same time, in upholding with equal conviction that Father, Son and Holy Spirit are each God, the church resisted the heretical tendency to deny that the Son and the Holy Spirit are truly God.

The language the church chose for its definition still remains the clearest and simplest way to describe the Trinity. There is one God within whom are three Persons. Each person shares a common "substance," that of God; and each has a different "subsistence," that of His person. Thus, God is one and God is three; God is triune.

The church has always confessed that the Trinity is a great mystery. No significant Christian theologian has ever suggested that a single explanation is adequate to show how the three can be one and the one three. And none has held that the doctrine of the Trinity can be reduced to a numerical system.[74] Revelation has given us the precious knowledge of God from a human stance; we struggle to articulate this knowledge in metaphors and analogies.

The Coequality of the Persons of the Trinity

The doctrine of Christ became the battleground of some of the fiercest debates in the early church. The creeds of the church state the Christian position unequivocally: The Word became incarnate in Jesus of Nazareth, ministered in Galilee and Judea, was crucified under Pontius Pilate and died, but was then raised from the dead and ascended into heaven. As such, He was the Son of God who is *homoousios*, that is, of the same substance with the Father. In the same manner, when the Spirit presently applies the provisions of Christ to our world, He, too, is of the same substance with the Father and the Son.

The Unique Relationship of Each Person of the Trinity to the Others

We use the language of the Scriptures in order to show that the relationship among the three persons is scriptural. The "Father," "Son" and the "Holy Spirit" are preeminently biblical terms, especially throughout the New Testament. No other terms could be adopted to show more succinctly and clearly the holy Trinity.

The Son is begotten by the Father, the Spirit proceeds from the Father and the Son. The Father is the source of the Trinity. This carries the idea of priority but only in regard to relationship. He did not exist without the Son or the Spirit nor is the being of the Father superior to the other Persons. Thus, we understand those passages in the Scriptures that speak of the Father's priority and those that speak of equality among all three Persons of the Trinity without doing violence to either set of passages.

That Each Person of the Trinity Shares in the Work of God while Each Has a Work Proper to Himself

The Apostles' Creed articulates belief in the Trinity, naming each Person in succession and the work in which each is involved. So the Father is named as the Maker of heaven and earth. The Son is declared to have been incarnate, to have suffered and died, to have been raised from the dead and received into heaven. The Spirit brings forgiveness and creates the church.

At the same time, all Persons of the Trinity are involved in each task. God created the world through the

Word (John 1:3), and the Spirit was hovering over the waters at creation (Genesis 1:2). God was in Christ reconciling the world to Himself (2 Corinthians 5:18), and He anointed Jesus of Nazareth with the Holy Spirit so that He went around doing good and healing all who were oppressed of the devil (Acts 10:38). Those who have received the Spirit of God have received the Spirit of adoption and cry out, *Abba*, Father (Romans 8:15f.); and the veil that remained from the time of Moses has been taken away in Christ so that where the Spirit of the Lord is there is freedom (2 Corinthians 3:14-18).[75]

SUMMARY: *The Holy Trinity*

1. The doctrine of the Trinity is the teaching that most distinctly characterizes the Christian faith. It has been embraced by nearly all Christians throughout the centuries, and provides the basis for other fundamental teachings such as the doctrine of salvation.

2. The doctrine of the Trinity is consistent with Old Testament statements about God, though the doctrine is nowhere explicitly taught there. The New Testament clearly speaks of the Father, Son and Holy Spirit, attributing to each the character of God, as in Christ's baptismal command (Matthew 28:19f.), which provides the source for the specific Christian articulation of the doctrine.

3. Within the early centuries of the Christian era, various heresies sprang up that veered from the conviction that God is one and at the same time three. The most important of these, Arianism, did so by weakening the deity of the Son and the Spirit.

4. Classic Christian teaching in both the East (Greek) and the West (Latin) came to describe the Trinity as one God in three Persons, each Person sharing the same substance but each having a different subsistence.

5. Each Person of the Trinity had a unique relationship to the others: The Father generates the Son, and the Spirit proceeds from the Father and the Son.

6. Though each Person of the Trinity is involved in the work of the whole, each also has a work peculiar to Himself: The work of the Father as the source of creation, the work of the Son atonement and reconciliation, and the work of the Spirit redemption and sanctification.

ENDNOTES

[1] Schaff, *CC* 2:12-41.

[2] Athanasius, *Councils* 3:35 (*NPNF* 2:4:469); Gregory of Nyssa, *Against Eunomius* 2:4 (*NPNF* 2:5:105); Pope, *CCT* 1:250f.; Wiley, *CT* 1:244-46.

[3] Ambrose, *EOF* 3:9 (*NPNF*, 2:10:251).

[4] The tenth letter of Pliny the Younger to Trajan (*DCC* 3-5); Oden, *WL* 53f.

[5] Wiley, *CT* 1:320-29; Erickson, *CT* 265-67.

[6] Collins, *FW* 16-20.

[7] John of Damascus, *EOF* 1:4 (*NPNF* 2:9:3).

[8] John of Damascus, *EOF* 1:11 (*NPNF*, 2:9:12f); Vriezen, *OOTT* 171-75.

[9] Athanasius, *IW* 3:3f. (*NPNF* 2:4:37f.); Thomas Aquinas, *ST* 1:93 (*BWTA* 1:885-901); Calvin, *Inst* 1:15:3 (1:162-64).

[10] Oden, *LG* 84-88.

[11] See Heschel, *Prophets* 221ff.

[12] Vriezen, *OOTT* 128-43.

[13] John of Damascus, *EOF* 1:5 (*NPNF* 2:9:4).

[14] Wesley, Sermon 120, "The Unity of the Divine Being" *WJWB* 4:61-71.

[15] Grider, *WHT* 118-20.

[16] Arminius, "Review of Perkins II" *WTA* 3:477.

[17] Arminius, "Public Disputations IV" *WTA* 1:440f.

[18] Origen, *Against Celsus* 2:20 (*ANF* 6:440); Arminius, "Discussion with F. Junius" *WTA* 3:66-68; Watson, *TI* 1:371-98.; Pope, *CCT* 1:315-19; Pinnock, *OG* 121-24; Hasker, *OG* 147-50.

[19] Watson, *TI* 1:353-59; Childs *BE* 76f., 82-89.

[20] Basil, *Hex.* 1:2-6 (*NPNF* 2:8:52-55) and Augustine, *Conf* 11:8-31 (*NPNF* 1:1:166-75); Vriezen, *OOTT* 180-83.

[21] Basil, *Hex.* 1:7-10 (*NPNF* 2:8:55-58) and Augustine, *Conf.* 12:17-18 (*NPNF* 1:1:182f.); Wesley, Sermon 118, "On the Omnipresence of God" *WJWB* 4:40-48.

[22] Snaith, *DIOT* 52f.

[23] Snaith, *DIOT* 72-74.

[24] Snaith, *DIOT* 100-106.

[25] Wesley, Sermon 55, "On the Trinity" *WJWB* 2:374-86.

[26] Irenaeus, *AH* 1:10:1 (Schaff, *CC* 2:13f.).

[27] Tertullian, *AP* 13 (Schaff, *CC* 2:19f.).

[28] Thomas, *ST* 1:27-43 (*BWTA* 1:274-425).

[29] Calvin, *Inst* 1:13 (1:108ff.).

[30] Arminius, *Twenty-Five Public Disputations* 5-6 (*WJA* 1:464-79).

[31] Wesley, Sermon 55, "On the Trinity" *WJWB* 2:374-86.

[32] Hodge, *OT* 164-99.

[33] Pope, *CCT* 1:255-86.

[34] Strong, *ST* 1:304-52.

[35] *NPNF* 2:1:3.

[36] Schaff, *CC* 2:58f.

[37] Schaff, *CC* 62f.

[38] *Profession of the Trindentine Faith* II (Schaff, *CC* 2:207).

[39] *The Orthodox Confession of the Eastern Church* V (Schaff, *CC* 2:279).

[40] *The Augsburg Confession* 1:1 (Schaff, *CC* 3:7).

[41] *The Thirty-Nine Articles of Religion* 1 (Schaff, *CC* 3:487f.).

[42] *The Westminster Confession* 2:3 (Schaff, *CC* 3:607f.).

[43] *The Articles of Religion* 1 (Schaff, *CC* 3:807).

[44] *BD 1989* §A/101 (9).

[45] Gregory of Nazianzus, *TO* 5:26, *NPNF* 2:7:326; Hilary, *Trin.* 4:16-18, *NPNF* 2:9:75-77.

[46] Tertullian, *AP* 12, *ANF* 3:606f. and Augustine, *Trin* 1:7 (14) and 7:6 (12), *NPNF* 1:3:24 and 113.

[47] Hilary, *Trin.* 4:78-81, *NPNF* 2:9:78-81; Watson, *TI* 1:483-93.

[48] Tertullian, *AP* 2, *ANPF* 3:598.

[49] *CCC* 1240.

[50] Athanasius, *DAA* 3:25, *NPNF* 2:4:399-407.

[51] Eusebius, *CH* 3:27:1-6, *NPNF* 2:1:158-60.

[52] Carrington, *ECC* 2:58-61.

[53] Irenaeus, *AH* 1:27:2-4, *ANF* 1:352f.

[54] Epiphanius, *Pan.* 62:1-4.

[55] Arius' *Thalia* and his letter to Alexander, the archbishop of Alexandria, are in *Councils* 2:15f., *NPNF*, 2:457f.

[56] Athanasius, *DAA* 3:26, *NPNF* 2:4:407-13.

[57] Athanasius, *DAA* 2:18, *NPNF* 2:4:364-66.

58 Epiphanius, *Pan.* 76:54:33.

59 Kelly, *ECD* 255-57.

60 Gregory of Nazianzus, *TO* 5:16, *NPNF* 2:7:322f.

61 Hilary, *Trin.* 6:13-19, *NPNF* 2:9:102-4.

62 Hilary, *Trin.* 9:2-15, *NPNF* 2:9:155-60.

63 *NPNF* 2:14:4; Simonetti, *ECC* 1:395f.

64 Ambrose *ECF* is devoted to the Trinity, *NPNF* 2:10:201ff.

65 Hilary refutes the heretics in a manner that reminds us of the Eastern teachers in *Trin., NPNF* 2:9:40ff.

66 Augustine, *Trin., NPNF* 1:3:17ff.

67 See Augustine, *CD* 1:2-6, *NPNF* 1:2:523f.

68 Shedd, *HCD* 362-72.

69 Schaff, *CC* 2:62f.

70 Schaff, *CC* 1:26.

71 See Barth, *CD* 1/1:541-57.

72 Schliermacher, *CF* 738-42; Berkof, *CF* 332-37.

73 Athanasius, *DAA* 3:26, *NPNF* 2:4:407-13.

74 Gregory of Nazianzus, *TO* 5:13-21, *NPNF,* 2:7:322-24.

75 Watson, *TI* 1:630-34.

CHAPTER

3

GOD,
THE CREATOR

SECTION I. THE CREATOR AND PRESERVER OF HEAVEN AND EARTH

1. God, the Sole Creator
2. False Cosmogonies, Ancient and Modern
3. Creation out of Nothing
4. The Creator of All Things
5. God's Preservation of the World by Sustaining, Directing and Overruling

SECTION II. THE NATURE OF CREATION

1. The Goodness of Creation
2. The Rationality of Creation
3. The Focus in the Scriptures on Knowledge of Living
4. The Rationality of Christianity and the Irrationality of Paganism

SECTION III. THE CREATION AS A MORAL UNIVERSE

1. The Human Being, a Moral Creature
2. The Doctrine of Retribution
3. The Interconnectedness of the Natural and Moral Realms
4. Results of Parental Deeds Visited upon Their Children
5. The Creator as the Lawgiver

THE GOD OF OUR SALVATION

SECTION IV. DISORDER IN CREATION
1. Sin as the Ultimate Cause of Disorder in Creation
2. Evil and Irrationality in a Disordered Creation
3. God's Delay as Opportunity for Repentance
   and Training in Righteousness

SECTION V. THE REDEMPTION OF CREATION
1. The Goal of Redemption
2. The Origin of Redemption in the Creator's Plan
3. The History of Salvation in the Scriptures
4. The Foundation of Trust and Prayer

he Apostles' Creed begins with the majestic affirmation: "I believe in God the Father Almighty, Maker of heaven and earth." This belief forms a logical beginning point for other teachings that are crucial to the Christian faith. From the foundational idea that God is the sole Creator, historic Christianity understands the panorama of the universe, its origin and its destiny.[1]

SPECIFIC TEACHINGS FOUNDED
UPON BELIEF IN GOD AS THE CREATOR

The world God has created is good and rational and purposeful. The shocking evil in the world has arisen because of sin, that is, the rebellion of God's creatures, not because God failed in His plan of creation or because some evil supernatural being made a flawed world against God's will.

This is a moral universe. God has granted human beings a limited freedom to obey or disobey Him. He created them with the power of moral choice. Thus, we live in a universe in which actions have consequences. The order God created within the world has been disordered by sin.

Still, God preserves the world He has created. He grants life and sustenance to those who are evil as well as to those who are good. He patiently judges evil and overrules its power. He is bringing the world to the ultimate destiny that He designed for it. The entire story of redemption (including the history of Israel, the incarnation of the Son of God, the present ministry of the Holy Spirit, the promised return of Christ and the hope of a new creation) arises from God's activity in redeeming His creation.

These teachings give foundation for Christian virtues. Because God is the sole Creator and Sovereign of the world, we trust God even while enduring cruel suffering. We obey God even when the positive results seem distant. We pray with confidence since we believe God's will toward us is benevolent and His power unlimited.

SECTION I. *The Creator and Preserver of Heaven and Earth*

1. GOD, THE SOLE CREATOR

Wherever we look in the Scriptures we see God alone as the Creator (Genesis 1:1; also Genesis 2:4; Isaiah 40:26; Malachi 2:10). Nowhere do the Scriptures say that angels or other supernatural beings created or assisted God in creation. In His speech to Job, God asks the suffering man several times, "Who created the world?" (Job 38:4-11). The answer is God and only God.

John states that the world was made through the Word (John 1:3; see also Colossians 1:16; Hebrews 1:2). Since the Word is the eternally existent Son of God, not some lesser deity, creation is the work of God.

Recognition of God as the only Creator is a fundamental human duty. Paul points out that when people neglect this obligation they plunge themselves into social chaos. Because they fail to glorify and thank God, which is His due, and because they serve the creature instead of the

Creator, God hands them over to their uncontrolled desires by which they make their own misery (Romans 1:19-25).[2]

2. FALSE COSMOGONIES, ANCIENT AND MODERN

Israel, the Church, and the Cosmogonies of the Nations

The ancient affirmation that God alone is the Creator was said in the face of other beliefs. Both Israel and the early church had to contend with false explanations of the world's origins.[3]

Most peoples of antiquity taught that the world and its creatures were somehow the offspring of the gods.[4] That is, the world was not something the supreme divine being made, but it was something that he generated or gave birth to. Thus the Greeks called these stories of the world's origins cosmogonies. The word cosmogony comes from two Greek words: *cosmos* (world) and *genos* (family or race).

During the early centuries of the Christian era the church met a variety of such cosmogonies. Some of them resembled the myths the Hebrews had encountered earlier during the Old Testament era. Others, such as the Gnostic myths of creation, had a different view.

The Gnostic Cosmogony: The Lower Aeons

Those who held to the various systems of the Gnostic movement of the first and second centuries prided themselves on their wisdom. They had a standard cosmogony. According to Gnosticism the material world was generated not by a supreme god but by lower supernatural beings. These beings were separated from the supreme and utmost god by a graduated series of aeons or gods. The lower gods did not know their origin and were miserable in their forgetfulness and ignorance. They longed for knowledge (*gnosis*), thinking that this would bring salvation and peace. Through their longing they accidentally gave birth to the material

162

universe we live in, a world inherently evil because it is material. Human beings are born within this evil world. Gnostics taught that most people are simply matter and have no higher spiritual principle within them. But they believed that a few have within their bodies a good spirit that belongs to the higher aeons. However, this good spirit does not know its origin, just as the lower aeons did not know theirs. But when they are told the Gnostic myth of creation, they gain knowledge (*gnosis*) of their origin and thus of who they really are.[5]

The New Age Cosmogony: Super-Terrestrial Beings

At the present time in history, new ageism, the popular religious movement that has gripped the modern mind, has some similarities to ancient Gnostic mythologies. For one thing, it also lays claim to wisdom about ultimate reality. Also, new ageism often asserts that the existence of our world and human life is explained as the work of some super-terrestrial beings or some quasi-supernatural life force.[6] Moreover, the ancient Gnostic said that salvation came from depending upon the Gnostic teacher, and new ageism makes people depend upon psychics. These psychics supposedly can see into the supernatural world and can give ordinary people insight into their true origins, their future and the best course of action they should take.

Ancient Philosophical Cosmogonies: The Demiurge

Ancient philosophers have also offered their opinions on the topic of the world's origins.[7] Some regarded the myths as superstitions. But generally these ancient philosophers stated that the supreme god of their system was not a creator. They generally asserted that the material stuff of the universe always existed; it is coeternal with the supreme deity. Instead of creator, they called this god a demiurge, a fashioner or molder. He took primordial stuff and shaped the world from it. The power of the demiurge is thus limited

163

and his skill finite.[8] This applies to the systems of Plato, Aristotle and the Stoics.[9]

Modern Philosophical Cosmogonies

Modern atheistic or agnostic philosophical systems have not offered fresh answers about origins beyond those given by the ancient systems. A rigid empiricism becomes the foundation for the modern philosophical denial that God is the sole Creator. This rigid empiricism proposes that we cannot know anything about the material world that cannot be scientifically tested. Logical positivism goes the next step and says that questions about the world's origins are meaningless. That is, when we talk about origins, we are talking about something that only evokes emotion; it does not give genuine knowledge about the world. Atheistic existentialism objects to serious concern about origins for another reason. It claims that the question about beginnings does not help us deal with the real task of life; hence, it is irrelevant.

3. CREATION OUT OF NOTHING

Early on, Christians had to address the question of whether God created the world out of nothing or molded it from preexisting material. The Gnostic myths taught that the world was generated from the lower aeons' very being – that is, out of themselves. The philosophical systems of antiquity all taught that the material stuff of the world was as eternal as the most ancient god.

Christian faith, by contrast, taught the doctrine of creation from nothing, *creatio ex nihilo*. In a version of the Christian rule of faith, Tertullian, around the turn of the third century, said that there is "one only God, and that he is none other than the Creator of the world, who produced all things out of nothing through his own Word."[10] The Christian teaching reflected in Tertullian's words contrasted with all cosmogonies of the ancient world except that in the Scriptures. The assertion that God created the world out of nothing has been adopted as a concise expression of one feature in the Christian understanding of creation and has enjoyed almost universal acceptance.[11]

Scriptural Support for the Teaching that God Created out of Nothing

The Scriptures nowhere say explicitly that God created the world out of nothing, though there are passages that imply it. The affirmation of the early church that God created the world from nothing draws together two things: First, it is the logical deduction from scriptural statements on origins. Second, it explicitly answers the erroneous views of Gnostic and philosophical systems.

In the New Testament, Hebrews 11:3 is an important example. It teaches that "by faith we understand that the universe was formed at God's command, so that what is seen was not made out of what was visible."

In the Old Testament, Genesis 1:1 states that the cosmos had its beginning when God created it. This passage uses the Hebrew word *bara'* to describe God's action, a word rarely used of anyone other than God. And even when *bara'* is used of someone other than God, it does not refer in their cases to their making something. The choice of this word, then, says something special about God's work of creation that distinguishes it from anything claimed for other deities.[12]

The magisterial picture of God's command, "Let there be," and the response that it was as He commanded, appears throughout the creation story (Genesis 1:3, 6, 9, 11, 14f. 20, 24). This further reflects the power of God who uniquely brings into effect what He wills.[13]

The church has used Genesis 1 as its main source to reject the view of paganism that the world was only shaped from a primordial stuff or was the unintended offspring of a lesser supernatural being. The church describes God as completely sovereign over the world. He did not have to strive to gain control over a noncompliant mass, nor did He accidentally generate a material world from His being. With purpose and freedom He created that which until then did not exist and shaped it as He pleased. Other scriptural passages that speak of the creation, such as Proverbs 8:22-30 and Isaiah 45:11-13, support the view that God is the sovereign Creator of the world, alone responsible for its existence.

4. THE CREATOR OF ALL THINGS

God created two comprehensive realms, heaven and earth. To the first belong the celestial creatures, the sun, moon and stars, and also supernatural creatures such as angels and Satan. To the second belong the world we inhabit, the earth with its rivers, plants, animals and humanity. God is the sole Creator of both realms (Genesis 1; Exodus 20:11; 2 Chronicles 2:12; Psalms 8; 124:8; Isaiah 37:16; Jeremiah 32:17; Acts 14:15; 17:24; Revelation 14:7).[14]

When speaking of only one realm, the Scriptures nearly always refer to the earth (Psalms 95:5) or humanity (Genesis 5:1). More attention is given to God as the Creator of the natural world, including humanity, than to the supernatural realm.

The Creator of All Things, Seen and Unseen

The Nicene Creed extends the area of God's creation beyond that identified in the Apostles' Creed. The Nicene Creed says: "I believe in one God the Father Almighty; Maker of heaven and earth, and of all things visible and invisible" (seen and unseen).[15]

These additional words in the creed are based on Colossians 1:15f., a passage from the Apostle Paul. He teaches there that Christ is God's express image and that God by His image, Christ, created supernatural beings. "He is the image of the invisible God, the firstborn over all creation. For by him all things were created: things in heaven and on earth, visible and invisible, whether thrones or powers or rulers or authorities; all things were created by him and for him." The apostle's words were chosen carefully. They exclude the idea that any supernatural angel or power had existence by itself or apart from its being created by God. Neither are these supernatural beings the "offspring" of God, as stated in Gnostic cosmogonies. Paul's comprehensive words deny that any creature in the natural realm was made by such beings.[16]

The intention of the Nicene Creed is clear in affirming that God is the maker of all things, visible and invisible. It refutes Gnosticism or any other cosmogony that believes in supernatural beings who have supposedly made the natural world and humanity. The Christian faith teaches that God is the sole Creator and that He has created all things, whether they are natural things we can investigate or supernatural things we cannot investigate.

5. GOD'S PRESERVATION OF THE WORLD BY SUSTAINING, DIRECTING AND OVERRULING

God continues to work powerfully in the world by preserving and governing it. Through this preservation and governance, God directs his world to achieve divine purposes. This work of God has several dimensions.

God Sustains the Existence of the World

The very survival of the world and everything in it depends not only upon God's existence but also upon His continuing support. Nature, unlike God, is not self-sustained. It is God-sustained. "He is before all things, and in him all things hold together" (Colossians 1:17; see Psalms 104:29f.; Acts 17:28; Hebrews 1:3). If God should cease to exist, all things would cease to exist, falling into immediate oblivion. But the eternal God does not cease to exist, and He continues to preserve what He created.[17]

God Sustains the Processes of Nature

The created world we live in requires a myriad of processes that are marvelously synchronized, and without this ordering, life could not continue. Vegetable life depends upon a proper mixture of light, controlled temperature, moisture and fertile soil. Animal life has a comparable dependency. Human life requires that this entire and complex process work consistently and dependably.[18]

But the grand and elaborate system does work, and we human beings enjoy life. God has not only created a world in which these various elements could come together but He faithfully sustains and directs it. "He has shown kindness by giving you rain from heaven and crops in their seasons; He provides you with plenty of food and fills your hearts with joy" (Acts 14:4; cf. Matthew 5:45; 6:26-32; Psalms 104).[19]

Nature, Secondary Causes; God, the Primary Cause

What we see with the naked eye and measure with instruments of physical science are the processes of nature. These are secondary causes. We can study the complex of secondary and efficient causes, but cannot see and study the primary and necessary cause, God. God's direction of nature through these causes is unseen and unseeable.[20]

Some note the regularity of nature and believe the system is totally independent of any direction beyond itself. We call such people simple materialists or naturalists. But the Christian view is that nature is dependable because God maintains and sustains its processes.

The work of God as Creator and Sustainer of our world occurs at a level the naked eye cannot see. To attribute to God this great work of forming and sustaining our world requires an act of thought, which moves from the seen to the unseen. It also requires an act of faith. "By faith we understand that the universe was formed at God's command, so that what is seen was not made out of what was visible" (Hebrews 11:3). To understand God as the Creator and

Sustainer requires both thinking and believing (cf. Romans 1:20).[21]

God Directs the World to Divine Goals

God's preservation of the world also addresses the issue of ultimate goals and the realization of original intentions. God maintains the world's existence and sustains its processes so that it can systematically move toward its divinely planned destiny.

God, the Creator, had an intention in mind when creating the world. He established a world in which the divine will could be achieved. He set things in motion so that they would advance toward the goal, and He continues to guide and govern its affairs to the end He designed. The movement from origin to present status to destiny does not depend solely upon the natural sequence of events. It depends upon the governing work of God. After Jeremiah noted that God was the Creator for whom nothing was too hard, the prophet said, "Great are your purposes and mighty are your deeds" (Jeremiah 32:18).

God Overrules Resistance to Divine Sovereignty

Evil, in its various dimensions, challenges God's sovereign direction of the world. The many evil things that happen within this world do not conform to God's creative plan or follow divine direction. Some of these evils we call natural evils because they occur within the world of nature. Others we call moral evils because they are committed by moral creatures whom God has made. In both cases, these evils clearly depart from God's creative plan and resist the divine will.

Any doctrine of divine creation and preservation that ignores evil cannot hope to be taken seriously. But the historic view of Christian teaching is precisely that God's will triumphs over evil. Paul articulates the Christian hope in the face of evil with the words: "And we know that in all things God works for the good of those who love him, who have been called according to his purpose" (Romans 8:28). He then lists particular expressions of evil. These include oppression by other human beings, natural disasters and supernatural powers (Romans 8:35-39). Nothing, he concludes, can frustrate God's ultimate plan and separate us from God's love in Christ.[22]

SUMMARY: *The Creator and Preserver of Heaven and Earth*

1. God is the sole Creator. No creature, natural or supernatural, assisted God in the creation of the world. Through the Word, God created all things from nothing, seen and unseen, natural and supernatural. Christian teaching sharply opposes contrary ancient mythologies and philosophies as well as many modern philosophies, particularly at this time that of new ageism.

2. The church has always taught that God created the world out of nothing – *ex nihilo.* This is a logical deduction from the Scriptures. Even when making specific creatures, such as human beings, He worked with materials He had already created. God did not create from primordial stuff with which He was forced to work.

3. God preserves His creation, sustaining the processes of nature through which it lives. He directs His creation toward its destiny and overrules when evils arise. Thus, creation will ultimately fulfill its divinely planned goals.

4. The secondary causes we identify in nature result from their primary cause, God. We cannot see God as we see secondary causes. But we can think about God and believe in Him as the true explanation for nature's dependability and rationality.

SECTION II. *The Nature of Creation*

1. THE GOODNESS OF CREATION

The creation account states that God assessed the work and judged it good, the last time adding that it was all "very good" (such as in Genesis 1:4, 10, 31). The assessment applied to the natural world as well as to the supernatural, for over the six days God created plants, fish and birds, animals and last of all human beings.[23]

Two Pagan Views of Nature

The emphasis in the Scriptures on the goodness of creation distinguishes the Christian view of nature from that of other religions such as ancient Manicheism[24] or Hinduism.[25] Manicheism was the form of Gnosticism that the late fourth century Augustine embraced in his pre-Christian life. It taught that human beings dwell in finite, material bodies, which a benevolent supernatural being could not possibly have made.

Hinduism, a very old religion with many adherents in the Far East, is polytheistic and pantheistic. That is, Hinduism teaches that there are many gods and that these gods make up everything that is. The good things in life arise from good gods and the evil from destructive gods.

The Christian View of Nature

The Christian view of nature is that nature as God created it is good. Humans may disorder and even abuse the gifts of nature that God has given for our good. But it is not true that the enjoyment of nature is sinful.

When our first parents disobeyed God's prohibition, they brought about a disordering of nature. Through the disordering of nature, we can experience it as a terror and evil.

But God has preserved nature from going completely awry. It gives to us far more good than evil. On the whole, when we adhere to God's plan for nature's use, it provides for our needs and grants us pleasure.

Paul observed that to the pure all things are pure (Titus 1:15). He did not mean that those who are pure can do anything that crosses their minds. This is not a license for amorality. But he does mean that God has made the world and anything in it, such as certain foods or marriage, for our good and enjoyment (1 Timothy 4:3-5).

2. THE RATIONALITY OF CREATION

This complex cosmos runs in an orderly, systematic way that amazes us with its regularity. Myriads of different components must be perfectly coordinated for human life to be possible.

The Christian faith teaches that the orderliness of the world reflects the mind of its Creator. The world's systematic nature witnesses to its infinitely wise Maker who fashioned it with such symmetry and sustains it with such dependability that it truly is a "uni-" verse.[26]

The Sciences and the Rationality of Creation

In order for the sciences to advance, nature must work in a systematic way. Physicists, chemists and physicians, to name three specialties, all engage in research that depends on the reliability of matter.

All of nature, whether animate or inanimate, sensate or insensate, is rational. That is, because it is rational we search after the logic by which it works. The entire cosmos, though extremely complex, follows multiple rules that are synchronized into its very being.[27]

The Human Capacity to Understand the Rationality of the Cosmos

The creation account notes that human beings are by nature rational. Of all animal life, we were the creatures made in the divine image and to whom God gave supremacy

(Genesis 1:26-30). God gave direct commands to our first parents, expecting them to understand and obey them (Genesis 2:15-17) and judging them for failing to do so (Genesis 3:8-24).

Within the Scriptures the wisdom tradition – especially the Proverbs – particularly talks about the human capacity for learning. Solomon's expertise in various sciences is celebrated (1 Kings 4:29-34).

Thus, among the creatures of this earth we human beings have been uniquely endowed by the Creator with the capacity to reflect upon the order that is in the world and, to some degree, to understand it. The world is so vast and complex that we will never understand any more than a small portion of it. But we can understand it to some degree and that is a wonderful gift.

3. THE FOCUS IN THE SCRIPTURES ON KNOWLEDGE OF LIVING

Scriptural discussions on knowledge focus on the way to live a good life, the life God created us to live. The book of Proverbs is a case in point. Thus, we should spend much time learning how to live as God intended.

We can learn much from our environment. For example, we can learn by observing animals (Proverbs 30:24-28; 6:6). We can learn even more from other human beings, studying what they do and noting the results. These careful observations teach us, for example, that laziness leads to poverty (10:4), pride to disgrace (11:2), goodness to a legacy (13:22) and a loose tongue to calamity (21:23). A structure is built into the universe so that when we do certain things, our actions tend to bring about certain results. It is this rational structure that we are to explore and discover.

But nothing of such knowledge will avail if we fail to begin our learning at the right point. The wisdom literature states several times that "the fear of the LORD is the beginning of knowledge" (Proverbs 1:7; 9:10; Psalms 111:10).

Learning piled upon learning of itself will not bring happiness or meaning even if our observations are accurate (Ecclessiastes 1:16-18).

4. THE RATIONALITY OF CHRISTIANITY AND THE IRRATIONALITY OF PAGANISM

While the Christian tradition has pointed to the regularity and hence reasonableness of nature and human behavior, pagan religions almost universally have accepted irrational explanations for whatever in life we cannot understand. To explain things, they offer such possibilities as the capricious will of the gods, a conflict between different gods or the movement of stars. The Scriptures deny these explanations and prohibit seeking knowledge by pagan methods such as sorcery, witchcraft, divination, mediums, omens or communication with the dead (Deuteronomy 18:10-12; Leviticus 19:31; 20:6). On occasion, the people of Israel fell from God's way and resorted to pagan means of knowledge (see 1 Samuel 28:7-19). When the Christian church first entered the gentile world, it met a penchant for turning to the occult and the irrational for guidance. Paul encountered such pagan impulses at Paphos (Acts 13:6ff.), at Philippi (Acts 16:16ff.), and at Ephesus (Acts 19).

The Rationality of Christianity and Modern Nihilism

Pagan appeals to the irrational did not cease with the beginning of the Christian era. They have continued into the present. Some modern philosophers argue that the world is not rational. They point to natural disasters and the inhuman treatment people inflict upon one another. This leads them to embrace a nihilistic philosophy. Nihilism literally means "nothing." A nihilistic philosophy argues that we can discern no overarching rationality and plan in the world; nothing makes full sense of the world and human life.

Wherever the Christian gospel has won converts, appeal to the irrational has been in retreat and confidence both that nature has order and life has meaning have been on the rise.[28] This is the case in spite of the fact that Christianity acknowledged that we live in a fallen and broken world. Wherever the Gospel declines, the irrational returns. The resurgence of the occult and philosophical irrationalism in the Western world witnesses to this pattern.

SUMMARY: *The Goodness and Rationality of Creation*

1. The world that God both made and sustains is intrinsically good. This judgment applies to its materiality as surely as it does to its spirituality.

2. Evil did not arise because God failed in His work of creation. Rather, it arose because of human disobedience to God's command. It continues when we disorder God's creation, departing from the divine intention.

3. The cosmos is both complex and rational. It reflects the mind of its Creator and Sustainer, who works in an orderly and systematic way. By studying the world of nature, we can come to understand, to some degree, its inner logic. We can engage in the sciences because of the rationality of creation.

4. Human beings have been uniquely gifted by God to think rationally, but there is a limit to how much we can learn and understand because our rational abilities are damaged by sin. And our world is fallen and flawed. Even so, we can study the world with the confidence that we can acquire genuine knowledge and gain wisdom from it.

SECTION III. *The Creation as a Moral Universe*

1. THE HUMAN BEING, A MORAL CREATURE

We human beings are moral as well as natural creatures. The universe has a moral factor built into it. We do not merely live by instinct within the natural order.[29] We also live by the moral decisions we make, and these decisions may bring good or evil into our lives.[30] Thus, acting out of our moral nature, we may bring upon ourselves certain diseases or may cause an alienation in our human relationships. For example, an intemperate man will damage or even destroy his body; an unfaithful wife can deeply wound a spouse and family.

The Universal Witness to the Moral Factor in Human Nature

Some suggest that the moral feature of human life is not intrinsic to human nature. For example, behaviorists claim that our actions are completely conditioned by influences beyond our control; therefore, whatever we do should not make us feel guilty before some absolute tribunal for such behavior. Ethical relativists assert that moral principles are only the creation of various cultures. They are not universal principles written into the very structure of human nature.

However, humans universally judge that some actions are good and others are evil.[31] They therefore feel either approval or shame for what they do (Romans 2:14f.). Augustine wryly noted that even pirates and tyrants have a code of ethics by which they hope to justify their behavior.[32] By one means or another, we humans seek atonement for sin and reconciliation for estrangement. This is strong evidence that there is a universal moral factor in human nature.

Human Beings Have a Limited Freedom

The moral factor within human nature arises because we human beings have moral freedom to choose and act. This freedom, however, is limited so that we cannot do anything we might wish. That is, for one thing, we can choose only from the possibilities our environment offers us. Moreover, we can act only within the limits of the power we possess as finite creatures. Habits we have formed by prior decisions limit even further our possibilities to act freely. But within these limitations we have a genuine freedom.

Historic Christian thought has always taught that moral freedom is limited.[33] The continuing disagreement within the Christian community on questions related to such doctrines as predestination should not obscure the large ground of common belief.[34] It is widely held that we humans make moral choices and that God is not the author of our evil choices. They are made from within the confines of our limited human freedom and therefore we are responsible for them.

2. THE DOCTRINE OF RETRIBUTION

One sign that the universe is moral is that our deeds are connected to their results. Just as there is a correspondence between cause and effect in the natural realm, so there is a correspondence between cause and effect in the moral realm.

Natural scientists point to the connection between causes and results in the material world. For example, the right amount of warmth and moisture will cause a planted seed to germinate and bear fruit. The combustion of fossil fuels can turn huge turbines that bring light and heat to our homes.

Even so, in the moral realm actions bring results (see John 10:23f.; Galatians 6:7f.). The connection is necessary; it is built into the nature of reality. God created our world along moral lines and He sustains it to moral ends.[35]

"Each Person According to What He Has Done"

The Scriptures, Judaism and historic Christianity all have taught that sin brings judgment. This is the doctrine of retribution: "Surely [God] will reward each person according to what he has done" (Psalms 62:12; cf. Proverbs 24:12; Matthew 16:27; Romans 2:6; 2 Corinthians 5:10; Revelation 2:23).[36] For those who sin judgment is inevitable, even though God may delay it. Unrepentant sinners who think they are escaping judgment will find they are not (Psalms 37:1f.; Luke 13:1-5; Romans 2:3f.). The judgment of our sin is certain.

The Wise and the Foolish, the Righteous and the Wicked

Jesus illustrated His teaching on retribution by comparing two ways of life. He likened those who heed His words and put them into practice to a wise man who builds his house on a rock. By contrast the one who fails to heed His word is like a foolish man who builds his house on sand. When the wind and rain and floods come, the house of the wise man stands the judgment of nature, and the house of the foolish man collapses (Matthew 7:24-27).[37]

Similarly, Psalm 1 contrasts the righteous with the wicked. The former make God's law their guide; the latter do not. God watches over the righteous, but the way of the wicked will perish.

These stories contrasting those who are the wise and righteous with those who are foolish and wicked tersely illustrate the course of a person's life. They condense the entire life with its numberless deeds and their ultimate ends into two possible modes of life and their inevitable results.

The Way of Life and the Way of Death

The doctrine of retribution articulates our human situation. What we choose today and carry into action determines what we will experience tomorrow. Moses exhorted the Israelites just before they entered the land of promise to choose between life and death. Their ultimate destiny depended upon the choices they made and the actions that followed from them (Deuteronomy 11:26; 30:19; see Jeremiah 21:8; Galatians 5:16-26; 6:7-10). The moral dimension of life looms large in these passages. The Scriptures articulate the fact that we humans must choose to act wisely and rightly because our choices have consequences. We cannot act foolishly and wickedly now and later manipulate the results so that they will be good. The results are in our hands to the same degree that the choices and actions are in our hands.

3. THE INTERCONNECTEDNESS OF THE NATURAL AND MORAL REALMS

Visible and Natural Consequences of Moral Failure

In historic Christian thought, deeds relate to what results. The results may not occur or even be evident immediately. Nevertheless, a consequence naturally results from a behavior: "The one who sows to please his flesh, will from that flesh reap destruction, and the one who sows to please the Spirit, will from the Spirit reap eternal life" (Galatians 6:8).[38] Sin always has disastrous consequences in life. The prodigal wasted his inheritance on sinful living and eventually could not even feed himself properly (Luke 15:13-16).

Punishment in Kind

Often the Scriptures describe the results of sin as judgment in kind. That is, the consequence bears a striking resemblance to the sin committed. For example, after David took Uriah's wife and then plotted his death to cover his deed (2 Samuel 11:11), his own household was visited with sexual sin and murder: His son, Amnon forced and raped David's daughter, Tamar. Later, in revenge for the deed, Amnon was assassinated by Absalom, another son of David

(2 Samuel 13). Then Absolom attempted to overthrow David by possessing his harem (2 Samuel 16:21f.) and plunging the entire nation into civil war (2 Samuel 17:1-18:18; see Matthew 26:52).

Primary and Secondary Causes in the Moral Realm

The Scriptures do not always identify God as a participant in the deeds-and-results pattern. For example, Proverbs 11:3 says: "The unfaithful are destroyed by their duplicity." This short version of the doctrine of retribution occurs often in the book of Proverbs.

But the inevitable results occur because of God. Just as nature sustains itself and is dependable because its unseen Lord upholds it, so in the moral realm actions bear results because God decrees them. God is the Sustainer of both the natural, physical world and of the moral, spiritual realm. "In his heart a man plans his course, but the Lord determines his steps" (Proverbs 16:9; see 15:25; 16:1, 4, 6; Romans 1:24, 26, 28).

4. THE RESULTS OF PARENTAL DEEDS VISITED UPON THEIR CHILDREN

One tragic effect of sin is the transmission of its results from parents to children. Those who sin are themselves affected by consequences but often so are their children. In solemn words to Moses after Israel had worshiped the golden calf, God announced that the Lord does not allow guilt to go unrequited but "punishes the children and their children for the sin of the fathers to the third and fourth generation" (Exodus 34:7).[39]

The awesome and fearful teaching that generations are tied together by moral cause and effect is not the last word. Ezekiel challenged a false understanding of this truth when he said that a son can escape the life pattern of his sinful father. If he observes the tragic results of his father's sin and turns from it and does right, he will live (Ezekiel 18).

But the central idea of the intergenerational linkage holds. What we do profoundly affects our children for good or ill. We are largely responsible for the moral formation of our children. The teaching of the Scriptures and Christian tradition, which grows from a rugged realism, agrees with the findings of social scientists – that the home environment is the single most crucial factor in moral development.

5. THE CREATOR AS THE LAWGIVER

The Scriptures describe the Creator as also the Lawgiver. The account of creation in Genesis 2 states that after God made the man, He planted a garden in the East. He then put the man there to care for it and take food from it with specific instructions about the one tree from which he was not to eat (Genesis 2:7ff.). There is no divergence between Creator and Lawgiver. The Creator made the world as rational and then gave a law that is rational. It makes sense. The will of God does not arise from a capricious monarch who wants to lord it over us in an unreasonable way. What He asks of us always makes sense, even when in our limited capacity we cannot fully understand it.[40]

Revelation of God's Will Still Necessary Due to Our Sin

The law reflects creation; it gives verbal form to the ways in which the Creator intended the world to work and be used. But we still need the written law because we still need explicit direction from God's revelation so that we can know His will. Sin is so subtle and our minds are so affected by self-centeredness that we need the will of God articulated in clear form.[41]

Thus, historic Christian thought states two ideas at the same time: There is perfect accord between the will of God revealed in the Scriptures and the will of God written into the fabric of the world, but because of our sinfulness and our finitude, we are unable to discover God's will in nature without the direction and explicit teaching of the Scriptures.

SUMMARY: *The Creation as a Moral Universe*

1. In our universe deeds have consequences. Human beings are preeminently moral creatures who, with limited freedom, must choose between good and evil and then act.
2. As God preserves the natural realm, so He preserves the moral realm. For human beings the world is one. So we live in a moral universe in which spiritual choices and actions may have physical as well as spiritual consequences.
3. Our choices and actions have intergenerational consequences. Our first parents' sin continues to affect their descendants as well as nature. The sins that we commit affect our children for whose spiritual formation we have great responsibility.
4. God, who created and sustains this moral universe, also has revealed His will to us through the prophets and apostles. The written expression of God's will within the Scriptures corresponds to the unwritten will of God within nature. Sin has become the normal human behavior. Because it blinds us so that we cannot interpret nature correctly, we need the revealed Word to know God's will accurately.

SECTION IV. *Disorder in Creation*

1. SIN AS THE ULTIMATE CAUSE OF DISORDER IN CREATION

The world in which we live is disordered. Wherever there is disorder we can look to sin as its ultimate cause. Evil and disorder surface in nature when a child is stricken with disease or a village is buried under lava. It also appears when humans treat one another inhumanely. The holocaust in which millions of Jews were exterminated is a case in point. Epidemic parental abuse of children is another.

The Scriptures attribute the ultimate cause of this disorder to sin.[42] Tragedies happen to innocent people because we live in a moral universe that has fallen from its original righteousness. Because of the interconnectedness of our world, the evil done by one person may bring tragedy into the life of another who does not deserve it. Sin continues to introduce ever-new forms of evil into the universe, each of which has hurtful results.

A Definition of Sin: Missing the Mark

The most common words for sin in both the Old (*hata'ah*) and New (*hamartia*) Testaments mean to miss the mark. The metaphor pictures an archer failing to hit the target with the arrow or a traveler taking a wrong path.

Sin arises when we fail to live as God ordained that we should. The consequence of sin is to bring disorder into our lives and our environment. Thus we cannot define any sin as an innocent little misdeed. Every sin creates disorder, and the cumulative effect of our many sins is the colossal disorder our world experiences.

A Definition of Judgment: God Surrenders Us to Ourselves

In Romans 1:18-32 Paul describes God's judgment against all godlessness and wickedness. He begins with the primal or initial sin and then moves to particular sins that show the disorder that humans make for themselves and in which they then must live.

The primal sin was a refusal to worship God. Paul says of the pagan world that they failed to glorify and thank God (1:21). In their arrogance they made an empty claim of

183

wisdom (1:22) and exchanged the glory (1:23) and worship (1:25) of the true God for that of a creature.

For this primal sin God gave them over to themselves (1:24, 26, 28). This was His judgment. Since they refused to worship God and obey His will, He surrendered them to the worship of self, which, as He shows, is a grave judgment. They took the creation that He had made and in multiplied ways disordered it (1:24b, 26-27, 28b-31).[43]

We cannot create an order in the world different from the order God created. He alone is the Creator. What we do when we fail to worship God and obey Him is to disorder the world He has entrusted to us. This can be done in persons, in communities and even in whole societies. Sin inevitably results in chaos.

The Curse Has Fallen Upon the World as Well as Upon Humans

When God judged our first parents for their sin, nature was included within the orbit of judgment: Childbirth would bring pain to the mother (Genesis 3:16), and the ground would grow thorns and thistles (Genesis 3:17f.). Thus, the sin of our first parents brought disaster upon creation as well as upon their descendants.

Paul comments upon this curse of nature, "Creation was subjected to frustration, not by its own choice, but by the will of the one who subjected it" and so "the whole creation has been groaning as in pains of childbirth right to the present time" (Romans 8:20, 22).

2. EVIL AND IRRATIONALITY IN A DISORDERED CREATION

Nature and Human Life Are Flawed by Evil and Irrationality

Some things that happen within the world seem illogical. The psalmist, for example, complains that often evil people succeed (Psalms 64:1-6) and righteous people must

endure suffering (Psalms 22:1f.; 44). Thus, the morally ordered universe in which goodness should prosper and wickedness should fail appears to have broken down.[44]

Evil Could Not Flourish in a Totally Evil and Irrational World

Evil could not flourish in a totally evil world. For evil to
succeed, the world must be largely good and rational. A lie
is effective only when people believe it, and they would
not believe it if they did not generally trust others to tell the
truth. We would not bother to plant crops or build houses if
we could not depend upon nature to honor our efforts with
predictable results.

The Limits of Understanding Creation from Within Creation

Still, we cannot look at the disordered features of the
present state of things and argue that this is how things
ought to be or how the Creator intended them to be. The
world is disordered. While it remains the Creator's work and
reflects its origin in myriad ways, what we actually see is
the Creator's work refracted through its present disorder.

The disciplines that study human behavior – sociol-
ogy and psychology, for example – are limited in understanding the Creator's intentions because they study them
from within a fallen world. Sociologists and psychologists
can only observe the behavior of sinful people, disordered
to one degree or another. They can do little more than
describe what people do and offer some explanations of
why they do it.

But many behavioral scientists go beyond this limit.
They not only describe what people do; they also prescribe
what they ought to do. Some even state that they can determine what the Creator intended by studying human nature
in its present state. From this perspective sin in its many
forms is no longer looked upon as a fall from the Creator's

design but as natural behavior. But what is natural in this sense is not what the Creator designed but what people typically do as fallen creatures.[45]

Because of Our Fallen Nature We Naturally Sin

In contrast to the more secular views, the Christian view has historically described each person as sinful by nature, and because of our sinful nature we sin. Human nature is not sinful because God created it sinful, but because it has been corrupted. Thus, in the classic language of the Church of England, all persons have departed from "original righteousness" and are "inclined to evil." As such, they naturally sin.[46]

3. GOD'S DELAYS AS OPPORTUNITY FOR REPENTANCE AND TRAINING IN RIGHTEOUSNESS

The Scriptures indicate that in the present time God delays judgment. He brings good into the lives of the evil as well as the good. "He causes his sun to rise on the evil and the good, and sends rain on the righteous and the unrighteous" (Matthew 5:45). This delay does not suggest that God is indifferent to sin. Rather, the delay grants time for repentance and additional opportunities to set things right.[47] Peter said of those who mocked teaching on the Lord's imminent return, "The Lord is not slow in keeping his promise, as some understand slowness. He is patient with you, not wanting anyone to perish, but everyone to come repentance" (2 Peter 3:9; see Luke 17:1-4; Romans 2:4).

But this delay in judgment will soon come to an end, and when the end comes, things will be made right. For those who respond to God, the ultimate end will be good; for those who do not, it will be judgment. "A righteous man may have many troubles, but the Lord delivers him from them all. ... Evil will slay the wicked; the foes of the righteous will be condemned" (Psalms 34:19, 21; see Psalm 37).

Even the suffering we endure is a sign of God's goodness. It does not come as the necessary result of our evil, and it can lead us to repentance (2 Corinthians 7:8-11). Or suffering can cause us to depend more upon God and less upon ourselves. Thus it is a means of spiritual growth (2 Corinthians 11:7-10).

SUMMARY: *Disorder in Creation*

1. The world in which we live, though created with goodness and rationality, has been disordered by sin. Thus, it possesses signs within it of evil and irrationality, though the evil does not arise from a flaw in the Creator's work.

2. When we sin, we miss the mark that the Creator designed for us, and we try to establish an independence from Him. God judges those who arrogantly and impenitently resist His will by surrendering them to themselves. This always leads to further disorder and chaos.

3. The judgment of God and the disorder of the world have fallen on nature as well as on the human race. The whole universe is marked by the Fall.

4. Human nature has been seriously affected by the fall of Adam and Eve and by personal sin. The current state of human beings is not one of simple nature but disordered nature.

5. God delays final judgment for sin to grant us time for repentance and spiritual growth.

SECTION V. *The Redemption of Creation*

1. THE GOAL OF REDEMPTION

The entire story of the Scriptures sets forth the belief that God has not abandoned His fallen creation nor is He unable to redeem it. The account of God's dealing with Adam and Eve after their fall holds the promise of redemption. And the final scene of the entire Scriptures pictures a restoration: Paradise Lost becomes Paradise Regained.[48]

The Crushed Head of the Serpent

The early teachers of the church pointed to the recorded curse that God laid on the serpent after the Fall in Eden: "I will put enmity between you and the woman, and between your offspring and hers; he will crush your head, and you will strike his heel" (Genesis 3:15). This is the *protoevangelium*, the first announcement of the gospel. It alludes to Christ, the offspring who would crush the head of the serpent, though in the process He would be wounded.[49]

A New Heaven and a New Earth

God's ultimate goal is the complete restoration of the world. In the present age, His redeeming work focuses principally on the spiritual recovery of lost sinners. But historic Christian faith has always held that the message of the Scriptures is one promising a completely restored cosmos. These two, the glorification of the children of God and the restoration of the material world are closely related. "For the creation waits in eager expectation for the sons of God to be revealed." It was subjected "in hope that the creation itself will be liberated from its bondage to decay and brought into the glorious freedom of the children of God" (Romans 8:19, 21).[50]

Jesus referred to this as the "renewal of all things" (Matthew 19:28). John describes it as the new heaven and the new earth (Revelation 21f.).[51]

2. THE ORIGIN OF REDEMPTION IN THE CREATOR'S PLAN

Before He created the world, the Creator in His infinite wisdom had established the master plan of redemption. What we see within the history of salvation recorded in the Scriptures is the execution of God's eternal plan. Thus, Paul says:

"For he chose us in him before the creation of the world to be holy and blameless in his sight. In love he predestined us to be adopted as his sons through Jesus Christ, in accordance with his pleasure and will" (Ephesians 1:4f.; see Romans 8:29f.)

3. THE HISTORY OF SALVATION IN THE SCRIPTURES

The full message of the Gospel is that God will make a new heaven and a new earth at the end of time. But the Scriptures focus on the redemption of human beings. The entire human race has been caught in the tragedy of evil, and God looks with pity and redemptive purpose on all the children of Adam and Eve.

The history of salvation within the Scriptures, then, centers on the grand drama of God redeeming the human race. First, He calls one family (that of Abraham) from whom He builds a nation. Then, through the unfolding of Israel's history, He narrows His work down further to the one Son of Abraham, who is the incarnate Word of God. From that point on the scope of God's redeeming ministry enlarges as He reaches out to bring the entire human family within the orbit of salvation through the ministry of the church.

Thus, the stories of Israel, of the incarnate Word and of the church all encompass the work of God in restoring the fallen world to Himself.

The Promise to Abraham and Israel's Ministry to the Nations

In the initial call of Abram, God promised him, "All peoples on earth will be blessed through you" (Genesis 12:1-3). From the start, the scope of the vision is universal.

Within Israel there was a tremendous battle to determine whether all the nations of the world would know God's saving compassion or whether the compassion was to be reserved solely for Israel. This battle is represented by Jonah who knew God was gracious but hated the Ninevites and hoped they would perish. For this reason, Jonah initially disobeyed God and refused to preach in Nineveh, knowing that without repentance they would perish. And when he finally preached to the Ninevites and saw them repent, he articulated God's purposes with clarity: "You are a gracious and compassionate God, slow to anger and abounding in love, a God who relents from sending calamity" (Jonah 4:2).

The Incarnate Word as the Redeemer of the World

The redemptive work of God reached a new stage with the incarnation of the Son of God. The New Testament explicitly states that He came into our world to rescue us from the tragic situation created by sin. Our Lord said: "For God so loved the world that he gave his one and only Son, that whoever believes in him shall not perish but have eternal life" (John 3:16). Paul states: "For God was pleased to have all his fullness dwell in him, and through him to reconcile to himself all things, whether things on earth or things in heaven, by making peace through his blood, shed on the cross" (Colossians 1:19f.).

The Church's Ministry of Reconciliation

In final words to His disciples, Jesus told them that they were to "go and makes disciples of all nations" (Matthew 28:19). When the preaching of the Gospel in Antioch brought into being the church among the Gentiles, the early church struggled over the gentile mission, but very soon it concluded that God "at first showed his concern by taking from the Gentiles a people for himself" (Acts 15:14). Paul's last words recorded in Acts are along this line: "Therefore I want you to know that God's salvation has been sent to the Gentiles, and they will listen!" (Acts 28:28)

The message of redemption from sin has, as its backdrop, the belief that the good things of life we enjoy come from our benevolent Sovereign. Paul counseled the citizens of Lystra not to treat him as God, saying, "We too are only men, human like you. We are bringing you good news, telling you to turn from these worthless things to the living God, who made heaven and earth and sea, and everything in them. ... Yet he has not left himself without testimony: He has shown kindness by giving you rain from heaven and crops in their seasons; he provides you with plenty of food and fills your hearts with joy" (Acts 14:15-17).

4. THE FOUNDATION OF TRUST AND PRAYER

The teaching that God is the Creator and Sustainer of the universe provides the foundation for Christian trust and prayer. This teaching is voiced by the psalmist (Psalm 65), by the prophets (Isaiah 44:6-8), and especially by our Lord (Matthew 6:25-34).

Seek First the Kingdom of God

Jesus illustrated God's care for us by comparing our condition to that of the birds of the air and the lilies of the field. Neither birds nor plants can worry as humans do, and yet their needs are met. Worry does not increase what we possess but only distracts us from what we should be doing, seeking God's kingdom and righteousness (Matthew 6:25-34). The Scriptures teach that after much effort and conniving, a fortune can be swept aside by disaster (Job 1:13-17) or sudden death (Luke 12:20).[52]

Christian trust does not counsel laziness. As we are able, we are to work with our own hands (1 Thessalonians 4:11f.; see 1 Timothy 5:8). But the gospel does teach us that there are things far more important than the accumulation of wealth (Philippians 4:10-13). And even those people who threaten us cannot take away from us that which is most precious. Thus Jesus advised us not to fear the one who could take our lives but to fear only the one who could take away our eternal destiny in heaven (Matthew 10:28).

The Foundation of Prayer in the Benevolent Will of the Sovereign

The practice of effective prayer depends upon a certain view of God. We believe that He is good, that His purposes are for our good and that He is sovereign. It also depends upon a certain view of human beings. We hold that they are moral creatures presently involved in the great drama of life. Thus, they must make choices and carry through with actions that reflect obedience to God's will.

The personal relationship we have with God, then, reaches its most acute form in prayer. Here we lay before Him, as the psalmist prayed, such matters as our humanity (116:15f.; 8), our failings (32:3-5; 130), our needs (107:4f., 10-12, 17f., 23-25), our trust (31:19-20; 61:3-5) and our petitions (86:1-4; 88:1-2, 13-18).[53]

Our prayers are vibrant to the degree that we trust God to be sovereign and good and we seek to obey Him. The belief that God's gracious plan will ultimately prevail over all evil makes prayer both possible and necessary.

SUMMARY: *The Redemption of Creation*

1. The Scriptures teach us that God has set in motion a plan of redemption for his whole creation. He ultimately will create a new heaven and a new earth.

2. This plan of salvation was designed even before the creation of the world. It was announced to our first parents when God judged them for their sin and it was repeated at the end of the Revelation to John, the Apocalypse.

3. The entire story of salvation history within the Scriptures is a gradual unfolding and execution of this plan of salvation – in Israel, in the incarnate Word and in the church.

4. Belief that God is the Sovereign of the universe, that He is good and that He will ultimately triumph over all sin and evil provides the foundation for

Christian trust in the midst of suffering in this fallen universe. It also gives the practice of prayer vibrancy and hope.

ENDNOTES

[1] Wesley on Hebrews 1:3, *ENNT* 586.

[2] Leibowitz, *FM* 45-47.

[3] Bickermann, *ELM* 20, 50f.

[4] Long, *ER* 4:94-99.

[5] Angus, *BQGRW* 220f., 356-59.

[6] Albanese, "The Magical Staff: Quantum Healing in the New Age," *PNA* 68-84.

[7] Angus, *RQGRW* 58 ff.

[8] Watson, *TI* 1:46-48.

[9] Watson, *TI* 1:21.

[10] Tertullian, *PAH* 13, *ANF* 3:249; 2 Maccabees 7:28 and Shepherd of Hermas *Mandate* 1, *ANF* 1:82.

[11] Irenaeus, *AH* 2:9, *ANF* 1:369; Theophilus, *Autolycus* 2:10, *ANF* 2:97f.; Athanasius, *IW* 3, *NPNF* 2:4:37f.; Augustine, *CG* 11:4, *NPNF* 1:2:206f; Thomas Aquinas, *ST* 1:45:1-2, *BWTA* 1:432-36; *The Heidelberg Catechism* 26, *CC* 3:26; *Dogmatic Constitution on the Catholic Faith* 1, Vatican 1 *CC* 2:239; Collins, *FW* 21.

[12] von Rad, *OTT* 1:141-44.

[13] Basil, *Hex.* 1, *NPNF* 2:8:52-58.

[14] John of Damascus, *EOF* 2:5, *NPNF* 2:9:21.

[15] *CC* 2:58.

[16] John of Damascus, *EOF* 2:3, *NPNF* 2:9:19-21.

[17] Ralston, *ED* 93-85; Leibowitz, *FM* 40f.

[18] Ralston, *ED* 85-90.

[19] Wesley, Sermon 67, "On Divine Providence," *WJWB* 2:538-48; Pope, *CCT* 449-55; Cannon, *TJW* 169f.; Collins, *FW* 26.

[20] Watson, *TI* 1:272-325.

[21] Oden, *LG* 281-83.

[22] Oden, *LG* 279-81; 286; 300-302.

[23] First Clement 20, *ANF* 1:10f.; Wesley, Sermon 56, "God's Approbation of His Works," I, *WJWB* 2:388-97.

[24] Augustine, *Reply to Fautus the Manichean* 31, *NPNF* 1:4:331f.

[25] Kloetzli, *ER* 4:107-11.

[26] Ralston, *ED* 68.

[27] Ralston, *ED* 69.

[28] Oden, *LG* 147-50.

[29] Fairbairn, *RLS* 35-49.

[30] Wiley, *CT* 2:275; Cannon, *TJW* 176-83.

[31] Fletcher, "Appeal to Matter of Fact and Common Sense" V.II-III, *WJF* 3:257-309.

[32] Augustine, *CG* 4:5 *NPNF* 1:2:66.

[33] Irenaeus, *AH* 4:4:3, *ANF* 1:466; John of Damascus, *EOF* 2:24-28, *NPNF* 2:9:39-41.

[34] John of Damascus, *EOF* 2:30, *NPNF* 2:9:42-44.

[35] Wesley, Sermon 99, "The Reward of Righteousness," I, *WJWB* 3:400-405.

[36] Sirach 35:19; Wisdom 11:5; 2 Maccabees 5:9f.; Philo *Flac.* 171-75, *Philo* 9:395-97.

[37] Wesley, Sermon 33, "Upon our Lord's Sermon on the Mount," XIII, III, *WJWB* 1:694-98.

[38] Cannon, *TJW* 190.

[39] Wesley, Sermon 111, "National Sins and Miseries" II, *WJWB* 3:572-76.

[40] Wesley, Sermon 34, "The Original, Nature, Properties, and Use of the Law," I.1-3, *WJWB* 2:6f.; Watson, *TI* 1:8f.

[41] Calvin, *Inst.* 2:8:12 (1:309f.); Wesley, Sermon 34, "The Original, Nature, Properties, and Use of the Law," I.4-II.6, *WJWB* 2:7-10; Lindström, *WS* 81.

[42] Gregory of Nyssa, *GC* 6, *NPNF* 2:5:488f.; Collins, *FW* 29ff.

[43] Wesley, Sermon 44, "Original Sin," I-II, *WJWB* 1:172-82.

[44] Dunning, *GFH* 250-55.

[45] Wesley, Sermon 44, "Original Sin," III, *WJWB* 2:182-85; Sermon 56, "God's Approbation of His Works," II, *WJWB* 2:397-99; Lindström, *WS* 19-26.

[46] *The Thirty-Nine Articles of the Church of England,* Article 9, *CC* 3:492f.; see Article Seven of the Free Methodist Church, *1989 BD* 11.

[47] Arminius, "Private Disputations," XXI, *WJA* 2:49.

[48] John of Damascus, *EOF* 3:1, *NPNF* 2:9:45f.; Pope, *CCT* 2:90-92; Dunning, *GFH* 266-72; Oden, *LG* 249f.

[49] Fletcher, "Socinianism Unscriptural," VII, *WJF* 3:507.

[50] Wesley, Sermon 60, "The General Deliverance," III, *WJWB* 2:445-50.

[51] Wesley, Sermon 64, "The New Creation" *WJWB* 2:500-510.

[52] Vriezen, *OOTT* 189f.

[53] Wesley, Sermon 16, "The Means of Grace," III, *WJWB* 1:384-87.

CHAPTER

THE
INCARNATE
WORD OF GOD

SECTION I. THE LIFE AND MINISTRY OF JESUS OF NAZARETH

1. The Gospel Accounts of Jesus Christ
2. Jesus, a Real Man
3. The Birth of Jesus
4. The Community of Jesus
5. The Ministry of Jesus, I.: His Preaching and Teaching
6. The Ministry of Jesus, II.: His Compassion and Miracles
7. The Suffering and Death of Jesus
8. The Burial, Resurrection, Appearances, and Ascension of Jesus

SECTION II. THE TITLES OF JESUS

1. The Son of Man
2. The Son of God
3. The Christ
4. The Servant of the Lord
5. The Word
6. The Lord

SECTION III. THE CLASSIC VIEW OF JESUS AND ANCIENT DEPARTURES FROM IT

1. Adoptionism
2. Rejection of Jesus' Full Deity: Arianism
3. Rejection of Jesus' Full Humanity

Jesus of Nazareth was a wonderful person. As an itinerant preacher and miracle worker, He brought insight, healing, and freedom to thousands of Jewish peasants. However, Jesus' influence has extended far beyond His own time in the first century. Though He wrote no books, His ideas have penetrated every corner of the globe. The disciples He gathered around Him and who worked with Him formed the initial core of the Christian church, which has become the greatest religious movement in human history.

Since its inception the church has explained this astounding influence of Jesus in two ways. First, it reports events from Jesus' historical life. Peter summed it up in his sermon to Cornelius, the first gentile convert, as follows. During Jesus' life, He went about doing good and delivering those who were oppressed of the devil. Then He was crucified and raised from the dead. These events God has made the instruments of salvation (Acts 10:37-43). Second, Christians believe this occurred in Jesus because He is a unique person. Jesus of Nazareth is the Son of God and the Son of Man, and this belief is the foundation of the church, which even the gates of Hades cannot overcome (Matthew 16:16-18).

SECTION I. *The Life and Ministry of Jesus of Nazareth*

1. THE GOSPEL ACCOUNTS OF JESUS CHRIST

The Oral Witness of the Apostles to Jesus

During the first two generations of the church, Jesus' disciples witnessed to His life, death and resurrection. Their preaching depended upon a living memory. But after they died the church had to depend solely upon their writings for firsthand, eyewitness teaching about Jesus of Nazareth (Luke 1:2).[1]

The Written Witness of the Apostles to Jesus: The Rejection of Apocryphal Gospels and the Acceptance of the Canonical Gospels

During the decades after the apostles were no longer living, many additional stories about Jesus circulated and ultimately found their way into writing. These writings were called apocryphal gospels – apocryphal meaning hidden. They were rejected by the church and never achieved widespread authority.[2]

Thus, the four canonical Gospels, Matthew, Mark, Luke, and John, offer us the primary sources for the life and ministry of Jesus. Anything the church has taught about Him as authoritatively to be believed depends upon what these Gospels report.

The Gospels as Historical Accounts

The Gospel accounts are not biographies of Jesus, though they contain biographical information. Instead they leave out large periods in His life, such as His youth and early manhood, and focus on His ministry, death and resurrection. Because of their very nature, the Gospels do not report the life of Jesus as a newspaper or chronicler would, or record His words as a stenographer would. Still the Gospels can be examined as historical documents. While scholars may adopt different views in reconstructing the historical situations of the Gospel stories, the church has always trusted them as historically reliable. The authors of the Gospels accurately remembered and faithfully reported and interpreted the significance of a real life – that of Jesus of Nazareth.

One Gospel, Four Gospels

In one sense we say that there is only one Gospel, that of Jesus Christ our Lord, reported four times by four evangelists. On the other hand, each account of the Gospel has its own integrity so that it is proper to call it a Gospel.

One might expect that after the four canonical accounts of the Gospel had been recognized by the church, someone would have gathered their various stories into a single account, letting each story be told once in sequence. This was done by Tatian, a Syrian of the second century.[3] But the church did not accept his book, called the *Diatessaron*,[4] as a substitute for the four canonical accounts of the Gospel.

The Fourfold Witness to the Gospel

The church received and continues to use the fourfold witness to the Gospel as authoritative. Therefore, we do not have one account, but four that are placed side by side allowing us to compare them with one another. Such comparison reveals remarkable things.

Matthew, Mark and Luke have great similarities. These three have been designated as the synoptic accounts, since they often describe events with language that is remarkably similar. Most students of the Gospels believe there is a literary relationship among the three. John, however, is quite different, even though he reports many of the same stories as the synoptics do.

Regardless of the literary relationship among the Gospels, each gives an unique witness to Jesus. Matthew emphasizes His role as the Messiah of Israel and as the Prophet who proclaims the full will of God. Mark describes Jesus as the wonderful teacher and healer, who suffers unjustly as the Servant of the Lord. Luke pictures Him as the friend of the weak, the poor, and the gentile, who brings salvation to all. John portrays Him as the incarnate Son of God, rejected by His people but bringing spiritual life to those who will believe.

Each account of Jesus offers us a legitimate picture of His life, death, and resurrection. He was a complex person, and His accomplishments were complex. Collapsing the four accounts into one, as Tatian did, would have completely obscured this. So in its wisdom, the church has kept the four separate accounts.

2. JESUS, A REAL MAN

The Gospel accounts make it clear that Jesus had the range of experiences that all humans have, though He did not experience everything that a human can experience.[5] No single person can have all possible experiences. One is limited by the fact that one is male or female, single or married, wise or foolish, good or evil. But with this limitation, one person can nevertheless genuinely know all of what it means to be human.

Jesus' Physical and Emotional Life Was that of a Real Man

Though Jesus' conception by a virgin was unique, His birth was typical of a birth to poor Jewish peasants (Luke

2:6f.). In infancy His life was under threat, a threat His parents took seriously (Matthew 2:13-23). As a child (Luke 2:49), He obeyed His earthly parents (Luke 2:51), even though He also became involved at an early age in His heavenly Father's affairs (Luke 2:50). The church wisely rejected apocryphal stories that pictured Jesus as a miracle-working wonderchild.[6] Instead, the Gospel simply tells us that as a child He "grew in wisdom and stature, and in favor with God and man" (Luke 2:52).[7]

Jesus slept (Mark 4:38) and ate (Luke 15:2) and drank (Matthew 11:19), as all humans do. The Gospels make it abundantly clear that He died as a man. It was His body that was crucified (Matthew 27:35; Mark 15:24; Luke 23:33; John 19:18) by being nailed to a cross (see Colossians 2:14). When the soldier pierced His side with a spear, blood and water came forth (John 19:34). He refused the drugged drinks offered to deaden the pain (Matthew 27:34; John 19:29). When He breathed His last, His death was real (Mark 15:37).

When criticized for healing the man with a shriveled hand on the Sabbath, He grew angry and deeply distressed (Mark 3:1-5). When disbelieved after doing so many wonderful works, He was amazed (Mark 6:6). He wept when His friend Lazarus died (John 11:35). When wearied by hard work with the masses, He needed to be alone with friends (Mark 3:7). Jesus even noted of Himself that the Son did not know the hour of the final consummation (Matthew 24:36).

Jesus' Spiritual Life Was That of a Man

Jesus traveled the spiritual road open to all humans, a journey of growth, piety, temptation, and prayer. This was true of Him during childhood (Luke 2:49); it was also true of Him as an adult.

His parents faithfully observed the customs of the law (Luke 2:21, 22, 39, 41f.). He continued the same pattern when He was an adult (Luke 4:16; 22:8). He even instructed others to do the same (Mark 1:44).

Before His public ministry, Jesus endured severe temptations in the wilderness (Mark 1:12f.). These trials closely tested His adherence to the divine plan of redeeming the world through humility (Matthew 4:2-11). Similarly, in Gethsemane He once again had to decide whose will would prevail, His or the Father's. He was "deeply distressed and troubled" and told His disciples that His "soul was overwhelmed with sorrow to the point of death" (Mark 14:33f.).

Jesus prayed, often alone: at His baptism (Luke 3:21), before choosing His disciples (Luke 6:12), after one day of hard work and before another began (Matthew 14:23; Mark 1:35), and at the time of His final hour (Matthew 26:39).[8]

Jesus, Perceived as a Real Man

Jesus' contemporaries thought Him remarkable but viewed Him in human categories, such as a prophet (Matthew 16:14) and teacher (John 3:2) or demon-possessed (Mark 3:22f.) and a deceiver (Matthew 27:63). Though He performed signs that should have led others to faith in His deity (John 10:34-39), He refused to prove Himself by performing signs upon demand (Matthew 12:38).

Jesus' family life also had features typical of a Jew of His time. He obeyed His parents as a child (Luke 2:51) and cared for His mother to the very end (John 19:26f.). During His life even His brothers did not believe in Him (John 7:2-5; see Matthew 12:46-50). Jesus' contemporaries explained with self-assurance that since His family, whom they knew, was unimportant; He could not be important (Matthew 13:55).

Jesus allowed Himself to be touched (Mark 5:27), entertained (Luke 10:38ff.), and lavished upon (Matthew 26:6f.). Some loved and adored Him deeply (John 20:10f.; John 11:5) and were so committed to His ministry that they supported it (Luke 8:1-3); He did not try to prevent this. But He also allowed Himself to be misquoted (Luke 20:20-26; 23:1f.) and even hated (John 15:18-25). Most astonishing of all, Jesus did not revile or curse His enemies (1 Peter 2:23) for the abuse and violence He suffered during and after His trials (Matthew 26:67f.; Mark 15:17-20).

3. THE BIRTH OF JESUS

In reporting Jesus' birth, Matthew and Luke describe different circumstances surrounding the event but both note its essential features. He was born in Bethlehem of Judea (Matthew 2:1; Luke 2:4-7), though His family was native to Nazareth of Galilee (Matthew 2:23; Luke 2:4). His parents were Joseph and Mary (Matthew 1:18; Luke 2:4-5), and Mary was a virgin when she conceived Him (Matthew 1:18; Luke 1:29-38).

His Birth in Bethlehem

The importance of Bethlehem, a small and insignificant village in Jesus' time, lies in its heritage as the city from which King David came (1 Samuel 16:1-13). The fulfillment of God's promise to David that a son of his would reign (2 Samuel 7:11b-16; Matthew 1:17) was marked by Jesus' birth in that place (Micah 5:2; Matthew 2:3-6; Luke 2:4).

Born of the Virgin Mary

The fact of the virginal conception became known when it was disclosed to Jesus' parents. Matthew describes Joseph's dream (1:18-25), and Luke describes Gabriel's visit to Mary (1:26-38). But the essential features remain the same: Joseph and Mary were betrothed but not married (Matthew 1:18; Luke 1:27) when Mary conceived the child by the Holy Spirit (Matthew 1:20; Luke 1:35). Both needed reassurance, though for different reasons. Joseph at first believed Mary had violated her vow to him; Mary knew she would not conceive in the usual way because she was a virgin (Luke 1:34).[9]

Conceived by the Holy Spirit

In answer to Mary's question concerning how it would be possible for her to give birth to a son since she was a virgin (Luke 1:34), Gabriel said: "The Holy Spirit will come upon you, and the power of the Most High will overshadow you. So the holy one to be born will be called the Son of God" (Luke 1:35; see Matthew 1:18). Thus, through the secret work of the Holy Spirit Jesus was conceived within the Virgin. The "man" Jesus was someone who had never lived before.

Clear distinctions need to be made here. The Father eternally generates the Son of God, the transcendent and eternal Word. What took place within Mary, then, was not the conception of the eternal Word of God but the incarnation of the Word in human flesh. The man Jesus was conceived through the Holy Spirit and the Word of God was united to that human life within the Virgin. Jesus was more than just the son of Mary, He was also the Son of God.[10]

Human beings can procreate other human beings, and so in one sense can share in God's work. But only God actually created the first human being (see Luke 3:38). So God also created the New Adam, Jesus the Christ, who is now both the Son of God and the Son of Man.[11]

The Implicit Witness of Other Scriptures

No other New Testament Scriptures explicitly teach that Mary was a virgin at the time she conceived Jesus. Neither the other evangelists, Mark and John, nor Paul refer to this teaching. Historic Christianity has, however, taught that other passages implicitly support this teaching, such as John 1:13 and Galatians 4:4.[12]

Immanuel, God with Us

Isaiah's prophecy (7:14) included the statement that the child born of the virgin would be called Immanuel, which means "God with us" (Matthew 1:23). He would rightly be called the Son of the Most High (Luke 1:35). Through the Virgin's conception of Jesus God became present with the human family in a unique way.

4. THE COMMUNITY OF JESUS

Jesus called disciples: "Come, follow me ... and I will make you fishers of men" (Mark 1:17; see Mark 1:16-20; Matthew 4:18-22; Luke 5:1-11; John 1:35-42). With this simple act Jesus initiated a community of people like a Jewish *haburah* – His close-knit community – that gathered around Him as their leader.

Soon Jesus designated the Twelve as *apostoloi*, the ones He "sent out" to extend His work (Mark 3:13-19). He gave them authority to do the things that He did, such as preaching and driving out demons. He charged them to witness against those who refused their ministry (Mark 6:10f.). He promised them that they would have a special place in the future kingdom of God (Luke 22:30).[13]

Though He had other followers whom He sent on missions (Luke 10:1), the Twelve were regularly with Jesus during His ministry. They traveled with Him (Mark 3:14), and it was with them that He ate the Last Supper (Matthew 26:20).

The Enlargement of the Community

Though Jesus established the Twelve as His apostles, He also extended the boundaries of His community. He called people to follow Him and lose their lives yet find them, for His sake (Matthew 16:24ff.). He welcomed into His fellowship and ate with those whom the religious authorities thought sinners. Jesus' policy of table fellowship characterized His work (Mark 2:13-16; Luke 15:1f.). The feedings of the 5,000 (Matthew 14:13ff.) and 4,000 (Matthew 15:32ff.) are two cases in which Jesus extended the door of entrance wide.[14]

The Fellowship of Jesus Formed the Core of the New Church

When the church was forming after Jesus' ascension, it grew from the core that had been established during His life. The 120 were together in prayer, obeying Jesus' directive to wait for the promise of the Father (Acts 1:1ff.; 2:1ff.). The Twelve, after Matthias had been added to the number (Acts 1:15ff.), gave leadership to the young church (Acts 2:42-47).

5. THE MINISTRY OF JESUS, I.: HIS PREACHING AND TEACHING

The greater portion of each Gospel discusses the ministry of Jesus, the Synoptics emphasizing His work in Galilee, John giving more attention to His ministry in Jerusalem. After His baptism and John the Baptist's imprisonment, Jesus began His work (Mark 1:1-14; see Acts 10:34-38).

All the Gospels report that Jesus both taught and performed acts of compassion, which were often miraculous. Both what He said and what He did set Jesus apart from other religious leaders of His time.

The Gospels report words Jesus spoke to people one on one (Luke 19:1-10) or in small groups, such as at meetings with the Twelve (Matthew 26:17-30). He also spoke in public settings, for instance, in synagogue meetings (Luke 4:33f.). Some occasions drew huge crowds of people who listened to His preaching and teaching (Mark 8:1).[15] It was said of Him that "he taught them as one who had authority, not as the teachers of the law" (Mark 1:22) so that "the large crowd listened to him with delight" (Mark 12:37).[16]

The Kingdom of God

Jesus' Preaching to the Masses. Jesus began His ministry to the general public by calling them to repent in response to the good news that the kingdom of God – the rule of God among men – was near (Mark 1:15; see Matthew

4:17). It was precisely in His ministry that the kingdom drew near. This was shown vividly when He cast out evil spirits (Luke 11:20; see Matthew 12:22-30; Mark 3:22-27; Luke 11:14-23). The theme of God's kingdom played a prominent role in Jesus' teaching and features in many of His parables (Mark 4:1-34; Matthew 13:1-52; Luke 8:4-18; 13:18-21).

The roots of teaching on the kingdom lie in the Old Testament. Some of its authors celebrate God as a mighty warrior who conquers His foes (Exodus 15:1ff.) and who is the reigning Lord of the universe (Psalms 93; 97-99). They acknowledge that in times of national oppression God's power seems concealed; and in the present time evil rulers hold sway, or seem to hold sway over the earth (Daniel 2:20f.; 4:34f.). But, they affirm, at the chosen time God will again conquer all such powers and set up a kingdom that will never end (Daniel 2:44). This Old Testament emphasis gives precedent to Jesus' teaching.[17]

The Sermon on the Mount. Jesus called those who chose to follow Him to a demanding way of life. His teachings on this call are spread across the Gospel accounts, but the Sermon on the Mount (Matthew 5-7) epitomizes them in a remarkable way.[18]

The Beatitudes (Matthew 5:1-12) identify the attitudes and actions that should characterize Jesus' disciples. He promised that those who adopt these basic qualities would be blessed and find true happiness. These "beatific" characteristics of Jesus' followers stand in sharp contrast to the world's understanding that pride, aggressiveness and self-interest pave the way to success.

In many respects what Jesus required was essentially found in the Old Testament, and in recognition of this He specifically said that He had not come to set the law aside (Matthew 5:17-19).[19] But He did emphasize the inner meaning of the law as well as the need for outward compliance, both in basic moral values (Matthew 5:21-48) and in acts of piety (Matthew 6:1-18). Whatever the cost we might have to pay, the kingdom of God – the rule of God – is the most priceless value, and faithfully God cares for those who seek His kingdom first (Matthew 6:19-34).[20]

The Return of the Son of Man. Jesus taught that at the end time the reign of God will achieve fulfillment. He shared this apocalyptic view of history with other Jews. This view taught that at some future time God will bring history to an end and introduce a new era in which evil and tragedy will be completely subdued. Jesus discussed different aspects of that critical moment (Mark 13; Matthew 24-25; Luke 21:5-37; 17:20-37) and identified Himself as the Son of Man whose return would signal the kingdom's arrival (Daniel 7:13-14; Mark 14:62; Matthew 26:64; Luke 22:69).

Controversies with Religious Authorities

Many of Jesus' basic beliefs were the same as those of Jewish authorities, especially the beliefs of the Pharisees, on such issues as the resurrection from the dead (Mark 12:18-27) and the priority of the love commandment (Mark 12:28-34). But He differed with them over a few questions, such as His practice of associating with those careless about the law who were referred to as tax collectors and sinners (Luke 15); and the strict interpretation of the commandment on Sabbath observance (Mark 2:23-3:5).

The sharpest controversy, however, arose over the authority Jesus assumed for Himself. In public He generally avoided taking to Himself a divine title, but His actions and words, though veiled, showed that He thought of Himself as divine (Mark 2:1-12; John 8:12-59). The Jewish authorities also sensed that this was what He thought of Himself, and they considered Him guilty of blaspheming against God and deserving of death (Mark 3:6; John 8:59). At His trial before the Sanhedrin, they posed the question directly, and Jesus' answer confirmed their suspicion (Matthew 26:63f.; Mark 14:61f.).

207

6. THE MINISTRY OF JESUS, II.: HIS COMPASSION AND MIRACLES

The Care of Jesus for the Sick, the Sinful, and the Common People

Jesus gave special attention to common people. Frequently the evangelists note this with comments such as, "he had compassion on them, because they were like sheep without a shepherd" (Mark 6:34; see Ezekiel 34).

Consequently Jesus responded to the needy people, especially to those on the margins of society or without power. [21] His heart went out to a widow who had just lost her son, and He raised the son from death (Luke 7:11-17). He also raised the daughter of a synagogue ruler (Mark 5:21-24, 35-43). He praised the costly offering a widow made in the temple (Mark 12:41-44) and criticized the Pharisees' rigorous but insincere adherence to the law (Mark 7:1-8). Jesus became notorious in the eyes of the Pharisees for eating with tax collectors and sinners or allowing them to touch Him (Luke 7:39).

The Miracles of Jesus

Jesus performed many miracles. They can be divided into four categories: miracles in nature, healing the sick, raising the dead, and delivering those possessed by evil spirits (Mark 4:35-5:43).

Nature Miracles. Fewer miracles of this kind occurred. However, even nature miracles show something important about the person, Jesus. Take, for example, the stilling of the storm (Matthew 8:23-27). This demonstration of His power over nature testified to who He was, as reflected in Psalms 107:23-32.

The Healing of the Sick. The greatest number of miracle stories reported in the Gospels concern Jesus' healing of the sick. He dealt with all kinds of diseases: birth defects (John 9:1-12), long-term infirmities (John 5:1-8), contagious diseases that gradually bring death (Luke 5:12-16), and short-term sickness that temporarily disable persons from performing tasks (Mark 1:29-31).

The Raising of the Dead. Each evangelist reports that Jesus raised someone from the dead (Matthew 9:18f., 23-26; Mark 5:21-24, 35-43; Luke 7:11-17; John 11:1-44). In reply to John's inquiry whether He was the one who was to come, Jesus said his ministry fulfilled Old Testament prophecies (Luke 7:22; Isaiah 29:18; 35:5; 61:1). He added one item, however, that Isaiah omitted, the raising of the dead – a particularly telling sign of His power and authority.

The Deliverance of Those Possessed by Evil Spirits. The synoptics report that Jesus on a number of occasions delivered someone who was possessed of an evil spirit. Three of these are reported in some detail. There was the demoniac in the synagogue at Capernaum (Mark 1:23-28), the man in the cemetery whose name was Legion (Mark 5:1-20); and the boy whose distraught father brought him to the disciples of Jesus (Mark 9:14-29). Each of these cases clearly illustrates the helpless condition of persons possessed by hostile supernatural beings. Two clearly state that when Jesus delivered the possessed, He was conquering the power of evil at a level beyond the capability of any mortal (Mark 1:24; 5:7).

7. THE SUFFERING AND DEATH OF JESUS

In spite of the importance of Jesus' teaching and miracles, the climax of His story comes in His death and resurrection.

The Humiliation of Christ

The Shadow of the Cross on the Life of Jesus. A deep paradox follows the course of His ministry. On the one hand, the masses responded positively to His work. On the other, certain persons in power developed a profound hatred for Him. This grew and finally ended with His death.

The determination to kill Jesus did not wait long; all the Gospels place it early (Matthew 12:14; Mark 3:6; Luke 4:28-30; John 8:39f.).

According to the Gospels the Jewish leaders were the first to decide to destroy Jesus, and they were the ones who developed the plan by which it was done. Initial scheming began quite early (Mark 3:6), but more systematic planning occurred at a date much closer to His actual death (John 11:53).

Jesus told His disciples at least three times what would happen (Mark 8:31-33; 9:30-32; 10:32-34). However, they did not grasp what He was saying (Mark 9:32) and were stunned when the event actually occurred.

The Trials of Jesus. Jesus was tried by two different kinds of courts. There was the Sanhedrin, the religious court of the Jews, and there was the civil court of Pilate and Herod.

Jesus was examined by the Jewish authorities twice, once during the night and once when day had broken. Since He was being tried for a capital offense, Jewish law did not allow a conviction during a night trial. We know this from sources written after Jesus' time.[22] The night trial, therefore, did not have official status, even though during this illegal event the Jewish authorities elicited from Jesus a statement that became the grounds for the false charge on which He was to be convicted (Mark 14:53-65). The next morning the process was repeated officially (Mark 15:1; Luke 22:66-71). The Jewish court decided that Jesus was guilty of blasphemy, a crime deserving death.

Jesus was then taken to the Roman procurator, Pilate. There He was judged on a civil matter – whether He claimed to be a king and was the leader of an insurrection against Rome (Luke 23:2-3; John 18:29-38). Pilate and Herod both believed Him to be innocent (Luke 23:4, 14f., 22), and Pilate attempted to force the Jewish leaders to acknowledge this by offering to free the prisoner of their choice, either Jesus or Barabbas. This decision should have been easy for them because Barabbas was a proved insurrectionist. Pilate's ploy did not work. The crowds, at the urging of the chief priests, took up the cry that Pilate should release Barabbas and crucify Jesus (Mark 15:11-14; Luke 23:18-23). He finally yielded to their demands and handed Jesus over for crucifixion (Matthew 27:24-26; Mark 15:15; Luke 23:24f.; John 19:16). For this act Pilate has the dubious honor of being the only human mentioned by name in the Apostles' Creed as the one responsible for Jesus' death.

The Mocking of Jesus and the Road to Golgotha. After Pilate reached the decision to have Jesus crucified, the soldiers mocked Jesus. Roman soldiers began the humiliation in the praetorium, the Roman garrison in Jerusalem. After Pilate had Jesus scourged (Mark 15:15), the soldiers picked up on what they had heard. They mocked the notion of His royalty by putting on Him a hastily woven crown of thorns and a purple robe; they affected salutations and prostrated themselves before Him (Mark 15:16-20a). They then led Him to the place where He was to be crucified, forcing Simon of Cyrene, a stranger who happened on the scene, to carry the cross (Mark 15:20b-21).

After affixing Jesus to the cross, having stripped Him of all clothing, He was again mocked, this time by the chief priests and scribes and by any who passed by. They challenged Him to save Himself, since they had heard that He supposedly could destroy and rebuild the temple in three days (Matthew 27:39-42). They hissed at Him to trust God who would surely save His Son (Matthew 27:43). Even the two malefactors crucified with Jesus reviled Him (Matthew 27:44), although one of them repented before his death (Luke 23:39-43).

The Scandal of the Cross

The Persians, as far as we know, devised crucifixion as an unspeakably cruel form of executing political prisoners,

211

and the Romans adopted it from them. It was both humiliating and merciless, with the intention of discouraging those who considered revolution. Those crucified were stripped of all clothing and nailed or tied to a cross, which was either a simple pole or a pole with a cross member at the top or somewhere in the middle. The victims' arms and legs were affixed so that the only way they could breathe was to push up with the legs and pull up with the arms. Death came very slowly from a set of factors such as exposure, shock, and loss of blood. But asphyxiation was the major cause of death because the one being crucified, through sheer fatigue, could no longer free the lungs to expand and draw in life-giving air.[23]

In the case of Jesus, the title on the cross, "This is Jesus, the King of the Jews," identified the crime for which He was crucified (Matthew 27:37). This was ordered by Pilate even though he had not been convinced of Jesus' guilt. The Jews protested to him that the title failed to mention that this was only Jesus' claim and not – as they charged – a fact (John 19:19-22).

Often drugs were given to those who were crucified to deaden the pain. Jesus refused such help (Mark 15:23, 36).

His actions and words on the cross were markedly different from those of the typical person being crucified. For example, rather than curse His executioners, Jesus prayed for them to be forgiven (Luke 23:34). To the repentant criminal crucified with Him He promised immediate entrance into paradise (Luke 23:40-43). From His cross, He attended to His mother's future (John 19:26f.). The cry of dereliction, "My God, My God, why have you forsaken me?" (Matthew 27:46; see Psalms 22:1) indicates how deep was His isolation in that hour (Mark 15:34).

These actions and words of Jesus evoked responses. A Roman centurion who watched Jesus die declared, "Surely this man was the Son of God" (Mark 15:39), and the people who had "gathered to witness" the torture "beat their breasts and went away" (Luke 23:48).

Jesus Died

Death is the universal experience of human beings. The Scriptures witness that Jesus truly died.[24] He "breathed his last" (Mark 15:37; see Matthew 27:50 and John 19:30). The early church consistently testified to the reality of His death (Acts 2:23; 1 Corinthians 15:3). After His death, Jesus' presence was no longer here on earth but in the place of the dead (1 Peter 3:18-19; 4:6). It was from there God returned Him when He raised Him to life (see Romans 10:7).

8. THE BURIAL, RESURRECTION, APPEARANCES, AND ASCENSION OF JESUS

The Burial of Jesus

After Jesus' death Joseph of Arimathea, a member of the Sanhedrin (Mark 15:43) and a secret disciple of Jesus (John 19:38) who had not approved of the crucifixion (Luke 23:51), asked Pilate for the right to bury the body of Jesus. When Pilate consented (Mark 15:44f.), Joseph wrapped a linen shroud around the body and placed it into a tomb newly hewn from a rock. A large stone covered the entrance (Mark 15:46).

The prediction of Jesus' resurrection alarmed Jewish authorities. They went to Pilate because they feared that the disciples might steal His body and claim that He had risen from the dead. In response, Pilate granted them soldiers to guard the tomb (Matthew 27:62-66; Matthew 28:4).

The Resurrection

On the third day after the crucifixion, on Sunday, the first day of the week, God raised Jesus from the dead. Women first discovered the fact when they found the tomb empty. Soon Peter and John confirmed the women's finding. Little by little, the truth sank in. The New Testament universally witnesses to the resurrection of Jesus. The tomb was empty, the body of Jesus was no longer there, for He had been raised (Matthew 28:6; Mark 16:6; Luke 24:1f.; John 20:1; Acts 2:24; 10:40; Romans 10:9; 1 Peter 1:3).[25]

The Empty Tomb

Women who came to the tomb were the first of Jesus' followers to hear of the resurrection. They had come to anoint the body and instead were greeted with the announcement that He had risen and the tomb was empty (Matthew 28:1-7; Mark 16:1-6; Luke 24:1-7).

The tomb was indeed empty, though no one at the time knew what to make of it. The women were frightened (Matthew 28:8; Mark 16:7f.), and the disciples at first could not believe (Luke 24:11). Peter and John ran to the tomb. Peter entered ahead of John, but John believed in the reality of the Resurrection before Peter when he first saw the place vacated where Jesus had lain (John 20:3-8).

Even the Jewish authorities were confused by the empty tomb. In order to suppress the news of the Resurrection, they paid the attending soldiers to say that His disciples had stolen the body. In response to the soldiers' apprehension, the Jewish authorities promised that they would intervene for them with Pilate, should the need arise (Matthew 28:11-15).[26]

The Appearances of Jesus

On the day of the Resurrection and over the next 39 days the risen Jesus appeared to many of His followers (Acts 1:3; 1 Corinthians 15:5-8). Since these appearances confirmed that God had fulfilled the ancient promises (Acts 2:24-35), those who saw the risen Lord were obviously the crucial witnesses to this wondrous action of God (Acts 1:22; 3:15; 10:40f.).

The Gospel accounts report many of the appearances. Jesus appeared to the women who had gone to the tomb (Matthew 28:9f.), to Mary Magdalene (John 20:14-17), to Cleopas and his companion while they were walking to the village of Emmaus (Luke 24:13-35), to the disciples on the first Sunday night when Thomas was absent (John 20:19-23) and then a week later when He was with them (John 20:24-29), and to the disciples by the sea of Tiberias (John 21:1-14).

Attempts have been made to dismiss the biblical reports of the post-resurrection appearances as imaginary while, at the same time, exonerating the authors of misrepresentation. This does not work. The simplicity and straightforwardness of the accounts are self-validating. The accounts exclude the views that the disciples merely saw a ghost (Luke 24:36-43) or that the writers meant only that the spirit of Jesus' faith in God was being revived (Luke 24:19-24).

The Ascension of Jesus

Before His ascension, Jesus gave final instructions to His disciples. According to Matthew the risen Christ said He had received "all authority in heaven and on earth." The disciples were in turn to "go and make disciples of all nations, baptizing them in the name of the Father and of the Son and of the Holy Spirit, and teaching them to obey everything I have commanded you." As they went about fulfilling this task they were promised the continuing presence of the Lord Himself (Matthew 28:16-20).

Jesus told His disciples they would be His witnesses, but before they took up that task they were to wait in Jerusalem for the pouring forth of the Holy Spirit (Luke 24:48f.; Acts 1:4-8). After giving these instructions Jesus was taken up into heaven (Luke 24:50f.; Acts 1:9-11), and they saw Him no more.

SUMMARY: *The Life and Ministry of Jesus*

1. The Gospel accounts focus on Jesus' ministry, death, and resurrection, though two of them include infancy stories.

2. Jesus was conceived by the Holy Spirit in the Virgin Mary before she and Joseph were married. By this divine act Jesus Christ of Nazareth is rightly called the incarnate Word and the Son of God.

3. Jesus experienced life and death as a real human being, and was perceived as doing so by His contemporaries.

4. Jesus formed a new community within the Jewish nation. He called disciples and chose 12 of them to work as His apostles. He freely invited people to become His followers, even people whom Jewish religious authorities considered sinful. The fellowship of Jesus formed the core of the new born church after Jesus' ascension.

5. Jesus' public ministry of teaching emphasized that in His person and work the kingdom of God had come near. Therefore, people should repent and believe. He taught that His followers must adopt a way of life distinct from that of the world and that He, the Son of Man, would return at the end of the age to reveal the kingdom in its fulness.

6. Jesus engaged in controversy with the Jewish religious authorities of His time. He differed with them over His assumption of His divine rights. His interpretation of Sabbath observance was distinct from theirs. And they disapproved of the attention He gave to those who seemed much too casual, even indifferent, about keeping the law.

7. Jesus showed compassion to all who had need, especially to the poor, the powerless, or those despised by religious leaders.

8. Jesus performed many miracles of various kinds. There were a few nature miracles. On at least three occasions He raised the dead. He healed many and delivered others from demon possession.

9. The threat of being killed shadowed Jesus during most of His public ministry. Toward its end, Jewish leaders' hatred led them to plot His death.

10. Jesus was tried by both religious and civil authorities. The religious leaders found Him guilty of blasphemy. They brought Him before Pilate as the leader of an insurrection, but Pilate found Him innocent of the charge. Still, upon the insistence of the people, Pilate ordered His crucifixion.

11. Crucifixion was a means of execution which Rome had adopted to punish political criminals. So Jesus was officially condemned and killed as an insurrectionist. During the trial and while *en route* to the place of crucifixion, and as He was hanged on the cross, Jesus was mocked and treated viciously.

12. On the third day God raised Jesus from the dead. Women found the tomb empty as did some of His special disciples. For 40 days the risen Lord appeared to many of His followers and then He ascended to heaven.

SECTION II. *The Titles of Jesus*

THE ORIGIN OF THE TITLE AND ROLES OF JESUS IN THE OLD TESTAMENT

Depending heavily upon the Old Testament, the New Testament writers adopted a number of titles for Jesus. These titles accomplished two things. In the first place they identified the character of His person, that is, they showed what He was really like. In the second place they indicated the tasks He accomplished.

MODIFICATIONS OF THE MEANING OF THE TITLES

But for Jesus' contemporaries, the application of Old Testament titles to Jesus was not always obvious. For one thing the Old Testament had not made it clear that these various titles applied to one person. For example, the Son of Man of Daniel 7:14 was not understood as the Servant of the Lord from Isaiah 52:12ff. or the Messiah of Psalms 2:2. When Jesus filled all the roles in His one person, He inevitably enlarged the meaning and significance of a title.

This enlargement modified the precise meaning of a title in the Old Testament and in Judaism of Jesus' time. Thus, in Jesus, the Messiah became more than a triumphant and righteous leader; He was also a suffering servant. Even the disciples, during Jesus' life, were confused with this complex set of titles and tasks that Jesus fulfilled.

Some of the titles are attributed to Jesus by His disciples during the course of His life, sometimes hesitantly, sometimes more vigorously. Others were attributed to Him by God as in the case of the voice from heaven, by demoniacs, or by Jesus Himself. The disciples were awakened by the Resurrection to the appropriateness of some titles, reflecting on Him as they did from that vantage point.

The significance of these titles is rather like the significance of the special names of God. In crystalized and succinct form they identify Jesus' character and tasks; they tell us who He is and what He has done and will do. In the titles we see his uniqueness in all of history.[27]

1. THE SON OF MAN
The Old Testament Use of the Title "the Son of Man"

The Old Testament used the term "the Son of Man" in three different ways. The prophet Ezekiel referred to himself in this term a number of times (Ezekiel 2:1, 3; 3:1, 3, 4). The title also appears in Daniel, applying to the apocalyptic – endtime – figure who will come with the clouds of heaven and be given power and authority by the Ancient of Days (Daniel 7:13f.). More generally, the term may simply signify the humanity of a person. The psalmist asks, "What is man that you are mindful of him, the son of man that you care for him?" (Psalms 8:4) Finally, rabbinic literature witnesses to the term's use as a surrogate for the speaker, which is a humble reference to oneself.[28]

Jesus' Use of the Title "the Son of Man"

The term "the Son of Man," with one exception (Acts 7:56), was used by Jesus of Himself. Jesus sometimes identified Himself as one who had typical human experiences, such as when He compared His life pattern to that of John the Baptist (Luke 7:34). Also, when Jesus claimed an authority exceeding that of any other mortal, this served as a self-designation. When He healed the paralytic, for example, Jesus said, "The Son of Man has authority on earth to forgive sins" (Mark 1:10; see 2:28). Jesus also used this expression when speaking of His humiliation. For instance, after Peter confessed that Jesus was the Christ, Jesus went on to teach His disciples that the Son of Man must suffer, be killed and after three days rise again (Mark 8:31; Matthew 8:20).

Finally, the term appeared in apocalyptic sayings that remind us of Daniel. When, for example, He was asked directly during the trial whether He was the Christ, the Son of the Blessed, Jesus answered that He was and that they would "see the Son of Man sitting at the right hand of the Mighty One and coming on the clouds of heaven" (Mark 14:62; see 13:16).

Through the centuries, the historic church has viewed the title "the Son of Man" as an especially clear expression of Jesus' humanity.[29] The significance of this is heightened when we remember the contexts from Jesus' life in which the term may occur, such as when He has typical human experiences, when He asserts His unique authority, when He speaks of His suffering and death, and when He identifies Himself as the apocalyptic figure who will return at the end of time.

2. THE SON OF GOD
The Old Testament Origins of the Concept of God's Son

The Old Testament is also the source of the concept of Jesus' sonship to God. The king of Israel by virtue of his position was designated as God's son. The promise of this favor is given to David (2 Samuel 7:14; 1 Chronicles 17:13). It is also announced as a fact in the important messianic psalm that celebrates the new king's installation: "You are my [God's] Son; today I have become your Father" (Psalms 2:7).

The idea of a divine king is not unique to Israel. It is part and parcel of royal ideology across the Ancient Near East. In other nations the king may very well have been thought of as in some way supernatural. However, that view is hardly adopted by the Old Testament. In spite of the promise that the coming king would be God's son, the possibility is also held out that he might sin grievously and be punished by God (2 Samuel 7:14b; Psalms 132:12). This son of God, the king who comes in the natural line from David, can never be anything but an adopted son of God.

The New Testament Use of the Term "the Son of God"

But it is clear from the very beginning that in Jesus' case He is truly the Son of God. The term "the Son of God" refers to Jesus' deity, just as the term Son of Man refers to His humanity.

The idea that Jesus is God's Son actually comes in various forms. Sometimes we see the shortened form Son (John 3:17). Elsewhere, the full form, Son of God, is used (Mark 3:11). Other variants also occur, such as Son of the Most High (Luke 1:32), my beloved Son (AV, Matthew 17:5), or the only begotten Son (AV, John 1:14). John, in this last example, uses the word *monogenes*, which means "unique Son." All of these forms imply a special relationship, one of sonship, that exists between Jesus and God and that sets Jesus apart as God's Son in a unique way.[30]

When the various forms of the term "the Son of God" appear for Jesus in the New Testament, He is clearly the Son of God in an incomparable sense. He is the genuine Son of God. This explains the significance the biblical authors give to:

- the Virgin Birth (Luke 1:35);
- the voice from heaven at Jesus' baptism (Mark 1:11) and at the Transfiguration (Mark 9:7) ;
- the devil's tempting of Jesus to use supernatural power (Matthew 4:3);
- Jesus' command that the demons not tell who He was (Mark 1:24f.);
- the knowledge of God that only He, the Son, could give (Matthew 11:27);
- the sending of the Son into the world (John 3:16);
- the Pharisees' concern that Jesus claimed a special relationship with the Father (John 10:25-39) and for this He deserved death;
- the charge under which the Sanhedrin judged Jesus as guilty of blasphemy and thus deserving of death (Mark 14:61f.);
- the revelation that Paul received that brought about his conversion (Galatians 1:16) and the message he gave in Damascus immediately afterwards (Acts 9:20);
- Paul's teachings that through the resurrection from the dead Jesus was declared to be the Son of God with power (Romans 1:4), that God had sent His Son in the likeness of sinful flesh (Romans 8:3), and that God has rescued us from the dominion of darkness and brought us into the kingdom of His Son (Colossians 1:13);

- the teachings of the author of the letter to the Hebrews that in the former days God spoke through the prophets but in these last days He has spoken through His Son (Hebrews 1:1f.) and that Christ is the faithful Son over God's own house (Hebrews 3:6);
- the teaching of John that the blood of Jesus, God's Son, purifies us from every sin (1 John 1:7).

3. THE CHRIST

The Messiah in the Old Testament

The Hebrew word "messiah" comes from the word meaning to smear or to anoint with oil. A messiah, then, is someone who has been anointed. In an official sense this applied in Israel to those in one of two positions, priests (Exodus 28:41; Leviticus 4:5) and political leaders, particularly kings (1 Samuel 2:10; 16:12). The inner significance of the anointing ritual is captured in the words that follow Samuel's anointing of David, that "from that day on the Spirit of the Lord came upon David with power (16:13). Thus, "messiah" served as another title for the king, emphasizing, as such, that He was God's chosen and divinely enabled person for a task of supreme importance to the nation (Psalms 2:2). The Messiah was the true son of David.

Jews of Jesus' time expected a messiah who would deliver the nation from its Roman oppressors. According to a Jewish book written during the first century before Christ, the Psalms of Solomon, the messiah was to be righteous and godly but also politically and militarily powerful (17:23-51).[31] The son of David was expected to be the Son of God as stated in Psalms 2:7, but when typical Jews used the term, they did not think of their messiah as a divine being.[32]

Jesus as the Messiah

All of these factors explain Jesus' caution in accepting the title for Himself. For example, He redefined its meaning to include suffering and rejection after Peter confessed Him as the Christ at Caesarea Philippi. Peter found the new meaning very hard to accept (Mark 8:29-33). But on other occasions Jesus expressed no such caution. Blind Bartimaeus addressed Him as the Son of David, a variant term for the same idea, and over protests Jesus called the blind man to Himself, thus accepting the title (Mark 10:47-49). He gave teachers of the law opportunity to expand their view of the messiah by asking them to consider Psalms 110:1. This passage implies that the messiah is to be divine. The Jews already considered Psalm 110 as messianic (Mark 12:35f.).

Questioning Whether Jesus Was the Messiah

Herod the Great, who ruled in Jerusalem at the time of Jesus' birth, was the first to question whether Jesus was the Messiah. Magi from Persia came to the Judea, led by a preternatural star, and sought out Herod to ask, "Where is the one who has been born king of the Jews?" This disturbed Herod and He called together chief priests and teachers of the law to ask where the Messiah was to be born (Matthew 1:1-6).

Much later, when Jesus was beginning His public ministry, Andrew, after spending a day with Jesus, sought out his brother Simon Peter. His message to his brother was, "We have found the Messiah (that is the Christ)" (John 1:40f.).

This title became the foundation for the charge the Jewish authorities lodged against Jesus when they brought Him before Pilate. All the Gospel accounts witness that Pilate questioned Jesus whether He was the King of the Jews, the gentile word for the Hebrew term "messiah" (Matthew 27:11; Mark 15:2; Luke 23:3; John 18:33-35). Moreover, the placard on the cross testified to the same title (Matthew 27:37; Mark 15:26; Luke 23:34; John 19:19). Though Pilate could not grasp what Jesus meant when He explained the nature of His kingdom (John 18:36-38), Pilate clearly understood that Jesus was a king of some kind.

The Title "Christ" As Applied to Jesus After His Resurrection

On the day of Pentecost, Peter proclaimed that through Christ's resurrection from the dead Israel could be assured that God had made Jesus both Lord and Christ (Acts 2:36). Paul uses the term "Christ" extensively. Generally he uses this title "Christ" in place of the name "Jesus" (Romans 1:16; 1 Corinthians 1:24; Galatians 1:6)) or combined with this personal name when emphasizing the title "Lord." Thus Paul writes of Jesus Christ our Lord (Romans 1:3; 1 Corinthians 1:2; Galatians 1:3).

4. THE SERVANT OF THE LORD

The Servant of the Lord in Isaiah

The middle portion of Isaiah's prophecy contains the four servant songs (Isaiah 42:1-4; 49:1-6; 50:4-11; and 52:13-53:12). The historic church has always seen the last of these prophecies as a particularly clear portrait of Jesus' vicarious suffering.[33] The prophet describes the Servant of the Lord as one whose appearance does not draw attention to Himself as a special instrument of God, who innocently suffers bitter abuse and finally death, and who through this suffering for others achieves their redemption.

Though Jews talked about the suffering servant of Isaiah, they never seemed to identify Him with the messiah whom they expected. Instead, some said that He was either the prophet himself, or some other person, or a collective term for the nation of Israel, which had suffered so.[34]

Jesus as the Servant of the Lord

Nowhere do the Gospel accounts directly call Jesus the Servant of the Lord (though this may be the intent in Acts 3:13; 4:27, 30). But Jesus attributes to Himself the tasks that the servant fulfills. The concept of the suffering servant is unmistakable, for Jesus states that He does not lord it over people, as gentile leaders tend to do, but suffers on their behalf and thereby wins their redemption (Matthew 20:27f., Mark 8:29-31). Thus, He reinterprets His role as a leader. The sacrificial death of Jesus on the cross, which brings salvation, is thus understood by the early church as a direct fulfillment of the Scriptures about the Servant of the Lord (Luke 24:25, 46; Acts 13:28f.; 1 Corinthians 15:3; see Acts 2:23; 4:10-12, 27-30; and 1 Peter 2:21-25; 3:18).

5. THE WORD

No title we have considered so explicitly states that the Second Person of the Trinity existed before the Incarnation. Some ancient heretics argued that there was no pre-incarnate Christ and that God the Father adopted the man Jesus as a son. They appealed for support to Psalms 2:7: "You are my Son; today I have become your Father." But important passages in the New Testament explicitly address the issue of the pre-incarnate Son.

Old Testament Anticipations of the Pre-incarnate Word

In two different ways the Old Testament witnessed to the pre-incarnate Word. First it did so in reporting the appearances of God to the ancestors of Israel. Second, it did so in recording the discourse on Wisdom in Proverbs.

Old Testament Christophanies. Two accounts of God's appearances to patriarchs describe Him as a man. He first appeared in this manner to Abraham (Genesis 18:1ff.) and then to Jacob (Genesis 32:22ff.). In each case, He appeared as a man while at the same time being divine. We call such appearances of God "theophanies." Early teachers of the church seized upon these passages as clear examples of the eternal Word appearing before He was incarnate in Jesus of Nazareth. Thus we refer to these as early christophanies, appearances of the divine Christ in human form.[35]

The Wisdom of God. The discourse in Proverbs 8:22ff. speaks of Wisdom personified as the companion of God before anything had been created. In fact, wisdom assisted God in the creation (see Proverbs 3:19f.). Before Jesus' time Jews had thought about these passages from Proverbs and had given a high and lofty place to Wisdom, though none had reached a view that set out wisdom as a distinct Second Person of the Godhead.[36]

The Pre-incarnate Word in the New Testament

However, two New Testament writers, John and Paul, specifically discuss the pre-incarnate Word. By doing so, they push our understanding of the Word back to the very beginning.[37]

John: The Word

John is the author who specifically uses the title "the Word." The prologue to John (1:1-18) witnesses to several crucial aspects of "the Word" previous to the incarnation of the Word (see also 1 John 1:1-3). It states that:

- the Word was with God from the very beginning and in fact was God (1:1f.);
- everything that has been created was created through the Word (1:3);
- the Word is the source of life and light in all humans (1:4f.).

The Incarnation, then, is described in the clearest language possible when John states, "The Word became flesh and lived among us" (1:14; see Hebrews 10:5). Since the Word has taken the form of flesh, several additional things can now be said of the Word as the incarnate one. He:

- was unrecognized by the world He had made and not received by His own to whom He came (1:10f.);
- has brought knowledge of the Father to us, because He is the one who is at the Father's side (1:18);

226

- has brought grace and truth (1:14, 17) so that those who receive Him become God's children (1:12).

Paul: The Image

Paul discusses the pre-incarnate Christ in two passages.

In Philippians 2:6-11 Paul describes a sequence that starts from Christ's pre-incarnate glory, moves to His self-humbling by taking upon Himself a human form, goes to His humiliation in dying a criminal's death, and ends with God's exaltation of Him. Christ was:

- in very nature God (or in the form of God);
- did not count equality with God a thing to hang on to (2:6) but emptied Himself and took the form of a servant; then, being made in human form (2:7-8a), He humbled Himself, becoming obedient even to the point of death on the cross (2:8b).

Thus, Christ truly possessed the glory that belonged to His being God but gave this up to become incarnated as a man.

In Colossians 1:15-20 Paul uses a title for Christ, "the image of the invisible God." Two themes appear here that remind us of the prologue to John's Gospel: Jesus' special eternal relationship to God (1:15; see also Hebrews 1:3) and His relationship to creation (1:16, 17). Thus, Paul makes the arresting affirmation that the Son is uniquely of God and through Him all things that exist – the entire universe – were created.

6. THE LORD

Pre-Christian Use of the Title "Lord"

The special importance of the title "Lord" derives from two quite distinct sources, one Old Testament and Jewish, the other gentile.

Jewish Use of "Lord" as a Divine Title. The Greek translation of the Old Testament generally renders the Hebrew name for God, Yahweh, by the Greek, *kurios*, Lord. And when Hebrew- or Aramaic-speaking Jews of Jesus' time read the name Yahweh in the Bible, the preferred name they pronounced out loud was *Adonai*, my Lord.

"Lord" as a Divine Title in the Gentile World. The Greek and later the Roman empires often referred to their emperors as "lord."[38] The title regularly carried the idea of deity, and the emperor or the emperor's genius was worshiped as divine. During the Maccabean revolt (167-142 B.C.) Jews fought bravely to be free from the requirement that they acknowledge the emperor's deity. Only slowly were they granted this privilege that was later extended to them by Rome as long as they prayed for the emperor. But this privilege was not granted Christians once it was clear that they were distinct from Jews.

New Testament Use of "Lord"

All portions of the New Testament witness to the title "Lord" applied to Jesus. During the course of Jesus' life, He could be called "Lord," and in many instances the idea of His deity is unmistakable. Jesus said of Himself, that "the Son of Man is Lord even of the Sabbath" (Mark 2:28). Those who wanted healing appealed to Him as the Lord who could deliver them from their afflictions (Matthew 8:2; 20:30f.; John 11:21).

The debate between Jesus and the teachers of the law about Psalms 110:1 was most significant (Mark 12:35-37). Jews of Jesus' time understood Psalm 110 as messianic, a psalm which talked about the future son of David who would deliver Israel.[39] When Jesus pointed the Jewish leaders to the leading verse of the psalm, He questioned them whether it did not obviously speak of His deity: "The Lord said to my Lord: 'Sit at my right hand until I put your enemies under your feet.'" Echoes of this debate are heard later in the New Testament (Acts 2:34; 1 Corinthians 15:25; Hebrews 1:13).

Peter declared on the day of Pentecost that the Resurrection had witnessed that God had made Jesus, whom the

Jews had crucified, Lord as well as Christ (Acts 2:36). The meaning here is not that He became something by the Resurrection that He was not before. It was rather that the Resurrection became the means to manifest clearly who He was. Paul said essentially the same thing in Philippians 2:9-11 and something similar of Jesus as God's Son in Romans 1:4.

Paul makes "Lord" a common title for Jesus. In 1 Corinthians 12:3 he states that the confession "Jesus is Lord" distinguishes Christians, and no one makes this confession unless enabled to do so by the Spirit. In stating this thesis, Paul sets the Christian confession opposite of both the Jewish refusal to acknowledge Jesus as Lord and the pagan ascription of the title to human monarchs (1 Corinthians 8:5f.).

SUMMARY: *The Titles of Jesus*

1. The Scriptures have a variety of titles that were applied to Jesus to define His person and His work. Before Jesus' coming, the various Old Testament titles were not understood as applying to one person. But as Jesus' did His work and God raised Him from the dead, these titles were drawn together in the New Testament to describe the rich nature of Jesus' character and His work.

2. The title "the Son of Man" was used by Jesus as a self-designation that referred to the apocalyptic figure Daniel described, who would introduce the future kingdom of God (Daniel 7:13); and that reflected Jesus' full humanity.

3. The title "the Son of God," on the other hand, signifies that Jesus is the unique Son of God. None other can share this title in the same way.

4. The messiah whom Israel expected was fulfilled in Jesus the Christ. He is the Son of David who will

triumph over all His enemies and of whose kingdom there will be no end.

5. Jesus predicted that He would suffer as the Servant who was foretold in Isaiah 52:13-53:12. Through His innocence and His suffering the Servant of the Lord would bring redemption and deliverance from sin to His people.

6. John's use of the title "Word" and Paul's use of the title "Image" both point to the pre-incarnate life of the Son of God. He existed with God from the beginning and God created the world through Him. Yet the eternal Word of God was incarnate within history in the person of Jesus of Nazareth who humbled Himself to take full human form.

7. During His powerful ministry, Jesus was acknowledged as Lord; and, as such, He delivered from sickness those who were sick. However, through His resurrection, Jesus' lordship was made even more clear.

SECTION III. *The Classic View of Jesus and Ancient Departures from It*

Christology has always wrestled with the question: How, at one and the same time, can Jesus be the Son of God and the Son of Man? The Gospels clearly portray Him as both.

Views with which the ancient church had to do battle and which it rejected as heretical resolved the question by minimizing either Jesus' deity or His humanity.

1. ADOPTIONISM

Adoptionism is the teaching that Jesus of Nazareth was the natural son of Joseph and Mary and was adopted as the Son of God at His baptism. Proponents of adoptionism embraced this idea for more than one reason.

Gnostic Adoptionism. Gnosticism was one of the earliest heresies to threaten the health of the church. A primitive

230

form of gnosticism was alive during the time of the apostolic church. The letters of Paul to the Corinthians, the Colossians, and the first letter of John respond to these early gnostics. The fully developed gnostic systems appeared in the second century.

Gnostics believed that matter is evil rather than being the creation of the most high God. Thus, they rejected the idea that the Word of God or the divine Christ could be truly united to human flesh.

In the place of the orthodox view of Jesus' incarnation, gnostics taught an adoptionism that has often gone under the name of doceticism from the Greek word *dokeo*, "to appear," suggesting that Christ only appeared to be a man. Cerinthus, an early gnostic teacher, explicitly taught that Jesus was the son of Mary and Joseph, conceived and born in a normal fashion. He taught that because of Jesus' virtue and wisdom, Christ, one of the supernatural aeons in the gnostic mythology, descended upon Jesus as a dove at His baptism. Through this endowment Jesus was able to perform miracles. However, before His death, the Christ, who was impassible – that is, incapable of being subject to human emotions and suffering – departed from Jesus so that Jesus, the mere man, had to suffer and die alone.[40]

A view similar to that of Cerinthus is condemned by the apostle John.[41] John may even have been responding to Cerinthus' error. In any case, this heresy denied that Jesus is of God and that the Christ has come in the flesh (1 John 4:3f.).

Gnostic adoptionism has reappeared in some modern views. Mormonism, which teaches about a pantheon of gods and holds that its members themselves can become gods, explains Jesus of Nazareth in a manner compatible with gnostic concerns. Similarly, at the present time some types of new ageism see Jesus as an ancient psychic or spirit person who, as such, could bring His contemporaries into contact with the supernatural world, where they would find their ultimate salvation.

Anti-supernatural Adoptionism. Paul of Samosata (third century) proposed another form of adoptionism. He utterly denied that the Son of God came or that Jesus was anything but an ordinary man, though he granted that He was holy and mightily used of God. His objection to the Incarnation did not arise from a gnostic bias.[42] Instead Paul of Samosata embraced an anti-supernatural view of Jesus and a unitarian view of God, thus denying any Trinitarian possibility.[43]

Paul of Samosata's view included ideas about Jesus taught by the Jewish-Christian sect, the Ebionites. The Ebionites looked upon Jesus as a merely human messiah, rejecting His deity altogether. Paul of Samosata's view also anticipated by well over a millennium the objection some modern scholars have to the acceptance of Jesus as divine.

At root, regarding several basic ideas common to Ebionism, Paul of Samosata, and modernism remain largely the same. All hold that Jesus was an ordinary human being. Hence, no preexistent Son of God became incarnate in Jesus. Instead, He was an exceptionally virtuous person who was inspired by God and so used by God to spread the divine message.

2. REJECTION OF JESUS' FULL DEITY: ARIANISM

During the third and fourth centuries, neither gnostic nor anti-supernaturalistic adoptionism gained a permanent foothold in the church. The reason was that their exponents failed to use the Scriptures carefully. But with Arius and his followers, the matter was different. They built their case on Scriptures that actually do describe Jesus as subject to the Father or dependent upon the Father. They objected to describing Jesus as having the same nature, *homoousios,* as the Father. Since this word was not in the Bible, they claimed, its use granted more to Jesus than the Scriptures did.[44]

Arius did not deny that Christ was truly incarnate (as gnostic adoptionists did) nor divine (as Ebionites and Paul of Samosata did). But Arius did teach that only the Father was truly God and the Son was a creature of the Father, coming after the Father, and was not to be worshiped as true God but was to be venerated as Redeemer.

The teaching of the modern Jehovah's Witnesses concerning Jesus Christ resembles that of Arius, though the old heresy had abler advocates than the modern sect does. Jehovah's Witnesses, on a strained reading of John 1:1 argue that the Scriptures describe Jesus as divine but not truly God. This is very close to the reasoning of the ancient Arians.[45]

3. REJECTION OF JESUS' FULL HUMANITY

Other teachers, who accepted that Jesus was the Son of God in the fullest sense, explained how He was also the Son of Man in such a way as to compromise His humanity. They had weak views of Jesus' manhood just as Arius and his followers had a weak view of his Godhood.

The Word of God Not United to a Complete Human: Apollinarius

Apollinarius (mid-fourth century) is a prime example of one whose Christology has a weak view of Jesus' humanity. His teaching begins with the view that human nature is trichotomous. That is, each human has a body, a soul (the vital principle that makes the body live), and a spirit (the mind and the will). Apollinarius taught that Jesus received a real human body and soul from Mary, but He received His spirit when the Word of God was incarnated.[46]

Thus, according to Apollinarius, Jesus never experienced the intellectual and spiritual life of a human being. Temptation was not real for Him, as it is for us, since temptation by definition seeks to overcome the will. Jesus did not have a human will. Moreover, prayer was not the same for Him as it is for us, for He never had to depend upon God's help for spiritual life.

The Word of God Overwhelmed the Human Spirit: Eutyches

The teaching of Eutyches (early fifth century) differed from Apollinarius in form but not in effect.[47] This teacher claimed that Jesus received a human body, soul and spirit from Mary. But in the incarnation the Word of God completely overwhelmed and absorbed the human spirit. Thus, there is a *confusion* of the divine and human.[48] After the Incarnation, Eutyches taught, Jesus really had only one nature. Hence, his doctrine is called monophysitism (a single nature).

Monothelitism, a view similar to monophysitism, was promoted a couple of centuries after Eutyches. Monothelitism (a single will) taught that after the Incarnation Jesus only had one will, which was divine.[49]

The net result of monophysitism and monothelitism is similar to the teaching of Apollinarius. Both views said that Jesus never really had spiritual experiences like ordinary humans have. He could not have been truly tempted or have truly prayed.

4. REJECTION OF THE FULL UNION OF THE DIVINE AND HUMAN NATURES: NESTORIUS

Nestorius (early fifth century) accepted the full deity and the full humanity of the Lord Jesus. Thus, he differed with Arius and his followers, teaching that the Son had the same nature as the Father. He also differed with Apollinarius, teaching that Jesus was truly human and had the experiences of a true human. But Nestorius did not unite the two natures into one person. For Him, Jesus had a kind of split personality.[50]

The Council of Ephesus (A.D. 431) rejected Nestorius' teaching that separated the natures and divided the person of Jesus.[51] The solution to the question raised by Apollinarius and others was not solved by Nestorius. The reason was that he separated the two natures so that they acted independently of one another. By contrast, the classic view was that our Lord's two natures related perfectly to one another in one person.[52] His flesh was not changed into deity nor His deity into humanity; but there was a perfect interchange between the two. The Latin term *communicatio idiomatum* expresses this mystery. That is, the attributes belonging to each nature interchange with the other.[53]

5. ESSENTIAL TEACHINGS ON JESUS CHRIST

Historic teachers of the church answered the heretics' errors on the nature of Jesus Christ. The need to respond to error, in fact, was good because it pushed the church to state its fundamental views sharply. Among the essential teachings are the following.

True God

Arianism forced the church to decide how boldly it would affirm the deity of Jesus Christ. From New Testament times forward the church did not hesitate to affirm Jesus' full deity, and it always resisted attempts to blunt this affirmation. But Arianism brought the question into sharp focus. Is the Son truly God so that when the Son was incarnate in Jesus Christ, God really came in human flesh? The church after thinking the question over from every possible angle, answered Arius with a resounding yes. He is truly God. This is the case in two respects:

First, historic church teaching underlines the unique relationship of the Son to the Father. He is the true Son of the Father, thus not a creature but the uniquely begotten. As such He is true God of true God.[54]

Second, historic church teaching points to the preexistence of the Son. He is coeternal with the Father; so there was never a time, even before the creation and before time existed, when the Son was not. He does not merely have a temporal existence like creatures with a beginning.[55]

True Man

Once the issue of Jesus' essential deity is settled, the next issue to present itself concerned His essential humanity. Apollinarius and Eutyches raised this issue sharply. Both taught that the true Son of God was incarnate, but that in the Incarnation His deity overwhelmed the human element of Jesus so that He was not truly human.

Earlier church statements had spoken to the issue when they made affirmations such as, "Who for us men and for our salvation came down [from heaven] and was incarnate and was made man."[56] This was good, but to exclude error additional statements were necessary.

The teaching of the historic church once again deals precisely with the question raised. It has taught that the Son could only heal and redeem the human family only by fully assuming human nature.[57] Thus the Word of God must be incarnate in a true human person. Our Lord Jesus Christ is perfect in His manhood. That is, He is like us in all things, yet without sin.[58]

One Person, Two Natures

The final issue concerns the relationship of our Lord's humanity to His deity. Nestorius raised this issue. Church teaching on this matter affirms that after the Incarnation our Lord was (and is) one person with two natures. Thus, Jesus has always acted as a single person: His deity and His humanity both complete and both are involved in His work. Neither nature suppresses or minimizes the other nor are they separated or divided from one another. In essence there is a perfect interchange of attributes from each to the other.[59]

SECTION IV. *The Classic View of Jesus of Nazareth and Modern Departures from It*

During the Middle Ages and the early years of the Reformation the church faced no new teachings on Christology that successfully undermined historic orthodoxy. Abélard (early 12th century) developed a low view of Christ's atonement which anticipated some ideas espoused in the modern era. Also later, the Socinius family denied His deity and taught a unitarian view of God, that is, they rejected the historic view of the Trinity.[60] But the overwhelming majority of Christians in Eastern Orthodoxy, Roman Catholicism, and Protestantism all agreed on the doctrine of Christ and essentially on their understandings of how our atonement is possible through Him.

This changed with the rise of rationalism in the 17th century, which programmed a line of thought that became a profound challenge to historic orthodoxy.

The Source of Modern Departure from Historic Orthodoxy in a Philosophical Pre-commitment: Thoroughgoing Naturalism

The naturalistic explanation of all things lies at the heart of the program in giving a new assessment to Jesus of Nazareth. By naturalism, we mean the view that all historical events can be explained from within the world of time and space. Thus, its proponents, to one degree or another, systematically reject the idea that God intervenes in the course of history. Rather, they hold that history is a self-contained unit.[61] We must note, however, that this is a philosophical proposition, not the result of historical analysis.[62]

237

The Reinterpretation of the Scriptures

If, as we believe, the Scriptures provide the norm for Christian theology, a new understanding of Jesus would naturally require a reinterpretation of the Scriptures. For a plain reading of the scriptural accounts of Jesus would acknowledge the large role that the supernatural plays within them. Likewise, the best exegetes of the ages understood the Scriptures to teach this same truth. The historic rule of faith and the historic creeds grow from an acceptance of this as foundational. Therefore, those who wish to redefine the Christian faith in a manner that departs from this historic rule of faith must reinterpret the Scriptures.

During the last two centuries, such a reinterpretation of the Scriptures has taken place. It has had two aspects. In the first place it has employed radical historical criticism. By its method radical historical criticism casts doubt on the historical accuracy of much that the Bible has to say about Jesus of Nazareth. It disputes claims that He actually did or said many of those things which the Gospels claim for Him.[63] At the same time this criticism also holds that fragments of the actual events or sayings of His life are buried within the Scriptures and we can, with careful scholarship, reconstruct true pictures of the historical Jesus. In the second place, this criticism says we are greatly assisted in our enterprise of reconstructing the life of Jesus by consulting accounts of other religious leaders, such as Mohammed or Buddha.

1. DENIAL OF GOSPEL REPORTS ABOUT JESUS' HISTORICAL LIFE AND TEACHINGS

The Denial of the Miraculous

For a naturalistic interpretation of the Scriptures, the work of reconstructing the life of Jesus generally begins with the denial of the supernatural in the story. Such things as Jesus' birth to a virgin, His miracles, and His resurrection are either denied or so restated that they no longer are supernatural events. Of course there are many variations in the way critics may estimate the authenticity of the items reported in the Gospels. Some deny outright that any miracle took place. Others are selective. They may vigorously affirm Jesus' resurrection from the dead but deny His birth to a virgin. Consider two explanations these critics offer for the inclusion of miraculous events in the Scriptures:

- the miraculous events (for example, the stilling of the storm at sea) really happened but they can be given natural explanations;[64]
- the authors, who wrote at a considerable time after Jesus lived, recast His story by (1) embellishing quite normal events so they would appear miraculous or (2) creating stories to nurture faith in Him as God's Son.

The Denial of Jesus' Teachings

Radical critics also deny that Jesus taught all the things the Gospels report that He taught. They may accept some of His teachings, such as His sayings about the kingdom of God or His differences with contemporary Jewish leaders, but they attribute other teachings to Christians of a later period. This applies not merely to a few isolated sayings but also to crucial teachings, such as the continuing authority of the Law (Matthew 5:17-20) or Jesus' self-understanding (John 6:43-59).[65]

2. THE CRITERIA USED TO REJECT THE GOSPEL ACCOUNTS

Radical critics often acknowledge that their understandings of the Gospel accounts do not grow from a straightforward reading of them. Some even admit that there is great agreement between what the evangelists believed about Jesus and what the historic church has understood them to have believed. Instead, the critics claim that we can no longer take the Gospels at face value. They are fallible documents, tainted with the biases and limitations of their authors. If we would really know the Jesus of history, we must get behind the Gospels as we have them.

The critics offer two ways of explaining why we cannot trust the Gospels to give accurate historical accounts of either Jesus' deeds or words. First, they say the evangelists who wrote the Gospels were too far from the events to have firsthand and precise knowledge of what they report. Second, the cultural milieu in which they wrote was credulous and thus people of the times accepted the miraculous and the supernatural in a way that modern people simply cannot.

Critics Deny that the Evangelists Were Disciples of Jesus or Were Associates of His Disciples or Worked with Material that Came from Eyewitnesses

Historic Christianity has always asserted that the Gospels came from people who were close to the events, either disciples of Jesus (such as Matthew and John) or associates of apostles (Mark and Luke).[66] Luke specifically states that he drew information from prior written material that had derived from those who were eyewitnesses and who were the initial preachers of the word (Luke 1:1-2).[67]

Critics frequently place the writing of the Gospels at a distance in time from the disciples of Jesus and from eyewitnesses of the events of His life.[68] They hold that both the evangelists who wrote and the Christian communities for which they wrote had interests and needs quite different from those of the historical Jesus. The stories of Jesus were retold and reshaped, so the critics suggest, to meet these needs and interests. Naturally, they go on, as the stories of Jesus were recast, a good deal was interpolated, which He simply did not do or say.

Parallel Accounts in Non-Christian Religions Supposedly Refute Reports of the Supernatural in the Christian

Critics also point to parallel stories, or what are asserted to be parallel stories, in non-Christian religions in order to neutralize the uniqueness of scriptural accounts. Greek and Latin myths, for example, have stories of visitations from heavenly beings,[69] miracle births, healings,[70] and the like. The credulousness of ancient peoples, the critics say, accounts for the popularity and acceptance of the stories in Christianity as well as in other religions.[71]

These critics claim that the supernatural and the miraculous are accretions to the Gospel, not its center. They say we can peel off the layers of superstitious belief and still have the essential person of Jesus and his message left. This, they hold, is what God has given us for our redemption.

3. THE RECONSTRUCTION OF THE HISTORICAL JESUS

After critics have removed the supernatural from the story of Jesus and from His sayings that teach that He is the unique Son of God and Son of Man, they reconstruct the story from what remains.[72] These reconstructions of the historical Jesus depart to one degree or another from the view of historic Christianity.

They may describe Him largely as an apocalyptic prophet,[73] a sage that criticized artificial religion,[74] a friend of the politically and economically powerless,[75] or something similar.[76] Or they may affirm only selected elements of classic Christian faith in Jesus.

However, in the process, those crucial teachings that historic Christianity has believed to be fundamental to our understanding of Jesus are subjected to ruthless scrutiny. They are often denied or reinterpreted so as to put new teachings in their place. For example:

- The belief that Jesus was born of the Virgin Mary is rejected as a mythical or legendary way to explain that He is indeed the Son of God;
- The belief that Jesus was in fact the incarnate Son of God is replaced with the idea that Jesus was the person in whom the sense of the divine was most fully formed;
- His miraculous healings of the sick or His deliverances of those who were demon-possessed are replaced with the idea that He was a wonderful counselor. The accounts of demon possession are often set aside as primitive explanations of psychological dysfunction;
- The Gospel statements about Jesus' self-understanding as the Son of God are explained as the projections of later Christians;
- Some of the teachings the Gospels report as His are accepted as His, while others are rejected as foreign to His thought and are attributed to early Christian communities;
- The reports of His resurrection are explained as the attempts of Christians to state in mythical terms their conviction that the cause for which Jesus' gave His life had not perished with His physical demise.

4. THE OFFICIAL POSITION OF CHRISTIAN BODIES

A genuine ecumenical council to deal with issues of orthodoxy or heresy has not been convened since the separation of Western from Eastern Christianity in 1054. However, there have been church councils or church statements since the rise of modernism that have systematically rejected the views of radical critics and agreed with the views of ancient Christianity. Though radical critics may claim that many professors of religion and bishops and pastors of orthodox churches support their views, key official church statements do not. This is true of Roman Catholics,[77] the Anglican Church, the evangelical movement in North America,[78] and virtually all Protestant denominations.[79]

SUMMARY: *The Historical Orthodox View of Jesus of Nazareth and Ancient and Modern Views that Depart from It*

1. The question about the Incarnation focuses on how Jesus of Nazareth can be the Son of God and the Son of Man at the same time.

2. Attempts to deny or minimize Jesus' deity have come in several forms. Ancient heretics simply denied His deity (Ebionism and Paul of Samosata), or denied that the Christ was truly incarnate in Jesus of Nazareth (Cerinthus), or denied that the Word of God was truly God (Arius). Modern critics explain that the evangelists did not know the historical Jesus and created accounts to nurture the faith of people quite removed from Him. They further contend that peoples in the time of Jesus were credulous or naïve and easily believed reports of miracles that modern people simply cannot accept.

3. Attempts to minimize Jesus' humanity have also come in various forms, most of them appearing in ancient times. These heresies have denied that the Word was incarnate in a full human being (Apollinarius) or claimed that, when the Word was incarnated, it overwhelmed the human mind (Eutyches) or the will (monothelitism) of the man Jesus.

4. The Nestorian view was heretical in that it failed to keep the union of the two natures of the one person fully joined.

5. Historic teaching on the incarnate Word has emphasized:

- that Jesus is true God, the very Son of the Father and of one substance with the Father, preexistent with the Father from all eternity;

- that Jesus is true man and that when the Son of God was incarnated and born of the Virgin Mary, He was like us in all respects, having a human mind and will, yet without sin;

- that our Lord Jesus Christ is one person with two natures, neither nature being diminished or compromised in the union and each nature sharing the properties with the other

SECTION V. *The Mediatorial Roles of Jesus Christ*

A mediator is one who goes between or represents one person to another. In His mediatorial roles Jesus represents God to the human family and the human family to God. He goes between the two as the chief representative of both to the other.[80]

Calvin referred to Christ's mediatorial works as divided into three classes, as prophet, priest, and king.[81] These classes organize His tasks into distinguishable but interrelated groups. As Prophet, Jesus spoke for God, declaring clearly what God wanted us to know. As Priest, Jesus intercedes effectively on our behalf, praying for us and offering to God the sacrifice of His own life for our sins. As King, Jesus will rule over all the world and bring it into total subjection to the will of God.

A time element has been indicated in Jesus' three roles: He did declare, He does intercede, He will rule. This distinction describes in the large sense the three major tasks of Jesus in the three periods since the Incarnation. During His earthly life, as a prophet, He spoke authoritatively of God's truth, during the present He is at the right hand of the Father interceding on our behalf, when He returns, as a ruling monarch, He will triumph over all enemies and bring them into subjection to God's will.

1. PROPHET

Jesus' ministry included a great deal of speaking. The topics of His preaching and teaching, such as the kingdom of God and the will of God, reminded people of the classic prophets of Israel. It is not surprising, then, that some considered Him a prophet like one of the prophets of old (Mark 8:28).

Others considered Him as the fulfillment of the prophecy that said that at the end of time God would send Elijah (Mal. 3:1).[82] It was, however, the coming of John the Baptist that actually fulfilled this prophecy (Luke 1:17; 9:8).

A Prophet Like Moses

The real prophetic model for Jesus was Moses. In fact, Moses had promised that the Lord would send a prophet like himself whom Israel should heed (Deuteronomy 18:15-19). This is an important prediction, given the authority of Moses in the Old Testament and his authority as generally recognized by the Jews.[83] Moses had given Israel the law to which the nation was perpetually bound. During the history of Israel no prophet had displaced Moses as the primary one to speak for God. To the best of our knowledge, only a few Jews ever discussed the hope that God would send a prophet like Moses at the end times.[84]

But the early church made precisely that comparison. In its earliest days Peter (Acts 3:22f.) and later Steven (Acts 7:37) explicitly stated that Jesus fulfilled the promise that one like Moses would come (see John 1:21; 6:14).

The Epistle to the Hebrews also compares Moses and Jesus. It states that Jesus, as "the apostle ... whom we confess" (3:1), "has been found worthy of greater honor than Moses" (3:3). Christ's superiority to Moses can be easily explained: Whereas Moses worked as a faithful servant (3:4f.), Christ is faithful as a Son (3:6).[85]

Similarly, Jesus stated that He alone could grant knowledge of the Father since, as the Son, He alone really knows Him (Matthew 11:27). In Christ, then, we have one truly speaking for God, who is in being God and not merely a human commissioned by God.

Jesus Ministry as the New and Final Prophet

The common people who heard Jesus were struck by His teaching. "He taught as one who had authority, and not as the teachers of the law" (Matthew 7:29; see John 7:46).

Jesus' method of teaching was distinct from that of the teachers of the law in several ways. For example, He did not preface His comments by listing the opinions of a series of rabbis in order to support His own view. Rabbinic authorities were famous for doing this.[86] Even some Pharisees noted that Jesus taught the "way of God in accordance with the truth," not being "swayed by men because [he paid] no attention to who they [were]" (Matthew 22:16; see John 3:2).

In part, Jesus' authority was greater than that of the teachers of the law because they were guilty of various hypocrisies (Matthew 23:3bff.). Jesus did not reject but affirmed the law of Moses (Matthew 5:17-19) and even said that the teachers of the law, "who sit in Moses' seat," were to be obeyed (Matthew 23:2-3a).

But another part of Jesus' authority arose from the way in which He went deeper into the law of Moses. The Sermon on the Mount (Matthew 5-7) is a virtual parallel to the revelation Moses received at Sinai. Yet in the sermon Jesus frankly stated that the righteousness of those who would enter the kingdom of God must exceed that of the Pharisees who were meticulous about the law given to Moses (Matthew 5:10). He also said, "You have heard that it was said to the people long ago ... but I tell you" (Matthew 5:21-48).

Thus, Jesus clearly assumed that His teaching was authoritative. He indicated this authority when He prefaced individual teachings of His with the expressions "verily, verily" (AV, often in John, 1:51; 3:3; 5:19; 10:1) or "I tell you the truth" (Matthew 8:10; 16:28; Mark 3:28; Luke 4:24). His is the definitive word from God.[87]

2. PRIEST
The Old Testament and Jewish Heritage on the Forgiveness of Sin

The problem of sin – the universal tendency to rebel against God with its attending results – is taken seriously in the Old Testament.[88] The law provides for offerings that remove guilt and reconcile the worshiper to God. There were the burnt offering (Leviticus 1:3-17; 6:9-13), the offering for the unwitting (unknown and unintended) sin (Leviticus 4:1-5:13; 6:24-30), the guilt offering (Leviticus 5:14-6:7; 7:1-10), and especially the offerings on the Day of Atonement (Leviticus 16). Penitential Psalms such as 32, 51, and 130 and portions of other Psalms such as 103:3, 8-12 describe the burden of sin and the relief that comes from its removal. Jews of Jesus' time had thought much about sin and forgiveness and had developed detailed teachings regarding these matters.[89]

When Jesus addressed the problem of sin, He relied on this rich heritage of teaching on guilt and forgiveness. But in His ministry and work He made an advance in two respects. First, He announced the forgiveness of sins to the guilty, and thus He spoke authoritatively to sinners of God's provision for the removal of their sin. Second, He offered Himself up as the sacrifice for our sins, and He now intercedes continuously on our behalf, pleading the merits of that sacrifice.[90]

The Gospels: Jesus, the One Who can Forgive our Sins

During His ministry Jesus asserted His authority to forgive sins. He specifically said to a paralytic man that his sins were forgiven (Mark 2:5). The teachers of the law knew that such authority belongs only to God but did not acknowledge that Jesus possessed such authority.[91]

Jesus also conferred on His disciples the authority to forgive sins when He breathed upon them the Holy Spirit after the Resurrection (John 20:23). Thus they were to carry on His work after His departure though their authority, since it was derived, would not be so absolute as His was.

The Gospels and Letters: Jesus, the Perfect Sacrifice to Provide for the Forgiveness of Sins

The writers of the New Testament described Jesus' death as the perfect sacrifice for our sins. At the Last Supper He told His disciples that the cup from which they drank was the "blood of the covenant ... poured out for many for the forgiveness of sin" (Matthew 26:28). Paul explicitly linked the death of Jesus and our sins when he said "Christ died for our sins" (1 Corinthians 15:3). He also linked Jesus' death and our atonement (Romans 3:25) and compared the Passover sacrifice with His death (1 Corinthians 5:7). Similarly John stated that Jesus is the "atoning sacrifice for our sins, and not only for ours but also for the sins of the whole world" (1 John 2:2), and that because of this "the blood of Jesus .. purifies us from every sin" as we walk in the light (1:7). Peter said "he bore our sins in his own body on the tree" (1 Peter 2:24; see 3:18).

The Epistle to the Hebrews: Jesus, the High Priest after the Order of Melchizedek, Who Offers the Perfect Sacrifice

The Old Testament Priesthood. According to the law Aaron and his successors were to serve as high priests for the people of Israel (Leviticus 8). On the Day of Atonement they were to enter the most holy place of the temple – the inner sanctum – to offer sacrifice at the mercy seat, which represented the presence of God (Leviticus 16:2).

Melchizedek, who also is designated as a priest, appears twice in the Old Testament. Genesis 14:18-20 states that he was a priest who served Abraham, the father of Israel. Psalms 110:4 describes him as a priest from an order different from that of the Levitical high priesthood. This is a messianic psalm that joins together two roles for the future messiah; he would be both king and priest.

Hebrews 4:14-5:10 and 7:1-10:28 take up the issue of Jesus' high priesthood. Although the activity of the Levitical priesthood provides the antitype for the priestly action of Jesus, Jesus nevertheless belongs to the priestly order of Melchizedek and not to that of Levi.

Jesus, a Priest After the Order of Melchizedek. The book of Hebrews notes several ways in which Melchizedek provided an order for Jesus' priesthood that was superior to that of Levi. Consider:

- Though no one, even Aaron, took the priesthood on himself; yet God called Christ His Son (Psalms 2:7) and declared to Him by an oath (Psalms 110:4) that He was a priest after the order of Melchizedek (Hebrews 5:4-6; 7:20-22);
- Since Melchizedek served as Abraham's priest, he was a greater priest than Levi who was Abraham's son. So Christ, who is of Melchizedek's order is greater than the Levitical high priest (Hebrews 7:1-19);
- Jesus' priesthood is permanent and will not be cut short by death, as the Scripture says, "You are a priest forever" (Hebrews 7:23f.).

Jesus, a Perfect Priest. There are still other respects in which Jesus' priesthood is superior to that of Levi:

- The Levitical high priests must first offer atonement for their own sins before they could offer sacrifices on behalf of the people (Leviticus 16:6-14). Jesus, who is blameless, needs no atonement for Himself (Hebrews 7:26-28);

- Because high priests continue to sin, they need to repeat the sacrifice. But Jesus' sacrifice remains effectual as given, once for all (Hebrews 7:27);
- The Levitical high priest offers sacrifices here on earth at the sanctuary, which is only a copy of the heavenly and eternal sanctuary. But Jesus has entered into heaven and there offered a perfect sacrifice in the very presence of God (Hebrews 8:1-6; 9:1-10).

Jesus, the Perfect Sacrifice. Levitical high priests did offer according to the law, and their sacrifices of the blood of goats and calves were effectual through the animals' deaths (Exodus 24:8). But the sacrifices were only copies of the real sacrifice, that of Jesus Himself who offered the sacrifice that would never need to be repeated (Hebrews 9:11-10:18).

Jesus, the Interceding High Priest. Jesus perfectly fulfills the priestly role, which requires full knowledge of human weakness. He experienced temptation (Hebrews 4:15) and suffering (Hebrews 5:8) and was thereby made perfect for His mediatorial role for humans who experience both sin and weakness.[92]

3. KING
David, the Model King

David, the second and greatest king over Israel, firmly established the monarchy. Though his work was marred by personal and glaring lapses into sin (2 Samuel 11; 24) and a near fatal failure to manage his own family (2 Samuel 13-21), David still had qualities that marked Him as a "man after God's own heart" (1 Samuel 16:7; see 13:14) and the ideal leader. Henceforth, David became the model of what a king should be.

Isaiah: The Hope for One Greater than David from the Line of David

But the ideal king was to exceed David's standard, though He would arise within David's line (Isaiah 11:1). This ideal ruler is anticipated most clearly in Isaiah. Names that are given this king indicate his character: Wonderful Counselor, Mighty God, Everlasting Father and Prince of Peace (Isaiah 9:6). He is to govern in a wonderful way because He is to be endowed with the Spirit of the Lord who gives wisdom, understanding, counsel, power, knowledge and the fear of the Lord (Isaiah 11:2-3a). Consequently, His judgments will be absolutely righteous, not merely righteous in appearance, and He will bring the wicked to perfect justice (Isaiah 11:3b-5). The result of this righteous leadership will be a restoration of the earth to pristine peace (Isaiah 11:6-9).

Jesus Redefined Kingship

Jesus redefined kingship. He observed that gentile kings lord it over their subjects. By contrast, following the pattern He had set before His disciples, leadership should be characterized by service (Luke 22:24-27). But His redefinition of kingship required that Jesus resist popular attempts to make Him a king.

After feeding the crowd at the Sea of Tiberias and knowing that the people would try to force Him to be king, Jesus withdrew (John 6:15). Similarly, when Peter rebuked Him for predicting His suffering and death, Jesus rebuked Peter for having human ideas in mind and not God's ideal (Mark 8:32f.).

Jesus did act as a conquering ruler in overthrowing the power of evil, especially in casting evil spirits out of people or in liberating them from their afflictions. He healed the woman who had been crippled for 18 years by freeing her from Satan's bondage (Luke 13:16). The evil spirit in the possessed man in the synagogue of Capernaum (Mark 1:24) and the demons in the man among the tombs called Legion (Mark 5:7-12) acknowledged that in Jesus they had met their master (Mark 3:11; Matthew 12:25-30; Luke 10:18f.).

As Jesus approached the Crucifixion, several events clearly suggested His royalty. There were the Triumphal Entry (Mark 11:1-11), the cleansing of the temple (Mark 11:12-18), the parable of the tenants (Mark 12:1-12), and His debate with the teachers of the law about the superiority of David's son over David (Mark 12:35-37).

Jesus' kingship and the way it was different from the common view of kingship appear sharply in His arrest in the Garden of Gethsemane and His trial before Pilate. He repudiated the fight that Peter put up in the Garden (John 18:10f.). Jesus restored the ear Peter had lopped off from the high priest's servants and then went on to say that He could have a host of angels rescue Him (Matthew 26:53). This line of thought continued later when Pilate interviewed Him. Jesus said to Pilate that His kingship was not of this world. If it were, He explained, His servants would fight as humans hungry for power typically do (John 18:35-37).

The Exaltation of the Risen Lord to the Father's Right Hand and the Returning Son of Man

After His resurrection Jesus was exalted to the right hand of the Father (Acts 2:33; 5:31). This exaltation marked the end of His earthly humiliation and the beginning of His royal dignity (Philippians 2:9f.). The current status of Jesus, then, is that He is at the right hand of the Father (Acts 7:56; Romans 8:34; Ephesians 1:20; Hebrews 1:3; 8:1; 1 Peter 3:22), where the honor and worship due the Father (Revelations 4:11) are also due the Lamb (Revelations 5:12-13).[93]

Not everything has, as of yet, been subjected to the risen Son (Hebrews 2:8). We presently have a paradoxical situation: On earth we have a continued rebellion against Jesus' reign; in heaven we have a full acknowledgment of His sovereignty. But this hidden and heavenly exaltation of the Son will soon (Revelations 1:1) become a visible fact on earth, a fulfillment of an ancient promise (Psalms 110:1). All will come in due order. First, He will triumph over all powers, including death, and thus put all enemies under subjection. Then, He will subject Himself to God the Father (1 Corinthians 15:20-28; see Revelations 20).[94]

The new day of this full subjection will be announced with the Son of Man's glorious return. He will come in clouds with power (Mark 13:26; Matthew 24:30; Luke 21:27; Mark 14:62; Matthew 26:64).[95]

SUMMARY: *Jesus' Mediatorial Roles*

1. Jesus brings together God and humankind. We see Him as the Son of God who perfectly represents God to humanity and as the Son of Man who perfectly represents humanity to God. His mediatorial person and work can be described under three heads. Thus, He fills the roles of speaking for God to humans, interceding with God for sinful people, and governing us.

2. As Prophet during His public ministry, Jesus perfectly declared God's truth. His authority as a teacher was obviously greater than that of the teachers of the law. He fulfilled the promise that another prophet, like Moses, would come. But since He is God's Son, He is greater than Moses. And, though He did not set the law aside, He stated God's Word in a clearer and more binding fashion than Moses had.

3. As Priest, Jesus perfectly intercedes with God for us. His priestly order is that of Melchizedek and hence is superior to the Levitical order. He is a perfect high priest, and the sacrifice He offered, His own body, was perfect. He also offered His sacrifice in heaven in the very presence of God.

4. As King, Jesus redefined the general understanding of royal power. Even so, Jesus exercised sovereign power over the demons. After His resurrection His days of humiliation came to a close. He was exalted to God's right hand. Soon He will return to subject all things to Himself and then, in turn, subject Himself to the Father.

SECTION VI. *For Us and For Our Salvation*

The purpose of Jesus' life, death, and resurrection was to bring us salvation. In Christ, God acted in a marvelous way to deliver humanity from the tragic wrong that had engulfed it and to a greater or lesser degree every human within the race.

There is no single explanation for how Jesus Christ triumphed over sin and brought redemption to us. The problem of sin is complex, so God's resolution of the problem is complex.[96] In classic Christianity there have been at least three important ways of seeking to understand how God achieves our salvation in Christ. One focuses on the guilt or debt that sin creates, which must be remitted. A second considers sin that binds us as a power from which we must be liberated. A third centers on the damage sin has done to the Creator's unique creature, the human being, who alone was made in God's image.

1. CHRIST, THE ATONING SUBSTITUTE

Through His sacrificial death Christ provided a vicarious or substitutionary atonement for our sin. That is, Jesus Himself, through His crucifixion, became a substitute for us so that the debt that sin incurs can be justly remitted.

This teaching is often associated with the late medieval scholar Anselm (early 11th century) and his great book, *Why the God-Man?* The book's ideas, however, saturate the New

Testament and turn up repeatedly in the writings of the classic teachers of the church during the early centuries.

The Guilt of Sin

Human sin incurs guilt, and guilt must be remitted; that is, forgiven or pardoned, before the relationship between God and humanity can be properly restored. It is important to note that sin produces real guilt, not simply guilt feelings, even though the latter may arise from real guilt (Psalms 32:3). This understanding of sin and the resulting guilt has several dimensions:

- Sin introduces real evil into the world (Psalms 51:3, 9, 14);
- Sin disorders the world and sets in motion a chain of evil (2 Samuel 11);
- Sin offends God because it violates His sovereignty and holiness (Psalms 51:4, 6);[97]
- As a result, sin disorders the relationship between humans and God (Psalms 32:4), between humans among themselves (Genesis 4:1-12), and it brings intrapersonal disorder, that is, disorders in persons' internal relationships with themselves (Psalms 32:4).

God's Holiness and Love and the Problem of Sin

The Scriptures clearly teach that God is both perfectly holy and perfectly loving.[98] The resolution of the problem of sin by redemption does not arise from meeting the demands of only one aspect of God's character, His holiness or His love. Both are involved. That is, God's love does not merely prevail over divine holiness nor divine holiness over divine love.

The divine reaction to sin results because God is holy. This appears in passages that describe God's wrath (Exodus 32:11f.; Psalms 88:6f.; especially Romans 1:18ff.; 3:4-8). Some modern[99] as well as ancient[100] theologians have rejected the teaching that God is literally angry at the sinner.

They complain that such an idea teaches a view of God that we would object to in humans, that He is an irate and vengeful being who would not forgive the repentant until a debt is paid.

But such an objection fails to take seriously the problem of sin. It presumes, in fact, that sin does not incur real guilt and real debt and that the tragedy of sin is only relational. As Anselm said to his interlocutor, Boso: "You have not as yet estimated the great burden of sin."[101] For God to remain who God is, perfectly holy, and to understand sin in all its ugly and destructive dimensions, guilt must be remitted. God's character will remain consistent, and His name will be vindicated.

The divine reaction to sin also includes redeeming love. That is, at the same time as the holy God inherently abhors sins, God also loves sinners. Through Christ's self-offering, God unites divine holiness and divine love. In Christ, God gives Himself to remit the penalty for sin, thus vindicating his holiness while at the same time setting before all humans the offer of an unearned and undeserved forgiveness. The New Testament echoes the theme, then, that the coming of Jesus Christ has its source in the great love God has for sinful people (John 3:16; Ephesians 2:4f.; 1 John 4:9f.). "But God demonstrates his love for us in this: While we were still sinners, Christ died for us" (Romans 5:8).[102]

The Old Testament Foundation for Christ as the Sacrifice

The shedding of blood embodies the central feature of the sacrificial system. Since life is in the blood, atonement is made for sin through the offering of blood, "For the life of a creature is in the blood, and I have given it to you to make atonement for yourselves on the altar; it is the blood that makes atonement for one's life" (Leviticus 17:11).[103]

The "mercy seat" (AV) or "atonement cover" (NIV) also figures in this discussion. The term literally stands for the mercy seat in the inner part of the temple, the most holy place. It represents the precise place where atonement for the people was to be made on the Day of Atonement (Leviticus 16:15-16, see verses 1f.).

The Old Testament Foundation for Christ as the Substitute

The concept of a substitute sacrifice for sins permeates the Old Testament. God provided Abraham with a ram in place of his son (Genesis 22:14). Later, the Passover lamb was offered in place of the firstborn son of Israel (Exodus 13:14-16). The Levitical sacrifices atoned for the sins of the people, sins that were transferred to sacrificed animals. This was done by laying hands on an animal's head prior to its being slaughtered (Leviticus 4:4) or, in the case of the scape-goat, before the animal was driven into the wilderness carrying upon itself the sins of the people (Leviticus 16:21f.).

Isaiah 52:13-53:12 is a key Old Testament passage that speaks of substitution. The Suffering Servant takes on Himself the infirmities (53:4) and sins of others (53:5-6, 8, 10-12); and His suffering brings peace, healing, (53:5) and justification (53:11) to many.[104]

The Sacrificial Death of Christ

The sacrificial death of Christ figures even more prominently in the New Testament than do sacrifices in the Old. Each Gospel reaches it climax at the death of Jesus because the writers believe His death is the premier divine redeeming act. Beyond this the entire New Testament makes repeated references to the death of Christ or the shedding of His blood as having saving effect (Mark 10:45; Luke 24:26; John 10:11; 12:24; Acts 8:32-35; Romans 3:25-26; 1 Corinthians 15:3; Galatians 2:20; Colossians 2:13f.; Hebrews 10:1-14; 1 Peter 3:18; 1 John 2:1f.; Revelations 5:9-12).[105]

The Rending of the Temple Veil. Mark (15:38) and Matthew (27:51) tell us that immediately after Jesus' death the temple veil was torn in two from top to bottom. This signified that through Jesus' death direct access to the atoning presence of God was made possible (Hebrews 10:20). This distinguishes the new covenant from the old covenant, for in the old only the high priest could enter into the presence of God and this only once a year on the Day of Atonement (Leviticus 16:2). Now the holy of holies is open to all who bring for their atonement the redeeming sacrifice of Jesus, the Christ.

Jesus' Statements at the Last Supper. The words of Jesus at the Last Supper (Mark 14:22-25; Matthew 26:26-29; Luke 22:15-20; 1 Corinthians 11:22-26) also indicate the significance He saw in His death. He referred to the bread as "my body" (Mark 14:22) "given for you" (Luke 22:19). The cup was "my blood of the covenant, which is poured out for many for the forgiveness of sins" (Matthew 26:28). Paul goes on to note, "Whenever you eat this bread and drink this cup, you proclaim the Lord's death until He comes" (1 Corinthians 11:26).[106]

A Curse for Us. In Galatians 3:10-13 Paul explains the meaning of Jesus' death drawn from the Old Testament understanding of the curse. Two Old Testament passages are cited. The first (Leviticus 18:5) states that a curse falls on whoever does not continue in all that is written in the law. The second (Deuteronomy 21:23) notes that whoever hangs on a tree is cursed. The first passage applies to us who are guilty of violating the law; the second to Christ who was crucified. Paul articulates the significance of this in a classic statement in which he says, "Christ redeemed us from the curse of the law by becoming a curse for us" (Galatians 3:13).[107]

Sin for Us. In 2 Corinthians 5:17-21 Paul describes the newness that has come through the message of Christ's reconciling work. The passage climaxes with the extraordinarily bold statement that "God made him who had no sin to be sin for us, so that in him we might become the righteousness of God." The idea of substitution in both directions is transparently clear. We receive from God a gift we have not earned (righteousness) because He has taken upon Himself a penalty He did not deserve (our sin).

Propitiation or Expiation. Two New Testament writers take up the Old Testament imagery of the mercy seat and apply it to Christ. The meaning of the words *hilasmos* and *hilasterion* includes the ideas of both propitiation (AV) and expiation (RSV).

"Propitiate" signifies that the divine anger for our sin has to be assuaged so that sinners can return to a favored relationship with God. "Expiate" signifies that the sin that created the estrangement has to be removed.

Careful study of the passages suggests that modern opposition to the idea of propitiation, just as modern opposition to the idea of God's anger, is not well-based. It is driven by a simplistic understanding of God's complex attitude toward our sin and our sinfulness. God intensely hates sin and is angry at the sinner. His holiness, that is, by its very nature, is diametrically opposed to sin; sin cannot survive in His presence. At the same time, His love for sinners is an intense and unrelenting love. His holiness and love meet at the cross where sin is forever judged and redemption for sinners is forever declared.[108]

In Romans 3:25f. Paul states that God put Christ forward as the expiating and propitiating sacrifice for sin. These benefits are granted to us through faith in His blood, for in this way God demonstrated the rightness of His prior forbearance of sin and the rightness of His present gift of pardon – complete remission of sin – to those who are justified by faith in Jesus.[109]

In 1 John 2:2 the apostle declares that Jesus Christ is the atoning sacrifice for our sins and also for those of the whole world (see 4:10). Such undeserved atonement avails and brings reconciliation, however, only to those who walk in the light (1:6). That is, to those who walk in obedience and who confess their sin (1:8). These remarks echo a theme of the ancient prophets, who said that sacrifices made by those who continue to sin do not bring atonement (Isaiah 1:12-17; Amos 5:21-24). But when we walk in the light (1 John 1:7) and confess our sins (1:9), we have an advocate a pleader, with the Father, Jesus Christ the Righteous One (2:1).[110]

The New Covenant. The epistle to the Hebrews offers us the most detailed exposition found within the New Testament of the sacrificial significance of Jesus' death.[111] Chapter 9:1-10 briefly describes the tabernacle and priestly actions of the first covenant. However, the apostle declares, Christ did not enter an earthly and creaturely tabernacle; He entered the perfect tabernacle (9:11). He did not gain access to God by shedding the blood of earthly animals but by shedding His own blood, which sacrifice cleanses the conscience at the deepest levels (9:12-14). Then, choosing an analogy from the legal realm, He says that a will takes effect only when the testator dies (9:16f.). So Moses ratified the old covenant with animal sacrifices (9:18-22), but Christ ratified the heavenly covenant, once for all, with His own death (9:23-28). If the old sacrifices had really effected what they signified, they would have cleansed the consciences, and repetition of the sacrifices would not have been necessary (10:1-10). But Christ's sacrifice genuinely brings forgiveness at the deepest levels (10:11-18). Therefore, the writer concludes, we have confidence and an invitation to enter the Most Holy Place through His blood, which is the curtain, that is, His body (10:19f.).

2. CHRIST, THE VICTOR

Guilt refers to the persisting wrong that exists as well as the debt this wrong creates long after the sinful deed was done. Guilt is brought on by the sinful deed and the sinfulness of the sinner who did the deed.

But there is another side to evil. In the life of every sinner, before any sin is committed, there is a prior condition. This is the problem of bondage or enslavement to evil, the condition that makes wrongdoing inevitable. The New Testament teaches that God, in responding to this bondage prior to deeds of sin, sent Christ, who delivers us from the power of evil. This view of atonement understands Christ as *Christus Victor* – Christ, the Victor.[112]

The Controlling Power of Evil

The Scriptures state that three forms of the power of evil have tremendous influence:

- The dominion of evil or the existence of supernatural powers controlling our world and influential in the very structures of civilization (1 Corinthians 2:6-8);
- The dominion of evil or the existence of supernatural spirits that can take control over individual people (Mark 9:14ff.);
- The dominion of sin in the flesh or the existence of a state of "fallenness" that shows its debilitating presence in all persons (John 8:34).

Supernatural Powers of Evil. Two of the forms of evil that hold us in bondage are described as supernatural powers. Rationalism, the modern philosophical school that teaches all things can be explained without reference to the supernatural, strongly resists the idea of such beings. It believes that the idea of a personal devil flourishes only in a prescientific milieu or in childish or emotionally disturbed minds. But this materialistic reductionism ignores certain unexplainable data.[113] Further, it ignores the recent increase of Satanism in the West with its devastating effects on some members of society.

The Scriptures and classic Christianity have always taught that the devil, a chief arch-rival of God, along with his minions, is at work in the world. The power of these beings is enormous, beyond anything humans – even Christians – can master without divine aid (Ephesians 6:11f.). They successfully deceive unbelievers (2 Corinthians 4:4) and would deceive even the elect, if that were possible, through the appearance of false christs (Matthew 24:24). The Gospels describe the demon-possessed as the most pathetic victims of Satan and his minions. These are people who have virtually lost all ability to direct their own lives (Mark 5:1-7). Their behavior is anti-God, antisocial, and even self-destructive (masochistic).

Personal Bondage to the Power of Sin. The New Testament also refers to sin as an inner power that enslaves and causes people, who otherwise function within the range of normalcy, to disobey God. Paul states that this inner sin invades the flesh – the mortal limited human frame – so it can dwell within us. Through the weakened flesh, sin renders our moral power helpless. A human decision to do what is right, of itself, cannot overcome this power of sin that dwells in the flesh (Romans 7:14-20). Those who are in the flesh and thus left to their own resources; that is, those who lack the work of Christ within, do not submit to God's law; indeed they cannot (Romans 8:7f.).

Old Testament Anticipations of *Christus Victor*

The Lord Is a Warrior. Several passages in the Old Testament anticipate the deliverance promised through Christ in the New. For example, after crossing the Red Sea Moses described God as a warrior who had triumphed over Egypt and would lead Israel on to still further victories in the Promised Land (Exodus 15:3-18). The image is one of great military clashes in which the people of God would be hopelessly inferior to their enemies except for God's intervention.

The Coming Kingdom of God. Apocalyptic literature, such as the book of Daniel and portions of certain prophetic books (Isaiah 24-27), describes a future triumph of God that will be of even greater proportions than those of the past during Israel's history. Then God "will crush all [earthly] kingdoms and bring them to an end, but it [God's kingdom] will endure forever" (Daniel 2:44). Not only will earthly kingdoms be defeated, but supernatural and spiritual ones will, too. The Lord will slay Leviathan (Isaiah 27:1f.).

The Triumph of Christ in His Ministry

The Gospels clearly teach that in Jesus' work the kingdom of God was coming and the power of Satan and evil were being overthrown. The accounts of Jesus healing the demon-possessed offer particularly clear testimony to this.

The Demons' Acknowledgment of Jesus' Power. In the Gospels, the evil spirits used their victims to speak to Jesus and beg for mercy. For example, the man at Capernaum said: "What do you want with us, Jesus of Nazareth? Have you come to destroy us?" (Mark 1:24; see Mark 5:7).

Jesus delegated this power over evil spirits to His disciples (Mark 3:15). When the 70 returned from their mission, they reported: "Lord, even the demons submit to us in your name" (Luke 10:17). Jesus then explained the collapsing power of evil: "I saw Satan fall like lightning from heaven" (10:28).

Jesus' triumph over Satan extended even to the realm of physical infirmity. When He healed the crippled woman, He said He was delivering her from a condition caused by Satan (Luke 13:16; see Acts 10:38).

Jesus, Stronger than Satan. The attempt of religious authorities to discredit Jesus led to strained explanations for His success in healing the demon-possessed. They claimed that He acted under the authority of Beelzebub, the prince of demons (Matthew 12:24). Jesus responded that their argument made no sense. If Satan followed this plan, He would destroy his own kingdom (12:25f.). He went on to say that the only logical explanation was that He, working by the Spirit of God, cast out Satan; so they should note that the kingdom of God had come. For, He continued, just as a robber who is stronger than the owner of the house can succeed in his thievery, so He, Jesus, was strong enough to spoil Satan's kingdom (12:28-29).

The Triumph of Christ's Death

The Cross as the Moment of Triumph. Some might argue that the cross of Christ was simply a defeat from which God rescued Jesus. During the Crucifixion some who watched Jesus die said that if He were the Christ (Mark 15:32) or the Son of God (Matthew 27:40-43) He would deliver Himself or at least that God would deliver Him (Matthew 27:43).

But the New Testament writers saw the Cross as a moment of triumph. Jesus "disarmed the powers and authorities, He made a public spectacle of them, triumphing over them by the cross" (Colossians 2:15). John repeatedly notes that Jesus' death on the cross was the point in time when He was literally and figuratively lifted up, that is, glorified (John 7:39; 12:26; 17:1; see 21:19).

The Liberating Power Through Christ's Death. Paul teaches that Christ liberates us from the power of sin in the flesh. In Romans 8:1ff. Paul talks about a new law that frees us from the law of sin and death, namely the law of the Spirit of life, which is through Christ Jesus (8:2). This law came into sight when God, sending His Son in the likeness of sinful flesh and for sin condemned sin in the flesh (8:3). Thus the death of Jesus, who was incarnate in human flesh, was a death to sin, once for all (see Romans 6:10).

The Triumph of Christ's Resurrection

The church's earliest preaching described Jesus' resurrection as God's reversal of Jesus' death (Acts 3:15; 10:40; 13:30). Peter even said that God freed Jesus from the agony of death, "because it was impossible for death to keep its hold on Him" (2:24).

Paul describes death as the last enemy (1 Corinthians 15:25f.). Thus, the resurrection of Jesus, the firstfruits of the ultimate resurrection of all (15:20), marks the triumph over the last enemy, death, which is the curse of sin (Genesis 2:17; 3:19). If He has been raised, then those who belong to Him will be raised, in due order (1 Corinthians 15:23).

Saving Works Accomplished in Jesus' Name

After the Resurrection and Ascension, Jesus' disciples began to perform mighty works in His name. Thus, Jesus' power was released to liberate people who, in various ways, were held down by sin and its curse. To cite only three, the lame man at the temple (Acts 3:6; 4:4:9f.), the possessed slave girl in Philippi (16:18), and the gift of the Spirit, which resulted in consequent miracles by Galatian Christians (Galatians 3:2-5). This corresponds to the promise of Jesus to His disciples that, if they would ask in His name, they would do greater things than He did, because He was going to the Father (John 14:12-14).

Deliverance from the Present Evil Age

The New Testament teaches that the present age is controlled by the power of evil from which only Christ's triumph brings deliverance. John observed that "the whole world is under the control of the evil one" (1 John 5:19), which leads to actual sinning (3:8). The precise reason for the coming of the Son of God "was to destroy the devil's work" (3:8). One's being born of God has a powerful effect on the problem of sin, for "no one who is born of God will continue to sin" (3:9).[114]

Similarly Paul said that the Lord Jesus Christ "gave himself to rescue us from the present evil age" (Galatians 1:4), and that the Father "has rescued us from the dominion of darkness and brought us into the kingdom of the Son he loves" (Colossians 1:12-14; Titus 2:13f.).

The Treasure in Jars of Clay

The final and decisive conquest of evil awaits the return of Christ. Between the present and the time of His return our situation is paradoxical. That is, the triumph of Christ is real and brings real victories within the present age, but there are other victories that will not be realized until the eschaton, the end time. We are delivered from sin, but it still threatens us (Romans 6:15-18); we have trouble in the world, but Christ has overcome the world (John 16:33); we may suffer oppression, persecution, and brutality but are not crushed, discouraged, or destroyed (2 Corinthians 4:8f.); we carry around the death of Jesus so that His life may be revealed in our mortal bodies (4:10f.); we may endure all kinds of maltreatment from nature, people, or demonic forces, but nothing can separate us from the love of God in Christ Jesus our Lord (Romans 8:35-39; see 1 Peter 4:12ff.; Hebrews 12:1ff.).

Salvation and Glory and Power Belong to Our God

When the end comes, all God's enemies will be put down. Satan and all his forces will lose their power over the church of God and even over the world; they will meet their well-earned judgment (Revelations 20:7ff.).

3. CHRIST, THE NEW ADAM

Historic Christianity also considered that Christ's redemptive work included His whole life – from the time of His birth through to His resurrection. The birth and childhood of Jesus were more than a prelude to His ministry, death, and resurrection. Rather, through experiencing the full range of His human life He brought healing and sanctification to human life.[115]

Christian theology has distinguished the work Christ does for us from that which He does in us. To consider Christ as the atoning substitute emphasizes the work He does for us. On the other hand, Christ as the victor emphasizes both the work that He does for us (conquering the powers of evil) and in us (liberating us from the enslaving power of sin). Finally, to consider Christ as the new Adam emphasizes the work He does in us.

The Word Became Flesh

Three great New Testament thinkers describe the Incarnation as a great change that happened when the pre-incarnate Word became a human being and dwelt among us. These were John, Paul, and the author of Hebrews. They showed that the change was real and permanent.

John states that "the Word became flesh and lived for a while among us" (John 1:14). Classic Christianity does not teach that He "became" flesh by being transformed from the Son of God into a human being but by *assuming* true human nature. That is, He did not change from being one kind of being into another, from being divine to being human. Rather, in the Incarnation humanity was united to deity, never again to be separated.

Similarly Paul states that "being in very nature God" Christ Jesus "made himself nothing, taking the very nature of a servant, being made in human likeness" (Philippians 2:6f.). Thus He shared all things that humans share, including death (2:8).

The letter to the Hebrews also makes clear that the incarnate Son's human nature provides the basis for His saving work. Since the children whom God has given Him have flesh and blood, He has "shared in their humanity" so that He might destroy him who held them in the power of death (Hebrews 2:13f.). "Because he himself suffered when he was tempted, he is able to help those who are being tempted" (2:18). In fact, "though he was a son, he learned obedience from what he suffered and, once made perfect, he became the source of eternal salvation for all who obey him" (5:8f.). The perfecting of the Son applies to His humanity. His capacity to bring salvation required that He fully share in our humanity.[116]

The Last Adam

Paul compares Adam and Christ as the heads of two streams of spiritual descendants (Romans 5:12-21 and 1 Corinthians 15:21f.).[117] Through Adam sin and death found their way into human life, and through Christ righteousness and life have come. The descendants of both Adam and Christ participate in the originators' acts and in the results of their acts[118]

Thus, Paul describes Adam as far more than the biological father of the human race. Rather, Adam through his sin, established the condition in which all of us live and eventually die (Genesis 3). Through Adam sin entered the world (Romans 5:12), condemnation fell on all (5:18), all became sinners in deed (5:19) and so all die (5:12; 1 Corinthians 15:22).

Christ's influence is more than a simple example because those who belong to Him are raised to a new condition. Christ's great act of obedience (Romans 5:19) brought its benefits. Through Christ comes God's grace (5:15), justification (5:16), life (5:17f.), righteousness (5:19), eternal life (5:21), and the resurrection (1 Corinthians 15:21f.).[119]

Prayer to God as Abba

Jesus taught His disciples to address God in prayer as "Our Father" (Matthew 6:9ff.). To a lesser degree Israel also thought of God as Father but did not use the familiar expression Jesus did when He appealed to God as "Abba, Father" (Mark 14:36). Paul also says Christians who have received the Spirit of His Son cry to God in prayer, "Abba, Father" (Galatians 4:6f.). When Jesus taught His disciples the prayer, the Aramaic term He used was this unusual and intimate one for God. We address God in prayer as Jesus did.

The right to address God as "Abba", just as Jesus did, is based upon our filial relationship to God. Christ is the unique Son of God, and we are the children of God (John 1:12), co-heirs with Christ (Romans 8:12-17).

Union with Christ

Those united to Christ share in all aspects of His saving work. At our initiation as Christians, we are baptized into his death (Romans 6:3f.). The work began in Christ and is then applied to us. When Christ died, He died to sin (Romans 6:10). His death to sin was not, of course, required by His own acts of disobedience. Rather, disobedience is our problem as persons who dwell in sinful flesh and who do sin. But Christ took our fallen humanness upon Himself (Romans 8:3) as well as our guilt.

His union with us brought Him to death; our union with Him will ultimately bring us to the resurrected life. But in the interim we share in His suffering. So Paul says that he wants to know Christ and "the fellowship of sharing in his sufferings, becoming like him in his death, and so, somehow, to attain to the resurrection from the dead" (Philippians 3:10f.).[120]

The Life of Discipleship

Dying to Sin. The union with Christ will reach its goal when we are raised from the dead. In the meantime we share with Christ in several respects. Our sharing begins with our death to sin. In our sharing in His death, we are to die to sin and put to death the sin that remains within us (Romans 8:13; Colossians 3:5; Hebrews 12:1; 1 Peter 4:1; 1 John 3:3).

Following Christ. Christ becomes our leader and model for life. He called His first disciples to follow Him (Mark 2:14). He said that those who would be His disciples were to take up their cross and follow Him (Mark 8:34). To those who indicated that they would be His disciples (Matthew 10:38; John 12:26)) or wanted to find eternal life (Luke 18:22), Jesus said much the same thing. John wrote that "whoever claims to live in him must walk as Jesus did" (1 John 2:6; see 1 Peter 2:21; 1 Corinthians 11:1).[121]

This includes suffering for Christ. Paul wrote that we shall share in Christ's future glory if we suffer with Him (Romans 8:17; see Colossians 1:24; 2 Timothy 2:11-13). Such an idea is also taught by Jesus (Matthew 10:16ff.), Peter (1 Peter 4:12ff.), and in the Revelation of John (7:14ff. and elsewhere).

We Shall Be Like Him

The time is coming when sharing in His glory will take its final step. When Christ returns, the "dead in Christ shall rise first" (1 Thessalonians 4:16). Thus, as the first Adam was a living being, so the last will be a "life-giving spirit ... And just as we have borne the likeness of the earthly man, so shall we bear the likeness of the man from heaven" (1 Corinthians 15:45, 49). "When he appears, we shall be like him, for we shall see him as he is" (1 John 3:2).[122]

Classic Teachings on the New Adam

Irenaeus referred to Christ's work of restoring human life to its intended form as "recapitulation." He meant by this that Jesus, through His incarnation and human life, has restored and sanctified all of human life. Irenaeus wrote,[123]

> For He came to save all through means of Himself – all, I say, who through Him are born again to God – infants, and children, and boys, and youths, and old men. He therefore passed through every age, becoming an infant for infants, thus sanctifying infants; a child for children, thus sanctifying those who are of this age, being at the same time made to them an example of piety, righteousness and submission;

a youth for youths, becoming an example to youths, and thus sanctifying them for the Lord. So likewise He was an old man [a mature adult] for old men, that He might be a perfect Master for all, not merely as respects the setting forth of the truth, but also as regards age, sanctifying at the same time the aged also, and becoming an example to them likewise. Then, at last, He came on to death itself, that He might be "the first-born from the dead, that in all things he might have the pre-eminence," the Prince of life, existing before all, and going before all.

Later, Athanasius referred to the restoring of the image of God. The Scriptures, he noted, teach that both human beings and Christ possess the image. However, with humans the image is damaged because Adam fell, and it is impossible for us to restore it ourselves. But the Son of God, who truly bears God's image, through His life, death and resurrection provided the means for the restoration of the image within us.[124]

Gregory of Nazianzus took up the question of how fully Christ shared in our nature. Gregory, a younger associate of Athanasius, responded to teachings of Apollinarius who had disputed that Christ had a human mind and will. But Gregory countered that Christ could heal only that which He assumed, and therefore, He assumed the whole human nature.[125]

These and other ancient writers[126] as well as Wesley[127] speak of the Incarnation, the union of God and man in Jesus Christ as a foundation for the restoration of human nature. In order for God fully to restore humanity to the original creative intention, there had to be this unique individual upon earth.

God created human beings without blemish or flaw to love and serve Him and to live in love and service with one another. But through sin the very nature of human beings has been disordered and flawed. Human nature therefore needs restoring.

Through the Incarnation the Word of God was united to human nature, not to its sinfulness but to its limited and broken state. In Jesus of Nazareth the perfect human life was lived, a life of obedience, service and the glorification of God. In Jesus' death there was a perfect death to sin. In Jesus' resurrection there was perfect restoration.[128]

Through the Spirit we also are united to God. Though not in exactly the same way and to the same degree that God and human nature are united in Christ, there is still a real union between God and humans and a real restoration of human nature to God's intention. The restoration is partial now and will reach its final stage only with the resurrection of the body. But even now we "are being transformed into his likeness with ever-increasing glory" (2 Corinthians 3:18). God has "predestined [us] to be conformed to the likeness of his Son, that he might be the firstborn among many brothers" (Romans 8:29).[129]

4. A COMPREHENSIVE VIEW OF CHRIST'S SAVING WORK

Variations in the Historic Teachings on Christ' Saving Work

Across the history of the church variations on the historic teachings of Christ's saving work have sprung up. These great themes have challenged the most skilled and devout theologians. We consider a few examples.

The Ransom Theory, An Elaboration of Christus Victor. During the early centuries some important teachers developed a form of the *Christus Victor* teaching that has gone under the name of the Ransom Theory (see Mark 10:44). They correctly saw that the Scriptures talk about humanity being under the power of evil and the devil and thus needing to be ransomed. At times, however, they stated that the devil was the one to whom the ransom was paid. Based on

272

this analogy, we might suspect that these teachers were thoroughgoing dualists – believing that God and the devil were equally powerful contestants joined in an eternal conflict that would never be resolved. Quite to the contrary, none of the major teachers endorsed the view that the devil and God were equally powerful.[130]

Subsuming Other Theories Under that of the Atoning Substitute. Within Western Christianity the view of Christ as the atoning substitute has in some circles completely displaced the other views as the one essential Christian view. Thus, some systematic theologies treat the entire topic of Christ's saving work by discussing only the teaching on Christ as the atoning substitute.[131] Other theologies consider other views as subtopics of the one large view, that of the atoning substitute.[132] While we dare not minimize the teaching on the atoning sacrifice, we also need the teachings of Christ as the victor and Christ as the New Adam to explain more fully his saving work.

The Moral Influence Theory, A Replacement of the Atoning Substitute. The Moral Influence Theory was first propounded by Abélard to replace the teaching that Christ was the atoning sacrifice.[133] A form of this viewpoint was adopted in the early post-Reformation period by Socinius[134] and has become in the modern era the predominant view of liberal theology (Schleiermacher and Bushnell).[135] This Moral Influence Theory teaches as follows.

Sin is a terrible evil that has engulfed the world and destroys humanity. God in His infinite love sent His Son to woo us away from our sin and back to Himself. By identifying Himself with sinful people and suffering the consequences of sin in his death, Christ moves and persuades us to repent and turn to God who is ready and able to forgive. His willingness to die also calms our fear that God is wrathful, and thus we return to God with confidence that we will be accepted. In this view the death of Christ does not accomplish an objective change in our relationship with God (the propitiation of divine wrath) but a subjective change (an ending of human rebellion and fear).

The Governmental Theory, A Variation of the Atoning Substitute. Grotius, a Dutch lawyer of the 17th century, offered a variation on the teaching that Christ is the atoning substitute.[136] he was followed in this by Richard Watson, a Methodist of the early 19th century. [137]The historic view insisted that the basic reason atonement was required lay in the character of God as absolutely holy. Sin had to be judged and His holiness vindicated. In place of this Grotius drew attention to the nature of the world that God had created. For God to maintain a well-ordered universe, which is to say, a moral universe, there had to be satisfactory atonement for the wrong within it.

While Grotius did point to an important fact, his theory was flawed. It shifted attention from one of the main features of the substitution view, that the estrangement between God and human beings must be resolved if there was to be real reconciliation. In classic thought, this alienation results not only from our turning away from God but also from God's offense at our sin.

Liberation Theology, A Variation of Christus Victor. A modern variation of the *Christus Victor* teaching looks at the way in which evil invades society. This is the case especially when the economic and political structures of a civilization harden so that they impoverish and disempower great masses of people. The result is that the masses live in want and misery with little or no hope of change. Some liberation theologians hold that this is real bondage from which liberation is needed. Those who adopt this theology point to Christ's compassion for the poor and His corresponding criticism of the rich and powerful. But in some forms of liberation theology the saving work of Christ is reduced to a this-worldly transformation of social structures.[138] Variant forms of liberation theology name themselves as black theology,[139] feminist theology,[140] or ecological theology.[141] Little is made in these theologies of crucial aspects in Christ's work, including the view that sin is an inner bondage of all classes of people or that the power of sin has supernatural features – a real Satan – against which the human race, in itself, is helpless.

The Relatedness of Christ as Atoning Substitute, as Victor, and as the New Adam

Many scriptural passages focus on only one or another aspect of Christ's saving work, since they give attention to a particular facet of the large and complex problem of sin. In other cases an individual passage, such as Hebrews 2:14-18., may have all three aspects together. Thus, this latter passage speaks of Christ's atoning sacrifice (2:17), His destruction of the devil's power (2:14f.), and His perfect humanity by which He is able to help us (2:16-18). The problem of sin is multifaceted and interwoven, so the salvation that God brought us in Christ is multifaceted and interwoven. The three different aspects of Christ's saving work relate closely to one another. Thus, none of the three should be neglected, and all should be kept in balance.

SUMMARY: *For Us and for Our Salvation*

1. The saving work of Christ has several dimensions because it responds to the complex situation that sin has created.

2. Christ is the atoning Substitute. His sacrificial death atones for our guilt, which is the result of our sinful behavior plus the enduring aftermath of debt since the deed was done.

3. Sin disorders the world. It also disorders the relationship between God and humanity. It offends God's righteousness and hence requires satisfaction and remission.

4. Because of His great love, God sent the Son who gave Himself as a substitute for us.

5. Christ is the Victor. All humans are victims of the power of evil. The devil and his minions exercise enormous influence over the universe. They work insidiously to propagate evil. Because of the power of sin, we sin even when we desire to do otherwise. We need to share in Christ's victory over evil.

6. Christ delivered the demon-possessed. His death was a triumph over the devil. Today, Christ liberates people from the power of sin and its tragic results. At His return He will complete His triumph over evil. Death, the last enemy, will itself be destroyed by the power of the Resurrection.

7. Christ is the New Adam. The effect of sin includes serious damage to humans made in God's image. The Son of God took our nature and thereby united God and humanity in His own person. He lived the perfect human life, enduring its temptation, suffering, and death. He was raised to a new, glorified life, no longer flawed by the effects of sin.

8. Christ's disciples are united to Him and so united to God. They are called to follow Him, and through union with Him they already die to sin and are freed from its enslaving power. They are being transformed into His likeness, and they share in the fellowship of His suffering. When He appears, they will be like Him, bearing the radiant glorified image of God.

ENDNOTES

[1] See Eusebius, *CH* 2:14-16, 21f.; 3:1, 4, 23-25, *NPNF* 2:1:115f., 123-25, 132f., 136-38, 150-57.

[2] See *ANF* 8:351-476 and *NTA* 1:71-531.

[3] See Ephiphanius, *Pan.* 46.

[4] *ANF* 10:43ff.

[5] Fletcher, "Vindication of the Catholic Faith of the Trinity" VI.XII, *WJF* 3:475-83.

[6] The Gospel of Thomas 1-5, *NTA* 1:392-94; The Gospel of Pseudo-Matthew 18-39, *ANF* 8:376-82; see Irenaeus, *AH* 1:20:1, *ANF* 1:344f.

[7] John of Damascus, *EOF* 3:21f., *NPNF* 2:9:69f.

[8] John of Damascus, *EOF* 3:23f., *NPNF* 2:9:70f.; Wesley, Sermon 20, "The Lord Our Righteousness" I.2-4, *WJWB* 1:452; Bruce, *HC* 237-90.

[9] Machen, *VBC*; Barth, *CD* 1/2 172-202.

[10] Ambrose, *ECF* 3:4, *NPNF* 2:10:246f.; Augustine, *Ench.* 38, *NPNF* 1:3:250f.; Barrett, *HSGT* 23f.; Oden, *WL* 108-12.

[11] Lactantius, *Inst.* 4:12, *ANF* 7:11f.

[12] Augustine, "Lectures on the Gospel According to St. John" 2:15, *NPNF* 1:7:18; Wesley's note on Gal. 4:4, *ENNT* 481; Oden, *WL* 142-44.

[13] Bruce, *TT*.

[14] Oden, *LS* 349f.

[15] Wesley, Sermon 21, "Upon Our Lord's Sermon on the Mount, I" 1-10, *WJWB* 1:469-75.

[16] Edersheim, *LTJM* 1:524-41; Manson, *TJ*; Stein, *MMJT*.

[17] Manson, *TJ* 16-41.

[18] Wesley, Sermons 21-33, "Upon Our Lord's Sermon on the Mount, I-XIII," *WJWB* 1:466-698.

[19] Wesley, Sermon 25, "Upon Our Lord's Sermon on the Mount, V" V, *WJWB* 1:551-53.

[20] Wesley, Sermon 48, "Self-Denial" *WJWB* 2:238-50.

[21] Wesley's note on Luke 16:20, *ENNT* 157.

[22] Sanhedrin 4:1ff., *Mish.* 386-88.

[23] Briant, *ABD* 1:1207-09, translated by S. Rosoff.

[24] John of Damascus, *EOF* 3:26, *NPNF* 2:9:71f.

[25] Oden, *WL* 483-501.

[26] Vermes, *JJ* 37-40.

[27] Fletcher, "Vindication of the Catholic Faith of the Trinity" VI.VII, *WJF* 3:431-40; Cullmann *CNT*; Taylor *PCNTT*; Dunn *CM*.

[28] Geza Vermes, *JJ* 163-168.

29 Ambrose, *ECF* 5:114, *NPNF* 2:10:298; Chrysostom, *The Homilies on the Gospel of St. Matthew* 29:2, *NPNF* 1:10:197; Wesley, note on Mt. 9:6 in *ENNT* 31.

30 Chrysostom, "Homily on St. John, LV," *NPNF* 1:14:199; Westcott, *GAJ* 2:28; Hoskyns, *FG* 348f.; Dodd, *IFG* 261.

31 *APOT* 2:649-651/

32 Moore, *Jud.* 1:89f.

33 Justin Martyr, *First Apology* 50, *ANF* 1:179; Chrysostom, *Homilies on the Gospel of St. Matthew* 36:3, *NPNF* 1:10:240; Augustine, *Lectures on the Gospel According to St. John* 35:7, *NPNF* 1:7:206f.

34 Hirsch, *JE* 11:204f.

35 Hilary, *Trin.* 4:23-33, *NPNF* 2:9:80-83; see Fletcher "Socinianism Unscriptural" Letter II, *WJF* 3:507-11.

36 Wisd. 7:22-30; Ben Sira 24.; Hengel, *JH* 153-75.

37 Oden, *WL* 66-74.

38 Foerster, *TDNT* 1049-58.

39 Murphy, *Jerome* 1:594f.

40 Irenaeus, *AH* 1:26:1, *ANF* 1:351f.; cf. Epiphanius, *Pan.* 28:2.

41 See Irenaeus, *AH* 3:3:4, *ANF* 1:416; Klijn, *EEC* 1:158f.

42 Eusebius, *CH* 7:29-30, *NPNF* 2:1:313-16.

43 Epiphanius, *Pan.* 65:5; Kelly, *ECD* 117-19; Simonetti, *ECC* 2:663.

44 Simonetti, *ECC* 1:396.

45 Stroup, *ER* 7:565.

46 Shedd, *HCD* 1:394f.; Kannengiesser, *EEC* 1:58f.

47 Di Berardino, *EEC* 1:340f.

48 Leo's *Tome*, *NPNF* 2:14:254, 257.

49 John of Damascus, *EOF* 3:17f., *NPNF* 2:9:65-67; Simonetti, *ECC* 568-570; Oden, *WL* 188-92.

50 Nestorius, "Letter to Celestine," *CLF* 346-48; "Third Letter of Cyril of Alexandria to Nestorius," *CLF* 349-54; "Counter-Statements of Theodoret," *NPNF* 2:3:26-31; Simonetti, *EEC* 2:594f.

51 See the third canon of the Council in *NPNF* 2:14:4.

52 John of Damascus, *EOF* 3:1ff., *NPNF* 2:9:62ff..

53 John of Damascus, *EOF* 3:17, *NPNF* 2:9:65f.; Wiley, *CT* 2:180f.; Oden, *WL* 180-83.

54 Lightfoot, *AF* 2:2:90-94.

55 Wesley, Sermon 77, "Spiritual Worship" I, *WJWB* 3:90-95.

56 The Nicene Creed, *NPNF* 2:14:3.

57 Gregory of Nazianzus, Epistles 101 and 102 (to Cledonius), *NPNF* 2:7:439-45.

58 See the Definition of Chalcedon, *CC* 1:62f.; Wiley, *CT* 2:167.

59   John of Damascus, *EOF* 3:3f., *NPNF* 2:9:46-8; Baillie, *GWC* 125-32; Berkower, *PC* 85-110.

60   Fletcher, "Vindication of the Catholic Faith of the Trinity" VI and "Socinianism Unscriptural" VII, *WTF* 3:392-97, 507-35; Zückler, *NSH* 10:488-92.

61   Bultmann, *JCM* 11-21, 35-44.

62   Oden, *WL* 217-28.

63   Borg, *ABD* 3:802-12.

64   Mann, *GAM* 274.

65   Funk and others, *FG* 140, 420.

66   See Eusebius, *CH* 3:39:15f., *NPNF* 2:1:172f.

67   Oden, *WL* 62-64.

68   Marxsen, *INT* 142f., 152f., 161, 251-56; see Guthrie, *NTI* 33-44, 69-72, 98-109, 241-71;

69   Bultmann, *HST* 297f.

70   Bultmann, *HST* 214f.

71   Kee, *MECW* 1-41, 290-96.

72   Bruce, *HC* 191-236.

73   Schweitzer, *QHJ*.

74   Mack, *MI*.

75   Horsley, *JSV*.

76   Borg, *SJ* 83-106.

77   *CCC*, 422-682.

78   Lee, *EA* 75-91.

79   See Oden, *DSWT* 59-62.

80   Stevens, *TNT* 498-505.

81   Calvin, *Inst.* 2:15 (1:425-31); see Augustine, Har. Gospels 1:3, NPNF 1:6:79; Arminius, "Public Disputations, XIV," *WJA* 1:550-64; Collins *FW* 44-66.

82   Moore, *Jud.* 2:257-362.

83   Moore, *Jud.* 1:269.

84   Qumran Documents, *Manual of Discipline* (IQS) 9, Vermes *DSSE* 87-89.

85   Bruce, *EH* 56-58.

86   Pirke Aboth 1:2-11, *Mish.* 446f.

87   Wesley, Sermon 36, "The Law Established Through Faith" I.6, *WJWB* 2:37f.; Pope, *CCT* 1:100-13.

88   Moore, *Jud.* 1:460-473.

89   Büchler, *SSA* 328-31; Moore, *Jud.* 1:445ff.; Sanders, *PPJ* 157-60.

90   Baillie, *GWC* 157-79.

91   Taylor, *GAM* 197.

92   Pope, *CCT* 2:236-42.

93 Pope, *CCT* 2:151-83.

94 Beker, *PA* 164-70.

95 Pope, *CCT* 2:252-55.

96 Lindström, *WS* 216-19; Oden, *WL* 412f.

97 Anselm, *CDH* 12-15, *Anselm* 203-10.

98 Arminius, "Orations" 1, *WJA* 1:28f.

99 Dodd, *EPR* 20-24.

100 Origen, *FP* 2:10:3-5, *ANF* 2:294f.

101 Anselm, *CDH* 21, *St. Anselm* 228.

102 Oden, *WL* 122-25.

103 Cave, *SDSA* 128-30, 143-57.

104 Wiley, *CT* 2:223-25.

105 Cave, *SDSA* 312-17; Denny *DC*.

106 Weiss, *BTNT* 1:421-23; Wiley, *CT* 2:228f.; Bruce, *CG* 163-67.

107 Wesley, Sermon 20, "The Lord Our Righteousness" II, *WJWB* 1:453-65.

108 Pope, *CCT* 1:348-51; Cave, *SDSA* 303-07; Wiley, *CT* 2:225-27, 282-90.

109 Cave, *SDSA* 296f.

110 Arminius, "Orations" 1, *WJA* 1:35-40; Berkower, *PC* 239-67.

111 Cave, *SDSA* 418-37.

112 Aulén, *CV* 22-35.

113 Peck, *PL* 182-85.

114 Lindström, *WS* 71-73.

115 Gregory of Nyssa, *GC* 15, *NPNF* 2:5:487f.

116 Wiley, *CT* 2:278f.

117 Stevens, *TNT* 392; Wiley, *CT* 2:130-34.

118 Fletcher Sermon 5 "Nature of Regeneration" *WJF* 4:133f.

119 Wiley, *ST* 2:185f.; Davies, *PRJ* 36-57; Barrett, *FAL* 68-91.

120 Stevens, *CDS* 451-69.

121 Turner, *VT* 131.

122 Stevens, *CDS* 484-91.

123 Irenaeus, *AH* 2:22:4; see 3:18:2, 7; 3:22:1-2, *ANF* 1:391, 446, 448, 454.

124 Athanasius, "On the Incarnation of the Word" 7-10, *NPNF* 2:4:39-42.

125 Gregory of Nazianzus, "Letters to Cledonius," 101 and 102, *NPNF* 2:7:439-45.

126 Leo the Great *Tome, NPNF* 2:12:40; Theodoret's "Counter-Statements" 1-4, *NPNF* 2:3:26-28.

127 Wesley, Sermon 62, "The End of Christ's Coming" 1-I.10, *WJWB* 471-477; Tyson, "Charles Wesley's Theology of Redemption," *WTJ* 20:17.

128 Oden, *WL* 103.

129 Augustine, "On the Spirit and the Letter" 52, *NPNF* 1:5:106.

[130] Origen, *Commentary on Matthew* 13:28, *ANF* 10:491; see Gregory of Nyssa *GC* 23, *NPNF* 2:5:493 but John of Damascus, *EOF* 3:27, *NPNF* 2:9:72.

[131] Strong, *ST* 2:728ff.

[132] Erickson, *CT* 802ff.; see Wiley, *CT* 2:241-51.

[133] Kürger, *NSH* 1:9f.

[134] Zöckler, *NSH* 10:492.

[135] Schleiermacher, *CF* 425-38, 451-66; Bushnell, *VS* 1:482-523.

[136] Joyce, *ERE* 6:441f.

[137] Watson, *TI* 2:91-96.

[138] Gutiérrez, *TL* 53-59.

[139] Cone, *BTL* 17-45.

[140] Daly, *BGF* 180-198.

[141] Moltmann, *GC* 13-19.

CHAPTER

5

THE INDWELLING SPIRIT

SECTION I. THE ADMINISTRATOR OF GOD'S
GOVERNING AND REDEEMING
WORK

1. The Spirit, the Presence of God in the World
2. The Indwelling Spirit
3. The Spirit of God as a Distinct Person in the Godhead
4. The Revelation of the Triune God in the Three
   Biblical Eras
5. The Administrator of Salvation
6. The Christological Foundation of the Spirit's Work
7. The Spirit Works in Both the Church and the
   Individual

SECTION II. THE PROMISE OF THE HOLY
SPIRIT

1. Prophetic Promises of the Spirit
2. John the Baptist: A Greater Baptism
3. Promises of the Coming Spirit in Jesus' Teaching

SECTION III. THE GIFT OF THE HOLY SPIRIT
TO THE CHURCH

1. The Gift of the Spirit to the Church as a Whole
2. The Gift of the Spirit to Each Person in the Church

SECTION I. *The Administrator of God's Governing and Redeeming Work*

1. THE SPIRIT, THE PRESENCE OF GOD IN THE WORLD

Jesus, the Historical Presence of God in Human Flesh

When the Son of God became incarnate in Jesus of Nazareth, God entered the world physically in one person. Jesus is both truly God and truly man. But as a historical person Jesus could live in only one location and in a given era. Since His ascension the man Jesus has no longer been with us as the visible Son.

The Enduring Presence of God in Spirit and Creation

But God has always been present to the world and to the human race in the Holy Spirit. First, God relates to the entire world, animate or inanimate, sensate or insensate. In the creation story, the statement that "the Spirit of God was hovering over the waters" (Genesis 1:2) suggests God's creative presence in the world through the Holy Spirit. At no time in its existence has creation been self-sustaining, for immediately upon its creation and from that time on God's Spirit has been here to sustain it (see Job 26:13).[1]

But God relates to human beings, among all His creatures, in a special way. The creation account gives special attention to the fact that humans receive life from God (2:7). Adam began to live when God breathed into Him (Genesis 2:7; see 6:3 and Job 33:4). The psalmist extends this idea and says that all creatures owe their physical lives to the Spirit's ever-renewing work (104:30).[2] But human beings consciously recognize God's presence. As the psalmist observed, "Where can I go from your Spirit? Where can I flee from your presence?" (Psalms 139:7) The universal testimony that people everywhere are aware of a divine being can be explained only by saying that God makes Himself universally known through His Spirit.

2. THE INDWELLING SPIRIT

The Spirit of God penetrates into the interior space of human beings and indwells Christians (Romans 8:9). The Spirit lives in us as in a habitation. In fact, since Christians are to serve God, their bodies are the temples of the Spirit (1 Corinthians 3:16).

This interpersonal intimacy has no equivalent. We cannot know the thoughts of others (1 Corinthians 2:11). But the Spirit, who knows the deep things of God (1 Corinthians 2:10), also searches our hearts (Romans 8:27).

The Spirit of God as the Breath of God

The scriptural words for the Spirit are full of significance. The Hebrew word *ruah*, the Greek word *pneuma*, as well as the Latin word *spiritus*, from which the English word derives, have the same range of meanings: wind, breath, and the spirit of a human or the Spirit of God (John 3:8; Acts 2:1-3). When used of God the term "Spirit" signifies the invisible God working and revealing His presence in the world and dealing with people at a deep interior level.[3]

Quenching the Spirit

Since the Spirit of God indwells and speaks from within the human being, all spiritual transactions are first of all inward. Through the Spirit we are made aware of God's inner voice. We cannot escape the call of God, even when we try.

When we engage in sin, that sin begins in the heart. All sins come from within (Mark 7:20-23) as we walk away from the leading of the inner Spirit of God. When we resist God, we resist first in the heart: We quench the Spirit (1 Thessalonians 5:19) or lie to the Spirit (Acts 5:3) or test the Spirit (Acts 5:9). We suppress or defy the inner prompting of God's Spirit.[4]

3. THE SPIRIT OF GOD AS A DISTINCT PERSON IN THE GODHEAD

Israel had fought for the belief that God is spirit and cannot even be represented by an image (Exodus 20:4-6). The battle with pagan mythologies and idolatries was intense, and Israel's lapses into Baalism were frequent, as the Old Testament attests. But by the time of Christ, the battle was long finished and belief in God's spirituality was firmly held among all Jewish peoples.[5]

The Christian doctrine of the Holy Spirit, however, advances the issue an additional step. This doctrine specifically teaches that the Holy Spirit is not only an aspect of God's character (see John 4:24) but also a Person within the Godhead.[6]

It would be incorrect to claim that Christian teaching on the Holy Spirit contradicts the Old Testament. Rather, what is somewhat hidden and undeveloped in the Old Testament is made plain in the New Testament.[7]

4. THE REVELATION OF THE TRIUNE GOD IN THE THREE BIBLICAL ERAS

The historic church has taught that the Father, Son and Holy Spirit were each active during the entire biblical time. We cannot state that the Old Testament is the era of the Father only, the Gospels of the Son only, and the time of the early church of the Spirit only.

However, God has revealed Himself distinctly in each era, so some demarcation is called for. The revelation of God as triune, three-in-one, arose through three historical eras as a divine pedagogy of the human race. Through gradual and developing education, God taught us about His triune nature.[8]

The foundation for the doctrine of God's oneness or unity lies in the Old Testament. The Old Testament sharply distinguishes its understanding of God from the polytheism and idolatry of Israel's neighbors (Deuteronomy 6:4; see Exodus 20:3).

During the life of Jesus of Nazareth, clear knowledge of the Son of God was revealed through the incarnate Word. In Jesus God was united to man in one person and became directly accessible through His material presence. Jesus of

Nazareth brought a new dimension to our understanding of God as both Father and Son, though one.

But full Trinitarian thought came during the era of the early church. After Jesus' ascension the living presence of God was known through the indwelling Spirit and the work He accomplished through the church. The Acts of the Apostles bears abundant witness to this.[9]

Knowledge of God's Spirit came early in the process of revelation. This knowledge pervades every part of Old and New Testaments. But clear articulation of the relation between the Spirit and the Father and the Son was not worked out until after Pentecost made the issue clear. Nevertheless, New Testament writers who teach us about the Spirit used the teachings of the Old Testament and Jesus.[10]

5. THE ADMINISTRATOR OF SALVATION

The overwhelming emphasis within the Scriptures falls on the work of the Spirit as the divine Person who works internally within God's people to perform His redeeming work. The key note here is God's superintendence through the Spirit in the grand scheme of salvation. Thus the Spirit's work is multifaceted.[11] He:

- inspired the prophets (Ezekiel 2:2) whose messages became Scripture (2 Peter 1:20f.);
- convicts of sin (John 16:8-11);
- renews with spiritual life (John 3:3-8);
- assures of adoption as God's child (Romans 8:15f.);
- enables us to obey God (Romans 8:4);
- directs us to know God's will (Acts 10:19);
- grants the graces of Christian life (Galatians 5:22f.);
- distributes spiritual gifts to the church (1 Corinthians 12:7-11);
- guides the church when it makes decisions (Acts 15:28).

The Spirit and the Plan of Salvation

The plan of salvation unfolds logically. This is so whether we look at it from the divine side within the mind of God (Ephesians 1:4ff.) or from its execution within history (Romans 8:29f.). And each Person in the Trinity has a principal role in the order of salvation: The Father initiates and sends, the Son comes and mediates, and the Spirit administers and applies.

In the classic Christian view, each Person of the Godhead shares in all the works of God. Thus, the Scriptures interchange the Persons of the Trinity as the subjects of saving action. The Father sanctifies (John 17:17), Jesus Christ sanctifies (1 Corinthians 1:2), and so does the Spirit (Romans 15:16). We are born anew of the Spirit (John 3:5f.) and born of God (1 John 3:9; 4:7). The Spirit intercedes for us (Romans 8:26f.), as does our high priest, Jesus (Hebrews 7:25). The interchange of Persons arises because the achieving of salvation and the unfolding of the plan of salvation are complex and many-faceted. The interchange is also accounted for by the fact that God is one and God is three; He is the triune God.

The Holy Spirit, the Spirit of God and the Spirit of Christ

Since the Spirit administers the plan of the Father for the world and the saving ministry of Jesus, His name is frequently linked with theirs. He may be called the Spirit of God (Matthew 3:16), the Spirit of Christ (Romans 8:9), or the Spirit of the Lord (Acts 8:39). Thus, the indwelling and ever-present Spirit works within the world and within people to accomplish divine goals.

6. THE CHRISTOLOGICAL FOUNDATION OF THE SPIRIT'S WORK

Christian teaching clearly bases the work of the Spirit on the person and work of Christ. There is a strong christological foundation for Christian Pneumatology (the teaching on the Spirit of God).[12]

The assurance that the Spirit gives us that we are children of God is founded upon the fact that we are joint heirs with Christ (Romans 8:16f.). The peace of an absolved conscience arises from the atoning work of Jesus' death (Hebrews 9:14). Our new life arises from our baptism into Christ, a baptism of death to sin and a raising to a new pattern of living (Romans 6:1-4). Our "attitude should be the same as that of Christ Jesus" (Philippians 2:5).

This implies more than that we should simply use Jesus' life as a model. Instead, it suggests that Christ's life, death, and resurrection establish the foundation for the Christian's life, death and resurrection. Because of Christ, the Last Adam, there are Christians who are reborn and obedient sons and daughters of God through the Spirit. What happened first in Him, now happens in us. "The first man Adam became a living being; the last Adam, a life-giving spirit" (1 Corinthians 15:45).

In Christ

The Scriptures can describe this christological foundation as an intimate relationship between Christians and Christ. Jesus told His disciples to remain (*meno*) in Him for spiritual life and fruitfulness (John 15:1-8). Paul speaks of being "in Christ" (Ephesians 1:11-14) or "with Christ" (Colossians 3:1-4). In bold language Paul says: I have been crucified with Christ, and I no longer live, but Christ lives in me" (Galatians 2:20a). This statement does not confuse the lines between the human person and the historical Jesus. The next statement clarifies that point: "The life I live in the body, I live by faith in the Son of God who loved me and gave himself for me" (2:20b.). The transformed life of the Christian results from the indwelling Spirit's work, and this is based on the saving life and work of Christ: Christ, the atoning Sacrifice; Christ, the Victor; and Christ, the Second Adam becomes the foundation and source of Christian redemption. The Holy Spirit effects within us the saving work of Christ.

7. THE SPIRIT WORKS IN BOTH THE CHURCH AND THE INDIVIDUAL

There are two foci to the work of the Spirit in God's people, He works in the church and He works in individual Christians. These two are inextricably united. The health and the growth of the church occurs through individual people within it; but people become and grow as Christians through the church. That is, there is a symbiosis of the two. A church that is filled with people who walk in the Spirit is a healthy church; and the church is the sphere in which God teaches us to walk in the Spirit within the body of Christ. Particular Scriptures may focus on the Spirit's work in the church or in individual Christians, but only together do they represent the sphere of the Spirit's work.

However, we do speak of a priority of the Spirit's work within the church.[13] This arises from the evangelizing and nurturing ministry of the church. We become Christians as we respond to the message the church proclaims, and we grow as Christians through the instruction and support the church gives. In turn, the Spirit enables the church to carry on the task given it by Christ so there will be more Christians who in turn build up the church.

SUMMARY: *The Administrator of God's Governing and Redeeming Work*

1. The Spirit is the sustainer of the material world and the giver of life to all creatures.

2. The Spirit is the invisible presence of God in our world, administering God's governing and redeeming work and making God's presence known.

3. The Spirit of God deals with us from within. He reveals God to the inner person and indwells the Christian. The breath of God, the Spirit, is not confined to space. When we yield to God, we yield to the promptings of His Spirit; and when we resist God, we resist the promptings of His Spirit.

4. Though the Spirit has always been at work, His personhood was not fully recognized until the time of the early church. This is a result of the divine pedagogy, which taught first about God's spirituality and oneness, then about the Son, and then about the Spirit.

5. The work of the Spirit is firmly grounded in the work of Christ. The Spirit's work in assuring, delivering and sanctifying the Christian is founded upon Christ and His life, ministry, death and resurrection.

6. Christian teaching has emphasized the work of the Spirit among God's people. He grants spiritual life to God's people and equips and enables them to do the work that God has assigned them. The Spirit administers and applies the work of God in the church and in individual lives.

SECTION II. *The Promise of the Holy Spirit*

1. PROPHETIC PROMISES OF THE SPIRIT

Peter said of the Spirit's coming on the day of Pentecost, "This is what was spoken by the prophet Joel" (Acts 2:16). His words imply a common belief of the Jews that in the last days God would send His Spirit in a fashion quite distinct from anything Israel had experienced before.

Three Old Testament prophets – Isaiah, Ezekiel and Joel – specifically speak of a future work of the Spirit, which the New Testament describes as fulfilled in Jesus and the church. These prophecies build upon Israel's experience when God sent the Spirit to equip leaders and to give them spiritual life.

Isaiah: The Spirit in the Messiah

Two of Isaiah's prophecies spoke of the Spirit's coming, which Jesus and the New Testament church saw as fulfilled in Jesus Himself. The prophet described an outpouring of the Spirit on the Messiah.

Isaiah 11:1-9 presented the future Messiah as endowed by the Spirit: "The Spirit of the LORD will rest on him" (11:2a). The specific task of the Spirit in this case was to equip the Messiah with the gifts that would enable Him to govern with skill and righteousness. Thus, the Spirit would endow the Messiah with wisdom, understanding, counsel, power, knowledge and the fear of the Lord (11:2b-3a). Because the Messiah would possess these necessary qualities, He would be able to judge with perfect equity so that the cause of the needy and poor would be met, judgment would fall on the wicked and tranquillity and peace would prevail on the earth (11:3b-9).

Much later the prophet spoke again of an endowment by the Spirit of God: "the Spirit of the Sovereign LORD is on me" (61:1a). The Spirit's anointing would lead to the proclamation of good news: to the poor, the brokenhearted, captives, prisoners and those who mourn (61:1b-2). Jesus explicitly referred this passage to Himself when He read the Scriptures in the synagogue in Nazareth (Luke 4:21).

Ezekiel: The Spirit and a New Heart

Ezekiel took up the question of obedience to God's law. He dealt with the question of the interior part of the human as the wellspring of moral action.

Ezekiel depended on Jeremiah's earlier discussion of Israel's persistent disobedience (Jeremiah 31:31-34). The ancestors of Israel had repeatedly broken the covenant made on Sinai, and Jeremiah said that the people would obey only after God made a new covenant with them, writing this law on the tablets of their hearts. Only when the law was interiorized would the people really obey God.

Ezekiel advanced to greater clarity the theme of a change of heart by specifically introducing the Holy Spirit. After giving new life to the people and returning them from exile (see 37:1-14), God would bestow additional blessings so that they would obey Him (Ezekiel 36:24ff.). The last of the additional acts was to be the following: He would put the Spirit within His people and move them to "follow [His] decrees and be careful to keep [His] laws" (36:27). Thus, the interior presence of God's Spirit would give them spiritual energy to obey God's law.

Joel: The Spirit of Witness

A final promise found in Joel concerns the gift of the Spirit to equip the people of God for their work as witnesses (Joel 2:28-32). The unique element here that advances it over the other prophecies in the Old Testament is the extent of this gift. Historically prophets were selected, called, and empowered by God to speak generally to the people of God. Therefore, only a few received the Spirit. But at the last days, Joel prophesied, God would send His Spirit upon all His servants: sons and daughter, young men and old men, men and women (2:28f.). As a result of this gift, they all would prophesy, dream dreams, and see visions.

2. JOHN THE BAPTIST: A GREATER BAPTISM

John the Baptist compared his baptism with that of the one who would follow him (Matthew 3:11f.; Mark 1:7f.;

Luke 3:15-18). He did not impugn his own work but recognized that it was limited: He could not transform the heart. But the one who would follow him was to be mightier and more worthy than he (Matthew 3:11), and His baptism would be superior to John's. He would baptize with the Holy Spirit, not simply in water (Mark 1:8). This Coming One would have the authority to bestow God's indwelling presence.

3. PROMISES OF THE COMING SPIRIT IN JESUS' TEACHING

Jesus clearly promised that the Holy Spirit would come only after His own ministry was completed. Some of His sayings are general in nature (Luke 11:13; John 7:37-39). Another saying deals with Jesus' teaching on the apocalypse, the revelation of the end of time. He warned His followers that among their trials they would be brought before various tribunals. No human preparation would be adequate for that time, but they should not worry. "Say whatever is given you in that hour," He taught, "for it is not you who speak, but the Holy Spirit" (Mark 13:11; see Matthew 10:19f.; Luke 21:14f.).

But Jesus gave His most detailed teaching on the Spirit in the final hours with His disciples. This is recorded in John 14-16.

The Gospel According to John: The Paraclete

In the last hours before His crucifixion Jesus told the disciples of the Paraclete – the Counselor or Comforter – one whom He would send and who would in fact take His place (John 14:15-17, 26; 15:26f.; 16:5-15). Two terms for the Spirit appear in the passages, "the Counselor" and "the Spirit of truth".

The Greek word *parakletos*, translated both "Comforter" (AV) and "Counselor" (NIV), literally means "one who is called beside [another]." Jesus said that though the disciples grieved at His imminent departure (16:6), it was good that

He should go. The Counselor could not come until such a time. But when that had taken place, the Spirit would come (16:7). And when the Spirit had come, He would live with them and would be in them (14:17). The term *parakletos* suggests, then, that the Spirit is a kind of surrogate for Jesus, somewhat like a legal representative or advocate. Further, there is an advantage in the Spirit's representing God because of the universality of that presence. The Spirit can be everywhere and always present with God's people.

Second, He is called the Spirit of truth because He would testify to the truth. That is, He would bring knowledge of divine things. The Spirit would witness to the disciples, who accepted Him, elaborating and explaining the things Jesus had said to them while He was with them (14:26). He would also enlarge their understanding of Jesus (15:26; 16:14). Thus, He would guide them into all truth (16:13). He would also witness to the world, which would not accept Him (14:17), by convicting it of sin, righteousness and judgment (16:8-11). Truth is that which corresponds to reality; and the term "Spirit of truth" suggests, then, that the Spirit would be responsible for spiritual illumination of believers. Through the Spirit, God can awaken in our minds understandings that have spiritual significance. This is true of those who believe and those who do not.

The Gospel According to Luke: The Promise of the Father

Luke's account of Jesus' promise of the Spirit dealt rather specifically with the missionary task of Jesus' followers after His departure. Luke reported that after the Resurrection and before the Ascension, Jesus gave His disciples instructions about the Spirit (Luke 24:48f.; Acts 1:4f., 8). These contained both a promise and specific directions.

The disciples' large task was to be witnesses (Luke 24:48; Acts 1:8). Before they could carry out that assignment, however, they needed power, namely the divine help given them by the Holy Spirit's coming upon them (Acts 1:8). Therefore, they were to wait in Jerusalem until they were clothed with power (Luke 1:49; see Acts 1:4), as promised by the Father (see Joel 2:28ff.).

SUMMARY: *The Promise of the Holy Spirit*

1. The teaching of the early church on the Spirit began with the promise of three Old Testament prophets plus John the Baptist and Jesus, all saying that in the last days God would pour out His Holy Spirit in an unprecedented way.

2. Isaiah, Ezekiel and Joel specifically addressed the future work of the Spirit. Isaiah said that the Spirit would come on the future Messiah, empowering Him for His governing and preaching work. Ezekiel said that God would put the Spirit within the hearts of His people so that they would obey His law. Joel said that God would pour the Spirit on all of His servants, young and old, men and women, to share in the work of prophecy.

3. John the Baptist, referring to Jesus, said that the one who would follow him would have a greater ministry of baptism than he did, because Jesus would baptize with the Holy Spirit.

4. Jesus taught His disciples that after His departure the Holy Spirit would come. He would be the Paraclete, the personal presence of God in place of Jesus' human presence. He would be the Spirit of truth to guide the disciples into all truth. And in the world He would convict those who did not believe. He would give the disciples the power to witness to Jesus, as He had commissioned them to.

SECTION III. *The Gift of the Holy Spirit to the Church*

The New Testament describes the gift of the Holy Spirit to the church in two different ways. The first treats the outpouring of the Spirit upon the entire church at one particular point in time. This "coming" functions as an initiating event. The second treats the giving of the Spirit to new Christians. As they come into the church through faith and baptism, they are each to receive the gift that properly belongs to the whole church.[14]

1. THE GIFT OF THE SPIRIT TO THE CHURCH AS A WHOLE

John: Jesus Breathed on His Disciples

John reports that in a certain respect the disciples were given the Holy Spirit at Jesus' meeting with them on the day of resurrection (John 20:19-22). After Jesus calmed their fears and commissioned them, He breathed on them saying: "Receive the Holy Spirit" (20:22). This giving of the Spirit anticipated His full outpouring on the day of Pentecost.[15]

Luke: The Day of Pentecost

Luke described this event (Acts 2:1ff.). He stated: "All of them were filled with the Holy Spirit and began to speak in other tongues as the Spirit enabled them" (2:4).

All of Them Were Filled. The Spirit was given to all of Jesus' followers who were in Jerusalem. The gift was not simply for the apostles who were to lead the church or any other select group of people, such as men as a class. Preceding the day of Pentecost and in obedience to Jesus' instruction, the disciples all joined together in prayer (Acts 2:4; see 1:13f.), so they were together when the Holy Spirit was poured out on the day of Pentecost (2:1). This, said Peter, fulfilled the prophecy of Joel (2:2ff.; Acts 2:16-18). Thus, the Spirit came upon the entire church.

The Holy Spirit came with phenomenal evidence: sound, sight and result (Acts 2:2-4). The sound was that of a violent wind and reminds us of the very meaning of the Hebrew and Greek words for "spirit". The sight was that of tongues of fire, separated and sitting individually on the heads of those present. This suggests the judging and refining work of redemption (Matthew 3:11f.; see Malachi 3:1-4). The prophesying in various tongues refers to the Spirit's enablement of the church to witness effectively to all peoples.

The Gift of Languages, The Reversal of Babel. The gift of languages enabled non-Aramaic-speaking pilgrims in Jerusalem to understand in their own languages the disciples' witness to Jesus (Acts 2:5-12). Historic Christianity has explained this gift as a reversal of God's judgment at Babel (Genesis 11:1-9). Recall that to prevent the nations from building a tower that would enable them to ascend to heaven, God confused their language so they could not understand one another. As a reversal, to enable the pilgrims in Jerusalem to understand the message of Jesus, God granted the gift of understandable tongues.[16] The judgment at Babel created disunity because of sinfulness; the gift at Pentecost brought harmony for the praise and honor of God (see Revelation 7:9f.).

The Revelation of God to the Nations, The New Sinai. In Judaism, Pentecost was the great festival that followed Passover and celebrated the giving of the Law at Sinai.[17] Rabbinic tradition states that the 70 nations of the world were at Sinai when Moses was given the Law, but only Israel received it.[18] Since that time, Jewish tradition says, the nations have been without knowledge of God and His will except for those who have become proselytes to Judaism. The eschatological hope of Israel was that knowledge of God and obedience to Him would become universal (Isaiah. 11:9; 45:18-25). In Christianity, Pentecost celebrates the gift of the Spirit who enables the church to proclaim the message of Jesus to all peoples.[19]

2. THE GIFT OF THE SPIRIT TO EACH PERSON IN THE CHURCH

Various authors within the New Testament witness that all who become Christians receive the Holy Spirit. The gift was not just for the first disciples then or for only present day leaders now, but for all. A Christian, by definition, is someone in whom the Spirit dwells. As Paul says: "If anyone does not have the Spirit of Christ, he does not belong to Christ" (Romans 8:9). The idea that each Christian has received the Spirit is implied in such passages as Galatians 3:2; Ephesians 1:13; Hebrews 6:4; 1 Peter 4:14; and 1 John 3:24 and 4:13.

Luke's Account of Conversions in the Early Church. Luke reports consistently that those who heard the witness of the church and responded with faith received the Spirit. In his sermon on the day of Pentecost Peter said to his listeners that they should repent and be baptized in the name of Jesus, and they would "receive the gift of the Holy Spirit." God had promised this to them, their children, and all who would call on the name of the Lord (Acts 2:38f.). Though the precise relation between repentance, faith, baptism, the laying on of hands, and the gift of the Holy Spirit can vary so far as time and sequence are concerned Luke describes these as factors in conversion and reception into the church (see Acts 8:12-17; 9:17f.; 10:44-48; 19:1-7).[20]

The Witness of the Spirit. Jesus taught His disciples to pray to God as Father (Luke 11:2). He taught that through faith in Christ we are given the right to become God's children (John 1:12f.). The Spirit effects this new birth (John 3:6) and also assures us of our new relationship to God as His children. Thus, the Spirit is the Spirit of adoption or sonship. He witnesses to our spirits. That is, He gives us an inner assurance that we are God's children. Through Him we cry, "*Abba*, Father," and thus receive the witness (Romans 8:14-16; Galatians 4:6).

Early Christian Confessions. No one says, "Jesus is Lord," (1 Corinthians 12:3) or confesses that Jesus Christ has come in the flesh (1 John 4:2f.) except through the Spirit. The public confession of Jesus was an important and costly part of conversion in early Christianity (Romans 10:8-10). Those who paid the personal cost, did so because they were persuaded that Christianity was true. The Spirit brought about this inner persuasion.

SUMMARY: *The Gift of the Holy Spirit to the Church*

1. In fulfillment of His promise, God sent His Spirit upon the early church after the ministry of Jesus was completed. The gift of the Spirit in the life of the church came in two respects: First, at Pentecost, the Spirit was poured out upon the waiting disciples generally as an initial and constitutive event. Second, the Spirit was given to each new person who believed and in doing so the person was made a member of the church.

2. The gift of the Spirit to the church in general came in two successive events: First, before His ascension, Jesus breathed on His disciples and said, "Receive the Spirit." This was symbolic and anticipatory. Second, on the day of Pentecost, the Spirit was poured out on all believers in Jerusalem who were together in prayer.

3. The coming of the Spirit on the day of Pentecost was attended with physical signs and the gift of languages. This event symbolized the reversal of God's judgment at Babel. It is also celebrated as an event in the life of the church corresponding to the giving of the Law at Sinai.

4. Each person who has come into genuine faith in Christ and His church since the day of Pentecost has also received the Spirit. Those who belong to

Christ, by definition, have the Spirit of Christ (Romans 8:9).

5. Luke includes the gift of the Spirit to new converts as a part of their story of conversion. Those who make an authentic Christian confession, through which they are converted, can do so only by the Spirit. And the Spirit witnesses to them that they are God's children. They cry, "*Abba*, Father."

SECTION IV. *The Ministry of the Spirit, J.: The Source of Enablement for Ministry*

The Holy Spirit works within the people of God to accomplish two things: to give them spiritual life and to equip them for the ministry He has for them.

The second of these has to do with the larger ministry of the church. The Spirit enables the people of God to carry on their God-given tasks. During the Old Testament era, this part of the Spirit's work focused on those in leadership, such as judges, kings and prophets. But within the New Testament era the work of the Spirit's ministry noticeably spread to all within the church. Everyone had an indispensable task to accomplish whether it was one of leadership or not. Therefore, the Spirit was poured out on all the church, so that all could perform the particular tasks that they individually had been given.

1. THE SPIRIT'S WORK DURING THE OLD TESTAMENT ERA

The Old Testament's most prominent presentation of the Spirit concerned His enablement of Israel's leaders to carry out their various tasks. In Moses' time, the Spirit of God filled Bezalel with artistic skill so that he could successfully make the tabernacle and its furniture and tools (Exodus 31:3). The Spirit that had rested on Moses was given to the 70 elders chosen to assist him in judicial work (Numbers

11:17, 25). Also, later the Spirit came on the judges so that they could deliver Israel from its oppressors (Judges 3:10; 11:29). Saul (1 Samuel 11:6) and especially David (1 Samuel 16:13) were anointed with the Spirit for their kingly roles, though Saul's disobedience led to the Spirit's departing from him (1 Samuel 16:14). And the Spirit's movings and enablings are mentioned by and of the prophets (Ezekiel 2:2; Micah 3:8; Zechariah 4:6; 2 Kings 2:9, 15f.).

2. THE SPIRIT AND JOHN THE BAPTIST

When the angel Gabriel announced John's coming miraculous birth to Zechariah, his father, he indicated the child would "be filled with the Holy Spirit even from birth" (Luke 1:15, see 1:5-25; 41). Thus, John was enabled, as were the prophets of old, to fulfill his mission (1:17).

3. THE SPIRIT'S DESCENT ON JESUS AT HIS BAPTISM

The account of Jesus' baptism and the Spirit's descent upon Him at that time offers an important insight into the relation of Jesus and the Spirit. John baptized Jesus, along with many others, in the Jordan. "When [Jesus] came up out of the water, immediately he saw the heavens opened and the Spirit descending upon him like a dove" (Mark 1:10; see Matthew 3:13ff.; Luke 3:21ff.; John 1:29ff.). There followed a voice from heaven that announced: "You are my Son; with you I am well pleased" (Mark 1:11).

Historic orthodoxy has explained that this descent of the Spirit endowed Jesus for the work He was to do as the Son of Man (see Acts 10:37f.; John 3:34).[21] It rejected the view, proposed by some heretics, that previous to this occasion Jesus was not the Son of God. Instead, it has taught that the baptism equipped Jesus for His public ministry.[22] His baptism was followed by His going into the wilderness, under the Spirit's direction. There His preparation continued through the 40 days of fasting and an attendant period of temptation (Matthew 4:1ff.; Mark 1:12f.; Luke 4:1ff.).

4. THE ASSISTANCE OF THE PRIMITIVE CHURCH

The New Testament makes many references to the Spirit's assisting the early church in fulfilling its work under trying circumstances. From the very beginning of the church, the Spirit played a significant role. Everyone within the church was expected to have the gift of the indwelling Spirit (see Acts 19:1-7), though being full of the Spirit was a necessary qualification for election to leadership (Acts 6:3; 13:4). Intimidation by Jewish leaders (Acts 4:8) or political powers (Acts 13:9) failed to silence Christians, because of the Spirit. When threatened, Christians prayed for divine assistance and "were all filled with the Holy Spirit and spoke the word of God boldly" (Acts 4:31). Also, the Spirit gave constant direction to the church, such as leading it on occasions when the proper course of action was difficult to discern (Acts 8:29; 16:6f.) or when a breakthrough in understanding God's will was required (Acts 10:19).

5. THE GIFTS OF THE SPIRIT

The New Testament speaks of the gifts of the Spirit to describe how God worked in equipping people for ministry (see Romans 12:3-8; 1 Corinthians 12-14; Ephesians 4:7-13; 1 Peter 4:10). A variety of ministry gifts were required because the church was a body. Healthy bodies must have various members or parts, each carrying out a function in order for the church to work properly (12:12-27). Thus, the Spirit distributes various gifts as He will to those within the church (12:7-11), for the good of the whole.[23]

The gifts of the Spirit may be looked at in different ways. Peter divides the gifts of the Spirit into two major categories, *to speak* or *to serve* (1 Peter 4:10). In one place Paul offered a list of gifts that emphasize certain tasks to be done in the church (Romans 12:3ff.). In another he identified positions or offices within the church to be filled (Ephesians 4:4:7ff.).

The crucial test of any gift is whether it edifies or builds up the church (1 Corinthians 14:1-5). Gifts are not for the celebration of one's personal spirituality or skill; they are grace gifts (*charismata*), given by the Spirit for the good of the whole church.

SUMMARY: *The Source of Enablement for Ministry*

1. The Holy Spirit works within the church to accomplish two things: to give spiritual life and to equip its members for the ministry He has for them.

2. During the Old Testament era, the Spirit was given to empower leaders: judges, kings and prophets. The gift at this time was not universally given to all the people of God.

3. The Spirit was particularly at work in the ministry of John the Baptist as he prepared the way for Jesus.

4. The Spirit descended upon Jesus at the time of His baptism empowering Him for His ministry as the Son of Man.

5. The primitive church was opposed by both Jewish and gentile authorities. In the face of this opposition, the Spirit gave the church boldness. When the church needed special guidance, the Spirit gave the help needed.

6. The Spirit continues to the present to provide for the church through the distribution of gifts. These gifts enable believers to fulfill their God-assigned tasks.

SECTION V. *The Ministry of the Spirit, &c.: The Source of Spiritual Life and Graces*

The Scriptures teach that the Holy Spirit is the source of spiritual life within humans. Before His renewing work, we are dead in our sins (Ephesians 2:1), and apart from His work we would remain dead.

Not only does the Spirit bring about new life, He also is the source of all spiritual graces. When Christians manifest such virtues as love or self-control, they do so because the Spirit is at work to create and nurture such graces within. The ability to overcome temptation and resist the power of sin also results from the Spirit's inner work.

In broad terms, the ministry of the indwelling Spirit of God brings about regeneration (the gift of new spiritual life) and sanctification (the shaping of our life and behavior after the model of Jesus).[24]

The saving work of Christ is administered by the Spirit. It is He who indwells and shapes Christians so that their lives conform increasingly to the Last Adam, Jesus Christ Himself. Paul wrote, "And we, who with unveiled faces all reflect the Lord's glory, are being transformed into his likeness with ever-increasing glory, which comes from the Lord, who is the Spirit" (2 Corinthians 3:18).

1. THE WITNESS OF THE OLD TESTAMENT

The Spirit as the Giver of Spiritual Life

The Old Testament rarely links the Holy Spirit specifically to the spiritual life of a person. But many Israelites had a vital relationship to God, as the Psalms confirm (see 23; 40:1-3; 62:1-2; 63). The idea that God's Spirit is essential for spiritual vitality is made explicit in one of the penitential psalms (Psalm 51). David begged God not to withdraw His Holy Spirit but to "restore to [him] the joy of salvation and grant [him] a willing spirit, to sustain [him]" (Psalms 51:11f.).

This passage explains the delicate relationship between the Spirit of God and the human spirit. God's Spirit effects the sense of spiritual well-being and enables the human spirit to remain faithful (see Ezekiel 36:27).

2. THE SPIRIT OF THE NEW BIRTH: REGENERATION

Historically, the church has taught that a decisive event occurs in the life of persons when God transforms them from being dead in sins to being alive in God. They now have spiritual life. The term for this, "regeneration", derives from several expressions found in the New Testament, such as born again (*paliggenesia*, Titus 3:5) and born anew or from above (*gennao anothen* or *anagennao*, John 3:3 and 1 Peter 2:23). Paul's description of a Christian in 2 Corinthians 5:17 as a new creation (*kaine ktisis*) is similar.

The Holy Spirit effects regeneration. He enters the interior space of humans and administers this wonderful change so that they have new life.[25]

John: The Spirit and the New Life

In conversation with Nicodemus (John 3:1-8), Jesus stated that one must be born again. This, He then explained, meant to be born of water (the ritual of baptism) and of the Spirit (3:5). The birth we have as humans is a natural birth, a birth of the flesh. The new birth which we need is a birth from God, made possible by the Spirit (3:8; see 6:35ff.).[26]

Apart from the renewing action of the Holy Spirit, we are dead in our sins. Jesus underscores the importance of this by stating the matter twice in slightly different forms. The first form, "Unless a man is born again, he cannot see the kingdom of God" (3:3), emphasizes the necessity of the new birth. The second, "Unless a man is born of water and the Spirit, he cannot enter the kingdom of God" (3:5), emphasizes the source of this new birth.

Paul: Renewal by the Holy Spirit

In Titus 3:5 Paul explicitly says the Spirit of God renews people who are dead in their sins. Here he links together several elements of this transformation. "[God] saved us through the washing of rebirth [*paliggenesia*] and renewal [*anakainosis*] by the Holy Spirit, whom he poured out on us generously through Jesus Christ our Savior." Paul mentions together baptism (the sacrament of entrance into the church), the grace granted through Jesus Christ (the energy of our regeneration), and the Holy Spirit (the agent of our regeneration). It is the Spirit who administers and effects the transformation so that we are reborn and renewed.

3. THE SPIRIT AND SANCTIFICATION

Sanctification is the action by which God separates people from a life of sin, separating them to Himself and a life of service. It encompasses the complex processes by which Christian character is formed and the resulting Christian behavior.

The entire work of sanctification has many aspects. Consider the major ones: The initiation came in the eternal plan of God (Ephesians 1:4). It was brought to the human race through the incarnation and sacrificial ministry of Jesus, the Perfect Man (Hebrews 2:10f.; 1 Corinthians 1:30). Sanctification is initiated in individual lives when persons become Christians through their saving relationship to Christ (1 Corinthians 6:11). That is, regeneration is sanctification begun. Christians are called to sanctify themselves, taking responsibility for purging out any remnants of sin (2 Corinthians 7:1) and offering themselves in full dedication to God (Romans 6:19; 12:1). A life of Christian fidelity can have a sanctifying effect on those close to believers (1 Corinthians 7:14). Sanctification is given concrete form when Christians obey God, living the life expected of them (1 Thessalonians 4:3-8; Hebrews 12:14). Finally, sanctification can reach a fulness and thoroughness through God's gracious work (1 Thessalonians 5:23).

The Sanctifying Spirit

As the Spirit is the Third Person of the Trinity who effects new life, so the Spirit is the Person who effects sanctification (1 Peter 1:2). The Spirit works in conjunction with the other Persons of the Trinity. As 1 Corinthians 6:11 states it: "But you were washed, you were sanctified, you were justified in the name of the Lord Jesus Christ and by the Spirit of our God."[27]

The Spirit of Freedom from the Law of Sin and Death

Understanding sanctification involves paying special attention to the Spirit's work in freeing Christians from a life of sin. The need for this lies in the enslaving power sin has over us. Normal human life follows a pattern of sin. The pattern is inevitable because of the subtle (James 1:13-15) and awesome power of sin (Romans 7:5-25). But the Scriptures say that the pattern is broken for Christians and should no longer characterize their lives (see Hebrews 12:1; 1 Peter 4:1-3; 1 John 3:7-10).

This change in behavior results from the liberating power of the Spirit. Romans 7:5-8:14 and Galatians 5:16-26 contrast living in the flesh and living in the Spirit. The flesh is weak and unable to overcome sin, because in the flesh we depend upon our own human strength. Even the gift of God's law, of itself, cannot enable us to overcome sin (Romans 8:3).[28] But the indwelling Spirit of God liberates us from this cycle of sin and death. "Through Christ Jesus the law of the Spirit of life has set me free from the law of sin and death" (Romans 8:2).[29]

Changes in behavior can occur then. We can walk or "live in the Spirit" and no longer do the works of the flesh (Galatians 5:16ff.). By the Spirit we can "put to death the misdeeds of the body" (Romans 8:13). We are led by the

Spirit (Romans 8:9) so that the "righteous requirements of the law might be fully met in us, who do not live according to the [flesh] but according to the Spirit" (Romans 8:4).[30]

4. THE SPIRIT AND THE GRACES OF A CHRISTIAN LIFE

A new way of living is made possible by the Spirit. Through Him the Christian graces can take shape within the person. Opposite a pattern of sin is a pattern of goodness.

Being Transformed into His Likeness

Jesus Christ established the pattern that Christians should follow. The Spirit of God does not lead us into uncharted territory but along the path that Jesus marked out (see Hebrews 12:2-3; 1 Peter 2:21-25; 1 John 2:6-8). The Last Adam sets the model for our lives, and the work of the Spirit enables progress in following the model. He mysteriously molds us to that pattern: "You show that you are a letter from Christ ... written not with ink but with the Spirit of the living God" (2 Corinthians 3:3). Thus we are "being transformed into [Christ's] likeness, with ever-increasing glory, which comes from the Lord, who is the Spirit" (2 Corinthians 3:18).

The Fruit of the Spirit

The Scriptures specifically identify the developing character and behavior of those who follow Christ. This appears in several lists of graces and deeds (2 Corinthians 6:6; Colossians 3:12-15; Galatians 5:22f.; 2 Peter 1:5-7).[31]

In one list, Paul called these graces collectively the "fruit of the Spirit" (Galatians 5:22f.). In concert with Jesus, he identified love as their summation (Mark 12:28ff.; 1 Corinthians 13; Romans 13:8-10; see 1 Peter 4:8; 1 John 3:16-24). Paul carefully chose the word "fruit" to signify the Spirit's life-giving role, since those who mature as Christians "walk in the Spirit" and follow the Spirit's leadership (see

Galatians 5:25). The Spirit enables; the Christian obeys. These graces are not humanly produced virtues nor Spirit-manipulated results.

5. THE SPIRIT OF PRAYER

Prayer is the most intensely spiritual of all activities. In this activity, people focus their attention upon God and converse with Him.

Because of prayer's very nature, however, we are less qualified for it than for any other activity. "We do not know what [or how] we ought to pray" (Romans 8:26). For this very reason, we need divine assistance in prayer.

In the very act of Christian prayer, the Spirit of God grants such assistance, interceding for us in ways that words cannot even express and drawing us into the deep things of God (Romans 8:26f.)

SUMMARY: *The Source of Spiritual Life and Graces*

1. The presence of the Holy Spirit within the Christian brings about a series of radical changes. A new pattern of life begins that is grounded in the indwelling presence of the Spirit.

2. The Old Testament testifies that there were people who knew a living relationship with God that arose from God's indwelling presence. Ezekiel testified that in the future God's Spirit would transform the inner life so that the people would obey the law of God.

3. The Spirit of God regenerates the inner life of believers, bringing them from spiritual death in sin to spiritual life. Through the Spirit they are given new spiritual life.

4. The Spirit sanctifies us, transforming our character. He frees us from the power of sin and calls us to consecrate our lives wholly to God. He enables us

to please and serve God. Those who live through His enablement will manifest the fruit and graces of the Spirit.

5. The Spirit assists us in prayer, the most intensely focused of all spiritual activities. He intercedes for us and draws us into the deep things of God.

SECTION VI. *Church Debates About the Spirit*

Debates about the Spirit across church history have focused on several large questions. How do we understand the Spirit in relation to the other Persons of the Trinity? How does the work of the Spirit relate to the institutional church and to the received, canonical Scriptures? Does the Spirit of God witness to us so that we are conscious of actually having to deal with God? Is there a fulness of the Spirit?

1. THE SPIRIT AND THE TRINITY

During the early centuries of the church, intense debates occurred on the place of the Spirit within the Trinity. A few contestants claimed that the Spirit was not a distinct person but only another way of describing God in terms of His activity. But this viewpoint never prevailed among more than a small minority.

The viewpoint of Eunomius and Macedonius, who were followers of Arius, was far more serious. They contended that the Spirit was a third-ranked divine being behind the Father and the Son. As a creation of the Son, He was not equal to either the Father or the Son. This position was condemned at the First Council of Constantinople (381).[32] The bishops of the Council enunciated the view that has become the historic one of the church in addition to the Creed of Nicea. It reads, "And I believe in the Holy Ghost, the Lord and Giver of Life Who proceedeth from the Father [and the Son]; Who with the Father and the Son together is worshipped and glorified."[33]

2. THE SPIRIT AND THE CHURCH
The Filioque Clause

A third historic debate concerned the procession of the Spirit. This debate has never been resolved and divides Eastern from Western Christianity to the present. According to the Eastern and older form of the Creed of Nicea, the Spirit is said to proceed "from the Father." In the Western form, the Spirit is said to proceed "from the Father and the Son." This debate concerns the relation of the Persons in the Trinity to one another both within the Trinity itself (the Eastern form) and the Trinity to the world (the Western form).[34] But it also concerns the foundation of the church.

A Pneumatological Foundation for the Church

There are two foundations for order within the church. The first bases the church on Christ, the second on the Spirit.

The Christological foundation for the church teaches that Christ instituted the church through His disciples. He appointed them as His successors in leadership and authority, and they in turn appointed their successors.

The pneumatological foundation for the church teaches that the Spirit, free of institutional forms, established and continues the church. He grants gifts of leadership to whom He will, and the church should recognize and follow His free movement.

Throughout the history of the church some have seen these two foundations for the church as in conflict. A church that emphasizes the christological basis may become rigid and hierarchical and suppress genuine spiritual vitality. A church that emphasizes the pneumatological basis may become unstable and volatile. Strong and gifted people may gain control of the church and lead it in almost any direction they choose.

The conflict is unnecessary. Christian orthodoxy has always emphasized that the work of the Spirit has a Christological basis. That is, it is the Spirit who gives life and vitality to the church, but the life the Spirit gives is the life of the ever-living Christ.

The Guidance of the Spirit and the Scriptures

Orthodoxy generally holds that the Spirit uniquely inspired the Scriptures that we recognize as canonical. Some have raised the question of whether the church can receive utterances from the Spirit that have the same authority as the biblical authors. During the late second century Montanus[35] criticized the church for suppressing prophetic utterances that he believed he spoke under the direction of the Spirit. He claimed for himself unique inspiration, making himself virtually equivalent in authority to Scripture authors. Montanus claimed that it was the Paraclete speaking through him.[36] In the 18th century George Fox, the founder of the Quaker movement, developed a different approach to the Spirit's enlightenment. Fox taught that an individual could find the will of God through the "Inner Light," which God gives to all and which was another form of revelation.[37]

Historic Christian teaching has rejected the view that the Spirit continues to give revelations that, in authority, can be set alongside the Scriptures.[38] The Spirit enlightens. The Spirit awakens to the meaning of the Scriptures. And the Spirit enables those who exposit and proclaim the truths of the Scriptures to do so with insight and power.[39] But the canon is closed and should not be challenged or weakened by claims that the Spirit continues to grant new revelations that may supersede or even equal the Scriptures.

3. THE SPIRIT AND CHRISTIAN SALVATION

A different debate concerns the initiative of the indwelling Spirit in bringing about Christian conversion and Christian living. The issue surfaced toward the beginning of the fifth century in the controversy between Augustine and Pelagius. This fundamental debate centered around the question: Is the action of the Spirit necessary for Christian salvation?

Pelagius taught that the crucial dynamic in Christian life was the determination, by the exercise of one's will, to obey God. He said humans could live without sin if they really wanted to. In his scheme, God's grace was limited. He taught that God forgave repentant sinners for their past sins. He also taught that God would give people new opportunities to obey Him. But he denied that God transformed people and gave them inner, spiritual assistance to live a new life. Repentance and a change of life came about from human effort.[40]

Augustine, on the other hand, argued that the will is so damaged and weakened by sin that we cannot obey God unless the Spirit works within to transform us. Any movement we make toward God arises only after God Himself has initiated a change.[41] We repent only when the Spirit of God moves us to repent.[42] And we love God and obey His will only as the Spirit moves and enables us to do so. We are commanded in the Scriptures to repent, love, and obey God, but these actions are made possible only by the Spirit. He secretly moves us and changes us from the inside so that we begin to hate the things we loved and love the things we hated.[43]

The issues raised in this debate are wide. At stake were questions about the depth of the roots of sin's and the degree to which God intervenes to set us on the right course. The results of this debate have left a permanent mark on Christian theology, especially in the West: Pelagius' views were repudiated. It is generally held that a change from rebellion and sin can occur only because the indwelling Spirit of God moves us toward change and gives us new life and energy to love and obey God.

4. THE SPIRIT OF WITNESS

Historic Christianity has taught that all Christians may know the presence of the indwelling Spirit. But the Enlightenment and the rationalistic approach it advocated cast doubt on this teaching. It doubted whether one could consciously experience the presence of God. In the 18th century, when the Enlightenment was in full bloom, John Wesley responded to this challenge. He taught that normal Christian experience included the Spirit's witness.[44]

Classic Christian thinkers have freely acknowledged that the teaching on the Christian experience of the Holy Spirit is a towering claim. They did not make the claim lightly. But with sober wonder the Christian church has historically taught that the Sovereign of the universe dwells within the hearts of finite and weak people through His Spirit. Through the Spirit He speaks to them so that they consciously know they are dealing with Him, and they are His children. The church has also taught that this communion with God can grow. It will reach its summation in the communion that awaits us after this life.

5. THE FULNESS OF THE SPIRIT

A persistent debate within Christendom concerns the degree to which a person can grow in sanctity within the present life. Some point to the limitations inherent in this life, saying that sin will always be our nemesis and cannot be mastered in this world. Others are more optimistic, not about human nature in itself but about the possibilities of God's grace. They teach an optimism of grace.[45]

The Scriptures set an ideal before us of a Christian life that is higher than the typical (Philippians 3:12-15).[46] The actual source of this cannot be in human resources; it must reside in the enabling work of the Spirit. The Spirit frees us from bondage to sin (Romans 8:3) and is the source of love (Romans 5:5). Thus, to reach the level held before us we are urged to be "filled with the Spirit" (Ephesians 5:18).

The Evidence of the Spirit's Presence

The fruit of the Spirit (Galatians 5:22f.) to some degree invariably attends the work of God within the human life. We may not point to some particular gift, say to prophecy or healing, and claim it as the evidence of the Spirit's ministry in us (1 Corinthians 12:7-11). But evidence of His fruit should be present in every Christian. In particular the evidence of fulness is the presence of love, the most excellent way (1 Corinthians 13). If we love, we live in God and God in us, and through this are made complete in love (1 John 4:13-18).[47]

SUMMARY: *Church Debates About the Spirit*

1. The historic church has firmly stated the belief that the Holy Spirit is a distinct Person within the Holy Trinity and of equal glory and substance with the Father and the Son.
2. The church has two foundations, a Christological one in the historical ministry of Jesus and His disciples and a pneumatological one in the ministry of the Spirit. The Christological foundation gives the church stability and continuity, the pneumatological foundation gives it vitality and freshness.
3. The guidance that the Spirit gives is always consistent with the Scriptures. The Spirit never grants a revelation that replaces the teachings of the Scriptures.
4. The awakening and energizing work of the Spirit is essential for spiritual life and growth. No one comes to God or grows in the Christian life apart from the

indwelling Spirit's work of regeneration and sanctification.

5. The indwelling Spirit of God witnesses with people in a way they can recognize. All Christians may receive the witness of the Spirit to their salvation and to God's ruling presence.

6. Christians should seek the fulness of the Spirit, which can move them to deep spiritual sanctity. The true sign of the Spirit's fulness is profound Christlike love.

ENDNOTES

[1] Cyril of Jerusalem, *CL* 16:4, *NPNF* 2:7:4.

[2] Eichrodt, *TOT* 2:47-50.

[3] Pope, *CCT* 2:329-31.

[4] Ambrose, *On the Spirit* 3:9, *NPNF* 2:10:143f.

[5] Novak, *JCD* 36-41.

[6] Gregory of Nazianzus, *TO* 5:1-12, *NPNF* 2:7:318-22; Wiley, *CT* 2:304f.

[7] Augustine, *CG* 7:32, *NPNF* 1:11:140f.; *Lectures on the Gospel According to St. John* 45:9; *NPNF* 1:7:252.

[8] Gregory of Nazianzus, *TO* 5:25-30, *NPNF* 2:7:325-328; Pope, *CCT* 2:101-05.

[9] Wiley, *ST* 2:305f.

[10] Fletcher, "The Portrait of St. Paul" II, *WJF* 3:166-69; Hogue, *HS* 52-70; Wood, *PG* 107-09; Oden, *LG* 209-12.

[11] Oden, *LS* 31-75.

[12] Fletcher, "Portrait of St. Paul" III.VIf., *WJF* 3:211-213; Barrett, *HSGT* 137.

[13] Snyder, *CK* 73f.

[14] Fletcher, "The Portrait of St. Paul" II, *WJF* 3:184-97.

[15] Chrysostom, *Homily 86 on John*, *NPNF* 1:14:325; Wesley, *ENNT* 271.

[16] Hilary, *Trin.* 25, *NPNF* 2:9:144.

[17] Moore, *Jud.* 2:48.

[18] Moore, *Jud.* 1:278.

[19] Cyril of Jerusalem, *CL* 17:15, *NPNF* 2:7:128; Bruce, *CBA* 59-61.

[20] McCown, "The Spirit in the Book of Acts," *SNA* 111-114.

[21] Barrett, *HSGT* 44f.

[22] Deasley, "Entire Sanctification and the Baptism with the Holy Spirit," *WTJ* 14:32f.

[23] Snyder, *CK* 76-96.

[24] Cannon, *TJW* 213f.

[25] Lyon, "Baptism and Spirit Baptism in the New Testament," *WTJ* 14:17-22.

[26] Gregory of Nyssa, *On the Holy Spirit*, *NPNF* 2:5:322; Wesley, Sermon 19, "The Great Privilege of Those That are Born of God" I, *WJWB* 1:432-35; Sermon 45, "The New Birth" I-II, *WJWB* 2:188-94.

[27] Ambrose, *On the Spirit* 1:5, *NPNF* 2:10:101.

[28] Wesley, Sermon 9, "The Spirit of Bondage and of Adoption" II, *WJWB* 1:255-60.

[29] Wesley, Sermon 9, "The Spirit of Bondage and of Adoption" III, *WJWB* 1:260-63.

[30] Wesley, Sermon 8, "The First-fruits of the Spirit" I, *WJWB* 1:235-37.

[31] Turner, *VT* 144-45.

[32] Canon one in *NPNF* 2:14:172; Gregory of Nyssa, *On the Holy Spirit*, *NPNF* 2:5:315-25; Ambrose, *On the Holy Spirit* 1:2f., *NPNF* 2:10:97-100.

[33] *CC* 2:59.

[34] Dayton, "Pneumatological Issues in the Holiness Movement," *SNA* 244-50; Collins, *FW* 61f.

[35] Eusebius, *CH* 5:16:6-16; 5:18:1-13, *NPNF* 2:1:231f., 235-37.

[36] Epiphanius, *Pan.* 48.11.6 (171).

[37] Braitwaite, *ERE* 6:142f.

[38] Hilary, *Trin.* 8:38, *NPNF* 2:9:148f.; Wesley, Sermon 37, "The Nature of Enthusiasm" 18-39, *WJWB* 52-60.

[39] Wesley, "A Letter to the Rev. Dr. Rutherford," *WJWB* 9:374-88.

[40] *DCC* 73-76; Augustine, "On the Grace of Christ" 1:14, *NPNF* 1:5:222f.

[41] Augustine, "On the Grace of Christ" 1:45-47, *NPNF* 1:2:234.

[42] Hogue, *HS* 143-160.

[43] Augustine, "On the Spirit and the Letter" 5, *NPNF* 1:5:84f.

[44] Wesley, Sermons 10 and 11, "The Witness of the Spirit, Discourses I and II" *WJWB* 1:267ff. and *FAMRR, I, WJWB* 11:147-150; Wiley, *CT* 2:431-39.

[45] Cell, *RJW* 347-362.

[46] Wesley, Sermon 40, "Christian Perfection," *WJWB* 2:99ff.

[47] Wesley, Sermon 89, "The More Excellent Way," *WJWB* 3:263-77.

GLOSSARY

Aeons. In gnostic thought, a hierarchy of lesser divine beings.

Agnosticism. The teaching that we cannot know whether God exists.

Ambrose. Late fourth century bishop of Milan, Italy who wrote various works on basic Christian teachings and who profoundly influenced Augustine.

Anselm. Twelfth century Archbishop of Cantebury who developed the ontological argument for God's existence and also wrote on the atonement.

Apocrypha. Books in the Greek Old Testament received as canonical by Roman Catholics and Greek Orthodox Christians but not by Protestants.

Apology. A reasoned defense and articulation of Christian faith against pagan accusations by early church teachers.

Arius. Fourth century priest from Alexandria, Egypt who taught that the the Word of God, though supernatural and superior to all other creatures, was himself a creation of God. Arius' teaching was rejected at the Council of Nicea and again at the First Council of Constantinople.

Articles of Religion. A set of succinct propositional statements that define basic beliefs in the Lutheran, Anglican, and Methodist traditions.

Athanasius. Fourth-century archbishop of Alexandria who spent his public life overcoming the influence of Arius.

Atheism. The belief that God does not exists.

Atonement. Means by which guilt is removed so that the enimity between God and humans can be removed and they can be reconciled.

Attributes of God. The characteristics of God.

Augustine. Late fourth- and early fifth-century North African bishop of Hippo who wrote many famous works and played a crucial role in the debate with Pelagianism.

Basil of Caeserea. One of the fourth-century Cappadocian fathers who wrote important works on the creation and on the Holy Spirit.

Biblical Criticism. The study of the Scriptures which uses historical critical methods.

Canon of Vincent. The rule of Vincent of Lerins that the true teaching of the universal church is that which is believed everywhere, always, and by all.

Canon or Canonical Scriptures. Those writings which the church has officially received as authoritative and normative – that is, the Bible.

Cappadocians. Three church fathers from Cappadocia, Asia Minor – Basil and Gregory of Nyssa, who were brothers, and Gregory of Nazianzus – during the late fourth century who opposed a variety of heritical teachings.

Catechesis. Instruction in the fundamental teachings of the Christian church.

Cerinthus. Late first-century and early second-century advocate of doceticism.

Chalcedon. City in Asia Minor of the fourth ecumenical council (451) which council condemned the teaching of Eutyches and offered the Definition of Chalcedon that has been widely adopted as the most complete statement on the nature of Christ.

Christology. The systematic study of Christ, His nature, and His work.

Communicatio idomatum. The interchange of attributes between the human nature and the divine nature of Christ.

Constantinople. The city of Asia Minor in which the second great ecumenical council took place (381) which rejected the teaching of Eunomius and Macedonius on the Holy Spirit and Apollinarius on the nature of Christ.

Cosmogonies. Ancient stories on origins that generally taught that the world emerged from the gods or was generated by them.

Cosmological Argument. An argument for the existence of God that reasons from effect to cause saying that God was the original and uncaused source of all that exists.

Cosmos. The entire world, including earthly and heavenly things.

Creed. A succinct statement that sharply defines what is believed.

Decalogue. The Ten Commandments of Exodus 20:1-17 and Deuteronomy 5:6-21.

Demiurge. The supernatural being who, according to many Greek philosophers, created the world by giving shape to already existing and material.

Didache. The early teachings of the apostles.

Doceticism. An early form of gnosticism that taught that the Word of God only appeared to be incarnate in Jesus of Nazareth.

Doctrine. A teaching or the teachings of the Christian Church.

Ecclesiology. The doctrine of the church.

Eschatology. The doctrine of last things including the resurrection, the judgment, heaven, and hell.

Eunomius. Fourth century heretic who followed Arius in his teaching of Christ and also specifically taught that the Holy Spirit was a creature made by Christ and inferior to him.

Eusebius. Fourth-century historian of the church from whom we gain important information about early Christianity.

Eutyches. An fifth-century heretic who propogated the view of Christ known as monopysitism.

Exclusivistic. A teaching that excludes other views as being equally possible.

Filioque Phrase. In Western Christianity, the added phrase in the Apostles' Creed "and the Son" on the procession of the Spirit.

Finiteness or Finitude. Having a limit or being limited.

General Revelation. The teaching that God has revealed Himself, to some degree, through the natural world. This revelation of God is available to all people at all times and does not require the Scriptures or the witness of the church.

Gnosticism. A widely dispersed movement of late antiquity that made significant inroads into the church. Gnosticism was dualistic – that is, it taught that matter is evil and spirit alone is good and that good is unable to overcome evil.

Gregory of Nazianzus. Cappadocian father who wrote against the teachings of Apollinarius and Eunomius and is sometimes known as "the Theologian."

Gregory of Nyssa. The most philosophical of the Cappadocian fathers.

Haburah. The Hebrew word for "fellowship" or "community," which describes groups such as formed by Jesus and His disciples.

Harmartiology. The doctrine of sin.

Hebrew Bible. The 24 books of the Hebrew Bible that have been adopted by Protestant churches as the Old Testament canon.

Heresy. A teaching that purports to be Christian but which the church has officially rejected.

Hermeneutics. The science of interpreting the Scriptures.

Hilary. Fourth century bishop of Poitiers, Southern France, who wrote important works on the Christ and on the Holy Spirit and is sometimes called the "Athanasius of the West."

Immanence. The teaching that God, though He transcends the world and is not limited to it, is everywhere present in the world, accomplishing His purposes.

Immutability. The teaching that God's essential nature does not change and that He remains constant in His purposes.

Irenaeus. Second century bishop of Lyons, France who wrote a crucial work refuting gnostic heresies.

John of Damascus. Teacher of the early eight-century whose work,

Exposition of the Orthodox Faith, summarizes the teachings of church fathers.

Kerygma. The proclamation of the gospel by the apostolic church that emphasized the life, ministry, death, and resurrection of Jesus.

Leo the Great. Bishop of Rome in the mid-fifth century whose *Tome* refuted the teaching of Eutyches and assisted the Council of Chalcedon in its work.

Logos. Greek for the "word" which John applied to the eternal Son who became incarnate and the early church adopted as its designation for the divine nature in Jesus.

Macedonius. A fourth century teacher who was accused of promoting a view of the Holy Spirit resembling that of Eunomius.

Manicheism. A form of gnostic teaching that influenced Augustine in his early years and was first propogated by Manes of Persia during the third century.

Marcion. A teacher of a gnostic heresy that for a few decades was adopted by many Christians.

Monophysitism. The teaching that after the incarnation of the Word, there was only one essential nature in Jesus – the divine.

Monothelitism. The teaching that after the incarnation of the Word, Jesus only had a divine will.

Montanus. Leader of a movement in the late second century who believed that the church has become too institutional and suppressed the free work of the Spirit.

Moral Argument. The argument for God's existence that states that the moral nature of human beings implies that they are made by a supreme moral being, God.

Nestorius. An early fifty century heretic who taught that Christ had two natures but they were not perfectly united.

New Ageism. A movement of the late twentieth century that teaches a number of items borrowed from the Eastern religions such as, the use of psychics and mediums, astrology, and reincarnations.

Nicea. The city in Asia Minor where the first ecumenical council was held that declared Arianism heretical (325).

Nihilism. The philosophical teaching that there is no meaninful explanation for the world.

Ontological Argument. The argument for God's existence that says He is the being of which a greater cannot be conceived.

Pantheism. The belief that God is everything but does not transcend the world.

Paraclete. The Greek word for "advocate" which Jesus uses of the Holy Spirit according to John.

Paul of Samosata. A third century heretic who taught that the Word of God only came upon Jesus of Nazareth as an adult.

Pelagius. A British monk who, around the year 400, taught that we do not inherit from Adam a bias to sin and that the grace of God does not internally transform us.

Pneumatology. The doctrine of the Holy Spirit.

Polytheism. The belief in many gods.

Quadrilateral or Wesleyan Quarilateral. The four elements we use in the development of theology – Scripture, tradition or historic Christian teaching, reason, and experience.

Rabbinic Literature. Documents written during the third through the sixth centuries of the Christian era that recorded the formative opinions of the great rabbis.

Reconciliation. The overcoming of the enemity between God and human beings created by sin.

Relativism. The teaching that there are no moral absolutes.

Retribution. The results including natural consequences and divine reward or punishment for deeds that have been done.

Revelation. God's disclosure to us of truths about Himself, His will and the world.

Rule of Faith. Within the early church a concise list of things believed.

Sanctification. The process by which God separates one from sin and unto Himself.

Septuagint. The first translation of Old Testament into Greek.

Shema. The Hebrew name that Jews give to Deuteronomy 6:4-9, the core of their belief.

Skepticism. The belief that we cannot really know and understand reality.

Soteriology. The doctrine of salvation.

Special Revelation. The belief that God has uniquely revealed Himself first in Israel, then in Jesus Christ, and finally in the church. Special revelation is mediated through the canonical Scriptures.

Stoics. Philosophers of late antiquity who taught that the events of the world was ruled by fate.

Tatian. Second century Syrian bishop who made a harmony of the four Gospels.

Teleological Argument. The argument for God's existence that points to the design

Tertullian. Late second and early third century church father who wrote important works against heresy.

Theogony. An ancient myth that explains the origin of the gods.

Theophany and Christophany. An appearance of God or an appearance of the risen Christ.

Third Council of Toledo. Council that officially adopted the *filioque* (589).

Transcendence. The teaching that God is greater than this world and cannot be contained with it.

Triune or the Trinity. The teaching that God is one and yet three – Father, Son and Holy Spirit.

Vicarious. In the place of another or as a substitute for another.

ABBREVIATIONS
AND REFERENCES

ABD   *The Anchor Bible Dictionary*. Edited by David Noel Freeman. Six vols. New York: Doubleday, 1992.

ABC   *Asbury Bible Commentary*. Edited by Eugene Carpenter and Wayne McCown. Grand Rapids, MI: Zondervan, 1992.

AC   *Augustus to Constantine*. Robert M. Grant. New York: Harper & Row, 1970.

AF   (1) *The Apostolic Fathers*. Translated by J.B. Lightfoot. Grand Rapids, MI: Baker, 1956 (originally 1891). (2) *The Apostolic Fathers*. J.B. Lightfoot. 2 parts in 5 vols. Reprint: Peabody, MA: Hendrickson, 1899.

AH   (1) *Against Heresies*. Irenaeus. Translated by Alexander Roberts and James Donaldson. *ANF* 1:315ff. (2) *Augustine of Hippo*. Peter Brown. Berkeley and Los Angeles: Univ. of California, 1969.

AM   *Against Marcion*. Translated by Dr. Holmes. *ANF* 3:271ff.

ANF   *The Ante-Nicene Fathers*. Edited by Alexander Roberts and James Donaldson; 10 vols. Revised for an American edition by A. Cleveland Coxe. Grand Rapids, MI: Eerdmans, 1989 reprint (originally 1885-1896). Cited by book, chapter and paragraph of the work and then volume and page of this edition.

Anselm   *St. Anselm*. Translated by Sidney Norton Deane. Chicago: Open Court, 1926.

AP   *Against Praxeas*. Tertullian. Translated by Peter Holmes. *ANF* 597ff.

APD   *The Apostolic Preaching and Its Developments*. C.H. Dodd. London: Hodder and Stoughton, 1936.

APOT   *Apocrypha and Pseudepigrapha of the Old Testament*. R.H. Charles. 2 vols. Oxford: Clarendon, 1913.

AS   *Anatomy of the Sacred*. James C. Livingston. New York: Macmillan, 1989.

AT   *The Treatise on the Apostolic Tradition of St. Hippolytus of Rome*. Gregory Dix. London: SPCK, 1937.

BD   *Book of Discipline*. Cited by year of edition.

BE   *The Book of Exodus*. Bervard S. Childs. Philadelphia: Westminster, 1974.

BGF   *Beyond God the Father*. Mary Daly. Boston: Beacon, 1985.

BM   *The Birth of the Messiah*. Raymond E. Brown. Garden City, NY: Image, 1979 (originally 1977).

BTL   *A Black Theology of Liberation*. James Cone. Philadelphia & New York: Lippincott, 1970.

BTNT   *Biblical Theology of the New Testament.* Bernhard Weiss. Translated by David Eaton. 2 vols. Edinburgh: T. & T. Clark, 1888.

BWTA   *Basic Writings of Saint Thomas Aquinas.* Edited by Anton C. Pegis. 2 vols. New York: Random House, 1945. Cited by part, question and article and then by volume and page of this edition.

CBA   *Commentary on the Book of the Acts.* F.F. Bruce. Grand Rapids, MI: Eerdmans, 1955.

CC   *Creeds of Christendom.* Edited by Philip Schaff, revised by David S. Schaff. 3 vols. Reprint. Grand Rapids, MI: Baker, 1990 (originally 1931).

CCC   *Catechism of the Catholic Church.* Chicago, IL: Loyola, 1994.

CCT   *A Compendium of Christian Theology.* William Burt Pope. 3 vols. New York and Cincinnati: Phillips & Hunt and Walden & Stowe, 1881.

CD   (1) *On Christian Doctrine.* Augustine. Translated by J.F. Shaw. *NPNF* 1:2:519ff. (2) *Church Dogmatics.* Karl Barth. Edited by G.W. Bromiley, et al. 4 vols. Edinburgh: T. & T. Clark. 1936-1969.

CDH   *Cur Deus Homo.* Anselm 177f.

CDS   *The Christian Doctrine of Salvation.* George Barker Stevens. New York: Scribner's, 1905.

CER   *A Commentary on the Epistle to the Romans.* C.K. Barrett. New York: Harper & Row, 1957.

CF   (1) *Christian Faith.* Hendrikus Berkhof. Translated by Sierd Woudstra. Grand Rapids, MI: Eerdmans, 1979. (2) *The Christian Faith.* Friedrich Schleiermacher. Edited by H.R. Mackintosh and J.S. Stewart. Edinburgh: T. & T. Clark; 1928.

CG   (1) *The City of God.* Augustine. Translated by Marcus Dods. *NPNF* 1:2:1ff. (2) *Commentary on Galatians.* F.F. Bruce. Grand Rapids, MI: Eerdmans, 1982.

CH   *Church History.* Eusebius. Translated by Arthur Cushman McGiffert. *NPNF* 2:1:81ff.

CK   *The Community of the King.* Howard A. Snyder. Downers Grove, IL: InterVarsity, 1977.

CL   *The Catechetical Lectures of St. Cyril, Archbishop of Jerusalem.* Translated by Edward Hamilton Gifford. *NPNF* 2:7:1ff.

CLF   *Christology of the Later Fathers.* Edited by Edward Rochie Hardy. Philadelphia: Westminster, 1954.

CM   *Christology in the Making.* James D.G. Dunn. Philadelphia: Westminster, 1980.

CNT   (1) *The Canon of the New Testament.* Bruce M. Metzger. Oxford: Clarendon, 1987. (2) *The Christology of the New Testament.* Oscar

Cullmann. Translated by Shirley C. Guthrie and Charles A.M. Hall. Philadelphia: Westminster, 1959.

Conf   *The Confessions of St. Augustine.* Translated by J.G. Pilkington. *NPNF* 1:1:45ff.

Councils *Councils of Ariminum and Seleucia.* Athanasius. Translated by John Henry Newman. Revised by Archibald Robertson. *NPNF* 2:4:451ff.

CT   (1) *Christian Theology.* Millard J. Erickson. 3 vols. bound as 1. Grand Rapids, MI: Baker. 1983-85. (2) *Christian Theology.* H. Orton Wiley. 3 vols. Kansas City, MO: Beacon Hill, 1940-1943.

CV   *Christus Victor.* Gustaf Aulén. Translated by A.G. Hebert. London: SPCK, 1970 (originally, 1931).

DAA *Four Discourses Against the Arians.* Athanasius. Translated by Archibald Robertson. *NPNF* 2:4:306ff.

DC   *The Death of Christ.* James Denney. Edited by R.V.G. Tasker. London: Tyndale, 1951.

DCC *Documents of the Christian Church.* 2nd ed. Edited by Henry Bettenson. London: Oxford Univ. Press, 1963.

DIHS *The Divine Inspiration of Holy Scripture.* William J. Abraham. New York: Oxford Univ. Press, 1981.

DIOT *The Distinctive Ideas of the Old Testament.* Norman H. Snaith. New York: Schocken, 1964.

DSSE *The Dead Sea Scrolls in English.* G. Vermes. Middlesex, England: Penguin, 1962.

DSWT *Doctrinal Standards in the Wesleyan Tradition.* Thomas C. Oden. Grand Rapids, MI: Zondervan, 1988.

EA   *Evangelical Action.* Edited by the Executive Committee. Boston, MA: United Action, 1942.

EAMRR *An Earnest Appeal to Men of Reason and Religion.* John Wesley. Edited by Gerald Cragg. *WJWB* 11:45-101.

EC   *The Earnest Christian.* Edited by B.T. Roberts, et al. Buffalo, and Rochester, NY: Roberts and Earnest Christian, 1860-1909.

ECC *The Early Christian Church.* Philip Carrington. 2 vols. Cambridge: Cambridge Univ. Press, 1957.

ECD *Early Christian Doctrines.* J.N.D. Kelley. 2nd ed.; New York: Harper and Row, 1960.

ECF *Exposition of the Christian Faith.* Ambrose. Translated by H. De Romestin. *NPNF* 2:19:201ff.

ED   *Elements of Divinity.* Thomas N. Ralston. Edited by T.O. Summers. Nashville, TN: M. E. Church, South, 1901.

EEC *Encyclopedia of the Early Church.* Edited by Angelo Di Berardino. Translated by Adrian Walford. 2 vols. New York: Oxford, 1992.

EG   *The Existence of God.* Edited by John Hick. New York and London: Macmillan, 1964.

EH   *The Epistle to the Hebrews.* F.F. Bruce. Grand Rapids, MI: Eerdmans, 1964.

EJ   *The Epistles of John.* Raymond E. Brown, S.S. Garden City, NY: Doubleday, 1982.

ELM   *From Ezra to the Last of the Maccabees.* Elias Bickerman. Translated by Moses Hadas. New York: Schocken. 1962.

ENCH   *Enchiridion.* Augustine. Translated by J.F. Shaw. *NPNF* 1:3:237lff.

ENNT   *Explanatory Notes Upon the New Testament.* John Wesley. San Francisco and Cincinnati: Carlton and Lanahan (Schmul reprint), n.d. (originally 1754).

EOF   *Exposition of the Orthodox Faith.* John of Damascus. Translated by S.D.F. Salmond. *NPNF* 2:9:1ff.

EPR   *The Epistle of Paul to the Romans.* C.H. Dodd. New York: Long and Smith, 1932.

ER   *The Encyclopedia of Religion.* Edited by Mircea Eliade. 16 vols. New York and London: Macmillan, 1987.

ERE   *Encyclopedia of Religion and Ethics.* Edited by James Hastings. 12 vols. New York: Scribner's, 1914.

ET   *Elements of Theology.* Luther Lee. Syracuse, NY: Crooks, 1869.

FAA   *From Age to Age. A Living Witness.* Leslie R. Marston. Winona Lake, IN: Light and Life, 1960.

FAL   *From First Adam to Last.* C.K. Barrett. New York: Scribner's, 1962.

FAMRR, I, II, and III   *A Farther Appeal to Men of Reason and Religon, Parts I, II, and III.* John Wesley. Edited by Gerald Cragg. *WJWB* 11:105-325.

FESP   *The First Epistle of St. Peter.* Edward Gordon Selwyn. London: Macmillan, 1947.

FG   (1) *The Five Gospels.* Edited by Robert Funk, et al. New York: Macmillan, 1993.(2) *The Fourth Gospel.* Edwyn Clement Hoskyns. London: Faber and Faber, 1940.

FM   *The Faith of Maimonides.* Yeshaiahu Leibowitz. Translated by John Glucker. New York: Adama, 1987.

GAJ   *The Gospel According to St. John.* Brook Foss Westcott. 2 vols., bound as one. Grand Rapids, MI: Baker, 1980 (originally 1908).

GAM   (1) *The Gospel According to St. Mark.* C.S. Mann. Garden City, NY: Doubleday, 1986. (2) *The Gospel According to St. Mark.* Vincent Taylor. London: Macmillan, 1966.

GC   (1) *God in Creation.* Jürgen Moltmann. Translated by Margaret Kohl. Minneapolis: Fortress, 1993 (originally 1985). (2) *The Great*

Catechism. Gregory of Nyssa. Translated by William Moore and Henry Austin Wilson. *NPNF* 2:5:473ff.

GFH   *Grace, Faith, and Holiness.* H. Ray Dunning. Kansas City, MO: Beacon Hill, 1988.

GR   *Graceful Reason.* J.V. Langmead Casserley. Greenwich, CT: Seabury, 1954.

GSM   *God in Search of Man.* Abraham Joshua Heschel. New York: Harper & Row, 1955.

GWA   *God Who Acts.* G. Ernest Wright. London: SMC, 1952.

GWC   *God Was in Christ.* D.M. Ballie. New York: Scribner's, 1948.

HC   *The Humiliation of Christ.* A.B. Bruce. New York: Hodder & Stoughton, n.d.

HCD   (1) *A History of Christian Doctrine.* Edited by Hubert Cunliffe-Jones. Philadelphia: Fortress, 1978. (2) *History of Christian Doctrine.* William G.T. Shedd. 2 vols. New York: Scribner's, 1863.

HETFAR *History and Exposition of the Twenty-Five Articles of Religion of the Methodist Episcopal Church.* Henry Wheeler. New York and Cincinnati: Eaton and Main, Jennings and Graham, 1908.

Hex.   *The Hexameron.* Basil the Great. Translated by Bloomfield Jackson. *NPNF* 2:8:52ff.

HJHBC *The So-Called Historical Jesus and the Historic Biblical Christ.* Martin Kähler. Philadelphia: Fortress, 1956

HS   (1) *On the Holy Spirit.* Ambrose. Translated H. De Romestin. *NPNF* 2:10:93ff. (2) *On the Holy Spirit.* Basil the Great. Translated by Bloomfield Jackson. *NPNF* 2:8:2ff. (3) *The Holy Spirit.* Wilson T. Hogue. Chicago, IL: Rose, 1916.

HSGT   *The Holy Spirit and the Gospel Tradition.* C.K. Barrett. London: SPCK, 1947.

HST   *The History of the Synoptic Tradition.* Rudolf Bultmann. Translated by John Marsh. Oxford: Blackwell, 1972.

IC   *On the Incarnation of the Word.* Athanasius. Translated by Archibald Robertson. *NPNF* 2:4:36ff.

IDB   *Interpreter's Dictionary of the Bible.* Edited by George Arthur Buttrick. 4 vols. with a supplement. New York and Nashville: Abingdon, 1962, 1976.

IFG   *The Interpretation of the Fourth Gospel.* C.H. Dodd. Cambridge: Cambridge Univ. Press, 1953.

Inst.   (1) *Institutes of the Christian Religion.* John Calvin. Translated by Henry Beveridge. 2 vols. Grand Rapids, MI: Eerdmans, 1979 (originally 1845). (2) *The Divine Institutes.* Lactantius. Translated by William Fletcher. *ANF* 7:9ff.

INT   *Introduction to the New Testament.* W. Marxsen. Translated by G. Buswell. Philadelphia: Fortress, 1968.

IOTG   *An Introduction to the Old Testament in Greek.* Henry Barclay Swete. Revised by Richard Rusden Ottley. Peabody, MA: Hendrickson, 1989 (originally 1914).

IPCT   *The Idea of Perfection in Christian Theology.* R. Newton Flew. London: Oxford, 1934.

IR   *Israelite Religion.* Helmer Ringgren. Translated by David E. Green. Philadelphia, PA: Univ. Press, 1988.

ITM   *Introduction to the Talmud and Midrash.* Hermann L. Strack. English Translation. Atheneum, NY: Temple, 1972 (originally 1931).

JC   *Jews and Christians.* Edited by George A.F. Knight. Philadelphia: Westminster, 1955.

JCD   *Jewish-Christian Dialogue.* David Novak. New York, Oxford: Oxford Univ. Press, 1989.

JCM   *Jesus Christ and Mythology.* Rudolf Bultmann. New York: Scribner's, 1958.

JE   *Jewish Encyclopedia.* Edited by Isidore Singer. 12 vols. New York and London: Funk and Wagnalls, 1905.

Jerome The Jerome Biblical Commentary. Edited by Raymond E. Brown, et al. 2 vols. bound in one. Englewood Cliffs, NJ: Prentice-Hall, 1968.

JH   *Judaism and Hellenism.* Martin Hengel. Translated by John Bowden. 2 vols. London: SCM, 1974.

JJ   *Jesus the Jew.* New York: Macmillan, 1973.

JJW   *The Journal of the Rev. John Wesley, A.M.* Edited by Nehemiah Curnock. 8 vols. London: Epworth, 1938 (originally 1909–1916).

Jos.   *Josephus.* Edited by H. St. J. Thackery, et al. 9 vols. Cambridge MA: Harvard Univ. Press, 1927-1942.

JSV   *Jesus and the Spiral of Violence.* Richard Horsley. San Francisco: Harper & Row, 1987.

Jud.   *Judaism in the First Centuries of the Christian Era: The Age of the Tannaim.* George Foot Moore. 2 vols. New York: Schocken, 1971 (first published in 1927).

JW   *John Wesley.* Edited by Albert C. Outler. New York: Oxford, 1964.

JWTT   *John Wesley's Theology Today.* Colin W. Williams. New York and Nashville: Abingdon, 1960.

LG   *The Living God.* Thomas C. Oden. San Francisco: Harper and Row, 1987.

LS   *Life in the Spirit.* Thomas C. Oden. San Francisco: HarperCollins, 1992.

LTJM   *The Life and Times of Jesus the Messiah.* Alfred Edersheim. 2 vols. New York: Longmans, Green, 1899.

MECW *Miracle in the Early Christian World.* Howard Clark Kee. New Haven and London, Yale Univ. Press, 1983.

Med. *The Mediator.* Emil Brunner. Translated by Olive Wyon. Philadelphia: Westminster, 1947.

MI *The Myth of Innocence.* Burton Mack. Philadelphia: Fortress, 1988.

Mish. *The Mishnah.* Herbert Danby. Oxford: Oxford University Press, 1933.

MMJT *The Method and Message of Jesus' Teaching.* Robert H. Stein. Philadelphia: Westminster, 1978.

Mono. *Monologium. Anselm* 35ff.

NHBR *New Horizons in Biblical Research.* London: Oxford Univ. Press, 1966.

NPNF *A Select Library of the Nicene and Post-Nicene Fathers of the Christian Church.* Edited by Philip Schaff and Henry Wace. 2 series, 14 vols. each. Grand Rapids, MI: Eerdman's, 1989 rep. (originally 1887-1900). Cited by series, volume and page number. Cited by book, chapter, and paragraph of the work and then by series number, volume, and page of this edition.

NSH *The New Schaff-Herzog Encyclopedia of Religious Knowledge.* Edited by Samuel MaCauley Jackson. 12 vols. New York and London: Funk and Wagnalls, 1908.

NTA *New Testament Apocrypha.* Edgar Hennecke. Edited by Wilhelm Schneemelcher. Translated by R. McL. Wilson. 2 vols. Philadelphia: Westminster, 1959.

NTH *The New Testament and Homosexuality.* Robin Scroggs. Philadelphia: Fortress, 1983.

NTI *New Testament Introduction.* Donald Guthrie. London: Tyndale. 1970.

OG *The Openness of God.* Clark Pinnock and others. Downers Grove, IL and Carlisle, England: InterVarsity and Paternoster, 1994.

OOTT *An Outline of Old Testament Theology.* Th. C. Vriezen. Newton Centre, MA: Branford. 1966.

OPR *The Origin of Paul's Religion.* J. Gresham Machen. Grand Rapids, MI: Eerdmans, 1925.

OS *On the Spirit.* Basil the Great. Translated by Bloomfield Jackson. *NPNF* 2:8:2ff.

OT *Outlines of Theology.* A.A. Hodge. Grand Rapids, MI: Eerdmans, 1928.

OTAE *The Old Testament Against Its Enviornment.* G. Ernest Wright. London: SCM, 1950.

OTT *Old Testament Theology.* Gerhard von Rad. Translated by D.M.G. Stalker. 2 vols. New York: Harper & Row, 1962.

OW   *Ordaining Women.* B.T. Roberts. Rochester, NY: Earnest Christian, 1891.

PA   *Paul the Apostle.* J. Christiaan Beker. Philadelphia: Fortress, 1984.

PAH   *The Prescription Against Heretics.* Tertullian. Translated by Peter Holmes. *ANF* 3:243ff.

Pan. *The Panarion of St. Epiphanius, Bishop of Salamis: Selected Passages.* Translated by Philip R. Amidon, S.J. New York, Oxford: Oxford Univ. Press, 1990.

PC   *The Person of Christ.* G.C. Berkower. Grand Rapids, MI: Eerdmans, 1955.

PCC   *Primitive Christian Catechism.* Philip Carrington. Cambridge: Cambridge Univ. Press, 1940.

PCNTT *The Person of Christ in New Testament Teaching.* Vincent Taylor. London: Macmillan, 1958.

PG   *Pentecostal Grace.* Laurence W. Wood. Wilmore, KY: Francis Asbury Publishing, 1980.

Philo *Philo.* Translated by Ralph Marcus et al. 10 vols. and 2 supplementary vols. Cambridge, MA and London: Harvard Univ. Press, 1929-1953.

PL   *People of the Lie.* M. Scott Peck. New York: Simon and Schuster, 1983.

PNA   *Perspectives on the New Age.* Edited by James R. Lewis and J. Gordon Melton. Albany: State Univ. Press, 1992.

PNT   *The Phenomenon of the New Testament.* C.F.D. Moule. London: SCM, 1967.

PPJ   *Paul and Palestinian Judaism.* E.P. Sanders. Philadelphia: Fortress, 1977.

PR   *Prophecy and Religion.* John Skinner. Cambridge: Cambridge Univ. Press, 1951.

PRJ   *Paul and Rabbinic Judaism.* W.D. Davies. 2nd ed. London: SPCK, 1955.

Prophets *The Prophets.* Abraham J. Heschel. Jewish Publication Society, 1962.

Pros. *Proslogium. Anselm* 1ff.

QHJ   *The Quest of the Historical Jesus.* Albert Schweitzer. Translated by F.C. Burkitt. New York: Macmillan, 1968 (originally 1906).

RHR   *Redemption and Historical Reality.* Isaac C. Rottenberg. Philadelphia: Westminster, 1964.

RJW   *The Rediscovery of John Wesley.* George Croft Cell. New York: Henry Holt, 1935.

RLS   *The Revelation of Law in Scriptures.* Patrick Fairbairn. Grand Rapids, MI: Zondervan, 1957 (originally 1869).

RQGRW *The Religious Quests of the Graeco-Roman World*. S. Angus. New York: Scribner's, 1929.

SCG *Summa Contra Gentiles*. Thomas Aquinas. *BWTA* 2:3ff.

SDSA *The Scriptural Doctrine of Sacrifice and Atonement*. Alfred Cave. Edinburgh: T. & T. Clark, 1890.

SH *Salvation in History*. Oscar Cullmann. Translated by Sidney G. Sowers. New York and Evanston: Harper & Row, 1967.

SJ *The Search for Jesus*. Edited by Herschel Shanks. Washington D.C., Biblical Archaeology Society, 1994

SM *The Servant Messiah*. T.W. Manson. Cambridge: Cambridge Univ. Press, 1966 (originally, 1953).

SNA *The Spirit and the New Age*. Edited by R. Larry Shelton and Alex R.G. Deasley. *Wesleyan Theological Perspectives*, vol. 5; Anderson, IN: Warner Press, 1986.

SP (1) *My Servants the Prophets*. Edward J. Young. Grand Rapids, MI: Eerdman's, 1952. (1) *Sex in the Parish*. Karen Lebacqz and Ronald. G. Barton. Louisville, KY: Westminster/John Knox, 1991.

SQ *The Sacred Quest*. Lawrence S. Cunningham, John Kelsay, R. Maurice Barineau, and Heather Jo McVoy. New York and Toronto: Macmillan, 1991.

SSA *Studies in Sin and Atonement*. Adolf Büchler. New York: Ktav, 1967 (originally 1927).

ST (1) *Summa Theologica*. Thomas Aquinas. *BWTA* 1:5ff.; 2:225ff. (2) *Systematic Theology*. Wolfhart Pannenberg. Translated by Geoffrey W. Bromiley. 2 vols. to date. Grand Rapids, MI: Eerdmans, 1991-. (3) *Systematic Theology*. Augustus Hopkins Strong. 3 vols. Philadelphia: Judson, 1907-1909. (4) *Systematic Theology*. Paul Tillich. 3 vols. in one. Chicago: Chicago Univ. Press, 1951-1963.

TDNT *Theological Dictionary of the New Testament*. Edited by Gerhard Kittel and Gerhard Friedrich. Translated by Geoffrey W. Bromiley. 9 vols. Grand Rapids, MI: Eerdmans, 1964-1974.

TI *Theological Institutes*. Richard Watson. 2 vols. New York: Nelson and Phillips, 1850 (originally 1823).

TJ *The Teaching of Jesus*. T.W. Manson. Cambridge: Cambridge Univ. Press, 1963 (originally 1931).

TJW *The Theology of John Wesley*. William R. Cannon. New York and Nashville: Abingdon-Cokesbury, 1956.

TL *A Theology of Liberation*. Gustavo Gutiérrez. Translated and edited by Sister Caridad Inda and John Eagleson. Maryknoll, NY: Orbis, 1973.

TNT (1) *Theology of the New Testament*. Rudolf Bultmann. Translated by Kendrick Grobel. 2 vols. New York: Scribner's, 1955. (2) *The*

Theology of the New Testament. George Barker Stevens. New York: Scribner's, 1927.

TO   *The Five Theological Orations* (Orations 27-31). Gregory of Nazianzus. Translated by Charles Gordon Browne and James Edward Swallow. *NPNF* 2:7:284ff.

Tome   *To Flavian Commonly Called "The Tome"* (Letter 28). Leo the Great. Translated by Charles Lett Feltoe. *NPNF* 2:12:38ff.

TOT   (1) *Theology of the Old Testament.* Walther Eichrodt. Translated by J.A. Baker. 2 vols. Philadephia: Westminster, 1961. (2) *The Theology of the Older Testament.* J. Barton Payne. Grand Rapids, MI: Zondervan, 1962.

Trin.   (1) *On the Holy Trinity.* Augustine. Translated by Arthur West Haddan. Revised by W.G.T. Shedd. *NPNF* 1:3:17ff. (2) *On the Trinity.* Hilary of Poitiers. Translated by E.W. Watson and L. Pullan. Edited by W. Sanday. *NPNF* 2:9:40ff.

TT   *The Training of the Twelve.* Alexander Balmain Bruce. 6th ed. Edinburgh: T. & T. Clark, 1901.

TTF   *Two Types of Faith.* Martin Buber. Translated by Norman P. Goldhawk. New York: Macmillan, 1951.

TWBB   *A Theological Word Book of the Bible.* Edited by Alan Richardson. New York: Macmillan, 1950.

VBC   *The Virgin Birth of Christ.* J. Gresham Machen. New York: Harper, 1930.

VC   *The Vicarious Sacrifice.* Horace Bushnell. 2 vols. New York: Scribner's, 1877.

VT   *The Vision Which Transforms.* George Allen Turner. Kansas City, MO: Beacon Hill, 1964.

WHT   *A Wesleyan-Holiness Theology.* J. Kenneth Grider. Kansas City, MO: Beacon Hill, 1994.

WI   *Wisdom in Israel.* Gerhard von Rad. English translation by James D. Martin. London: SCM, 1972.

WJA   *The Writings of James Arminius.* Translated by James Nichols and W.R. Bagnall. 3 vols. Grand Rapids, MI: Eerdmans, 1977 (originally 1856).

WJF   *The Works of the Reverend John Fletcher.* 4 vols. New York: Carlton & Porter, n.d.

WJW   *The Works of John Wesley.* Jackson edition. Peabody, MA: Hendrickson, 1991 (originally 1872).

WJWB   *The Works of John Wesley.* Edited by Frank Baker, et al. Bicentennial edition. 15 vols. to date. Nashville: Abingdon, 1975-.

WL   *The Word of Life.* Thomas C. Oden. San Francisco: Harper & Row, 1989.

WQ   *The Wesleyan Quadrilateral.* Donald A.D. Thorsen. Grand Rapids: Zondervan, 1990.

WS   *Wesley and Sanctification.* Harald Lindström. London: Epworth, 1946.

WTH   *The Wesleyan Theological Heritage. Essays of Albert C. Outler.* Edited by Thomas C. Oden and Leicester R. Longden. Grand Rapids: Zondervan, 1991.

WTJ   *Wesleyan Theological Journal.* Marion, IN and others: Wesleyan Theological Society, 1966-.

BIOGRAPHICAL INDEX

SUBJECT INDEX